P €15·75  9C

# Multicultural Education

## A Teacher's Guide to Content and Process

**Hilda Hernández**
*California State University, Chico*

MERRILL PUBLISHING COMPANY

A Bell & Howell Information Company
Columbus • Toronto • London • Melbourne

*Cover Illustration: Brian Deep, Frank Hernández*

Published by Merrill Publishing Company
A Bell & Howell Information Company
Columbus, Ohio 43216

This book was set in Palatino

Administrative Editor: David Faherty
Production Coordinator: Julie Higgins
Art Coordinator: Gilda Edwards
Cover Designer: Brian Deep

Credits: Thanks to the following individuals for their contributions to this book—Frank Hernández for the artwork on the Part Openers; John McNamara for the use of his photographs; and to Sŏ Sang-U, who drew the map depicted in Figure 6-2.

Library of Congress Catalog Card Number: 88-63836
International Standard Book Number: 0-675-21006-2
Printed in the United States of America
1  2  3  4  5  6  7  8  9—92  91  90  89

*Para mi familia*
*con todo mi amor y cariño*

# Preface

Incorporating multicultural education in the classroom is in some ways analogous to putting together an elaborate jigsaw puzzle. Although the vision of what the final outcome should be is clear, fitting the pieces together is not always an easy task. Some relationships are obvious; others are more difficult to recognize. Slowly, as pieces fall into place, the total picture becomes apparent. The purpose of this book is to help teachers see the big picture of multicultural education and to provide them with the means to make it a truly integral part of teaching and learning in their classrooms.

In this book, I approach multicultural education from a dual perspective that encompasses both content and process. Content is the substance—the visible aspect of curriculum and instruction. Process is the less visible curriculum—the interactional, organizational, social, and management dimensions involved in teaching and learning. From this dual perspective, teachers can better understand the many facets of education that is multicultural. They can see the connections to their own classrooms, whatever the level, setting, or school population. They can integrate and apply the precepts of multicultural education in their teaching and in the learning environment they create.

This is a book for all teachers: elementary and secondary, beginning and experienced. It is for those preparing to enter the profession as well as for educators continuing their professional development at the graduate level. It is for teachers dealing with a diversity of student populations in settings that are urban, suburban, and rural.

As the title suggests, the intent of the book is to provide teachers with a guide to content and process in multicultural education. The chapters are divided into two parts. Part I consists of two introductory chapters designed to provide the basis for those that follow. The first chapter describes what multicultural education is and why it must encompass both content and process. The second examines the cultural, societal, and school contexts in which education takes place.

Part II is the heart of this book. Chapters 3–8 explore different facets of content and/or process in education that is multicultural. Combining theory and practice, they offer a synthesis of contemporary scholarship complemented by strategies and techniques teachers can readily apply in K–12 classrooms. Each chapter begins with a statement of objectives and concludes with a summary of the major ideas presented.

That the text is designed for use by teachers is evident in the areas featured. In Chapter 3, the focus is on classroom processes—the "hidden" curriculum comprising the interactional, organizational, managerial, and societal aspects of the instructional environment. The two chapters that follow focus primarily on how classroom content and processes can be adapted to meet the unique needs and abilities of individual learners. Chapter 4 draws attention to bilingualism in American society and provides teachers with a foundation for working with language-minority students. Chapter 5 deals with the relationships between multicultural, special, and gifted education. In the next two chapters, consideration is given to the content of curriculum and instruction. In Chapter 6, instructional materials are examined from a multicultural perspective. Historical and contemporary views on the treatment of diverse groups in school textbooks, guidelines for the analysis of materials, and activities that can be used in the classroom are presented in this chapter. The integration of multicultural perspectives into the curriculum is the primary focus of Chapter 7. The curriculum development model presented encompasses needs assessment, educational goals and learning outcomes, implementation, teaching strategies, and evaluation. Finally, Chapter 8 assists teachers in going beyond the classroom to incorporate home, neighborhood, community, and societal elements as integral components of education that is multicultural.

## Acknowledgments

I gratefully acknowledge the contributions others have made in the preparation of this book. First, I am deeply indebted to John McNamara for the artistry of his photographs, which beautifully complement the text. I also want to thank the teachers, parents, and students—most especially those in the New Haven Unified School District—who allowed their photographs to be included as part of this book. If a picture is worth a thousand words, theirs certainly speak volumes. Special thanks go to Frank Hernández for the graphic designs that capture the theme of multicultural education.

This project was initiated during my tenure as a Spencer Fellow with the National Academy of Education. My debt to members of the Academy is considerable: for the influence of Nathaniel L. Gage, Lee S. Shulman, David Tyack, and others in shaping the direction of my work and for the generous support provided in the preparation of this manuscript.

I sincerely appreciate the contributions of those who reviewed the text at various stages of development. Especially warm thanks to reviewers Ivan Banks, University of Kentucky; Patricia Larke, Texas A&M University; Ralph Carter, Texas Tech University; Donna Deyhle, University of Utah; Ernest Washington, University of Massachusetts; Pamela McCollum, University of Colorado-Boulder; Michael Williams, Wright State University; and Gilbert Cuevas, University of Miami. A very special thank you to Carlos Cortes, University of California-Riverside, for his influence in shaping my perspective on multicultural education and for his encouragement and feedback.

I also want to express my gratitude to colleagues at California State University-Chico for their interest, advice, and support. For suggestions based on various drafts of the chapters, I am most grateful to Bonnie Johnson, David Bauer, and Mary Jensen, California State University-Chico; Kay Heath, Marysville Unified School District; and Dennis Parker, California State Department of Education. I also acknowledge the very useful and insightful comments provided by student teachers in the elementary and secondary basic credential programs at California State University-Chico. I thank all of my students—past and present—for everything they have taught me about education that is multicultural.

Special thanks to David Faherty, my administrative editor at Merrill Publishing Company, through the major part of this project. He is everything an author could ask for in an editor: positive, helpful, supportive, and patient. Thanks, too, go to Marianne Taflinger, Jennifer Knerr, and Beverly Kolz for their assistance, and especially to Amy Macionis, developmental editor at Merrill.

For their generosity, I thank the individuals, publishers, and school, state, and government agencies who granted permission for the use of materials reproduced in the book. Their contributions are most gratefully acknowledged.

Finally, I thank my family for the support and encouragmeent I needed to begin such an undertaking, and for the understanding and patience they offered me in seeing it through to the end.

# Contents

# P A R T

# 1

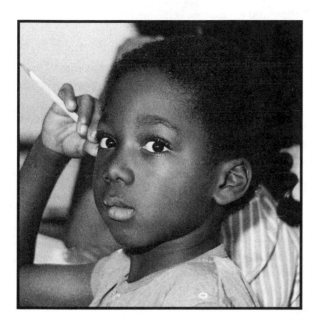

# 1
# Introduction to Multicultural Education

*Reality happens to be, like a landscape possessed of an infinite number of perspectives, all equally veracious and authentic. The sole false perspective is that which claims to be the only one there is.*

*Jose Ortega y Gasset*

Teaching, to be effective, must be multicultural. In a nation characterized by cultural diversity, schooling must serve all students. In a society that is pluralistic, educators must provide increasingly heterogeneous student populations a classroom environment that meets the diverse needs and develops the unique abilities of students from many different backgrounds.

The intent of this text is to introduce teachers and prospective teachers to the dynamic and multifaceted world of multicultural education. This chapter begins with definitions of the concept and approaches used in providing education that is multicultural. It explains why the focus on both process and content is central to implementation of multicultural education. It also describes the goals of multicultural education, identifies the competencies needed to attain related objectives, and presents a clear rationale for integrating multicultural perspectives at all levels for all students. Finally, this first chapter provides an overview of the content and organization of the entire book.

After completing this chapter, you will be able to

1. Define *multicultural education* and explain its relationship to classroom processes and curriculum content.
2. Describe the approaches most commonly associated with multicultural education.
3. Explore basic assumptions underlying multicultural education.
4. Identify related goals and teacher competencies.

## Definitions of Multicultural Education: An Overview

*Multicultural education* has been defined in numerous ways by various groups and individuals. Some definitions reflect perspectives of specific disciplines, such as education, anthropology, sociology, and psychology. Others represent the views of accrediting agencies and professional organizations concerning what teachers need to teach and what students need to learn. A third type of definition consists of statements developed and adopted by practitioners within schools and at district, county, and state levels. As a result, teachers routinely are confronted with a kaleidoscope of differing views that describe multicultural education as everything from "educational practice" (Pacheco, 1977) to "interdisciplinary process" (*Planning for Multicultural Education as a Part of School Improvement*, 1979).

The differences among definitions are more than a question of semantics. In the final analysis, what teachers do in the name of multicultural education depends upon their point of view. Recognizing the importance of clarity, some have proposed that the term *multicultural education* be replaced with labels such as "education that is multicultural" (Grant, 1977) or "the multicultural facet of education" (Frazier, 1977). These, they argue, better communicate the substance and meaning of the concept. At present, however, *multicultural education*, in spite of its limitations, remains the most common and accepted term.

There are two formal definitions of multicultural education that describe dimensions of the concept important for teachers. The first defines the essence of multicultural education as a perspective that recognizes (a) the political, social, and economic realities that individuals experience in culturally diverse and complex human encounters; and (b) the importance of culture, race, sexuality and gender, ethnicity, religion, socioeconomic status, and exceptionalities in the educational process (National Council for Accreditation of Teacher Education, 1986).

Recognizing the multiple realities existing within the contexts of school and society places certain demands upon teachers. First, it implies that students must learn to communicate and interact with people of different cultural backgrounds. In this sense, multicultural education is a process through which individuals develop ways of perceiving, evaluating, and behaving within cultural systems different from their own (Gibson, 1984). Second, it requires consideration of those forces that exert a powerful influence on schooling, directly and indirectly. These forces include societal and school factors affecting the priorities and directions of education nationwide and at the state and local levels. Also included are the social and cultural factors that influence how teachers teach and what they teach; how students learn and what they learn.

To complement this perspective, a second definition is needed to focus attention on multicultural education as an instructional approach. According to Suzuki (1984), "Multicultural education is a multidisciplinary educational program that provides multiple learning environments matching the academic, social, and linguistic needs of students" (p. 305).

Two essential attributes emerge from this definition. First, from a teacher's point of view, the focus is on learners as individuals characterized by a unique combination of abilities and instructional needs. Addressing their needs requires the creation of instructional environments genuinely sensitive to many kinds of diversity. Second, from a programmatic standpoint, multicultural education is integrated across disciplines with a strong emphasis on academic achievement as well as social and personal development.

In the final analysis, multicultural education is simultaneously *about* multiple cultures, *in* multiple cultures, and *of* students from different cultural backgrounds. It is education *for* all students (Higgins & Moses, 1981).

## Historical Development and Typologies

Several approaches mark the evolution of multicultural education from the 1960s to the late 1980s. According to the typology developed by Sleeter and Grant (1988), these can be labeled as follows: Teaching the Exceptional and the Culturally Different; Human Relations; Single-Group Studies; Multicultural Education; and Education That Is Multicultural and Social Reconstructionist. Except for the first, these approaches are intended for all students. The following summary of these approaches is based on the discussion by Sleeter and Grant (1988).

Initiated in the 1960s, the approach called **Teaching the Exceptional and Culturally Different** is characterized by efforts to promote the academic achievement of students from minority ethnic groups and lower socioeconomic levels, those with limited English proficiency, and those with other special educational needs. Central to this approach is the adaptation of instruction in regular classrooms to individual differences. Practices focus on the use of culturally relevant curricula, basic skills development, and sensitivity to individual learning styles.

Desegregation efforts provided impetus for **Human Relations**, an approach that emphasizes intergroup relationships and self-concept. This approach is intended to reduce intergroup conflict, promote greater tolerance of individual differences, and foster positive interaction among students. The curriculum and instruction associated with this approach focus on addressing stereotyping and name-calling, teaching about individual differences and similarities, and recognizing group contributions.

Another approach developed during this period—**Single-Group Studies**—is marked by in-depth study of particular groups (e.g., ethnic and women's studies). This approach attempts to raise social consciousness and promote social action on behalf of specific groups. The perspective of group members is integral to this approach, and instruction centers on the group's history, culture, and concerns. Minority groups are presented as distinct entities and usually are treated separately.

In the 1970s, **Multicultural Education** emerged as a more comprehensive approach. With cultural diversity and equal opportunity as its cornerstones, this approach examines and takes into account the relationships among culture, ethnicity, language, gender, handicap, and social class in developing educational programs. Of all the approaches, this is the most prevalent and the one used in this text. In the classroom, content is structured around the contributions and perspectives of different groups. Instruction emphasizes critical thinking skills and uses culturally relevant materials and curricular adaptations. As in other approaches, use of other languages, learning strategies, and cooperative learning is prominent.

A more recent (and controversial) approach—**Education That Is Multicultural and Social Reconstructionist**—represents an extension of multicultural education in the direction of more definitive social action. Compared with the other approaches, this one incorporates a much greater curricular emphasis on active student involvement in social issues (e.g., racism, sexism, classism) and on development of problem-solving and political action skills. In addition to curricular adaptations and cooperative learning, instruction emphasizes development of decision-making skills.

## Content and Process

Implementation of multicultural education in the 1990s will require educational reform. To fully realize the possibilities of innovations in education, changes must encompass not only content but also process (especially human interaction) and organizational structure (Hunter, cited in Lee, 1983). This task means looking beyond curricular content and instructional materials to the context of classroom life and the processes enacted by teachers and students as individuals and members of larger groups.

Content and process represent two sides of the coin that is the world of the classroom. By considering both dimensions, teachers can relate seemingly disparate elements into a comprehensive, cohesive, and meaningful whole. From this holistic perspective, the influence of larger social and cultural contexts on classroom processes and content is most easily understood.

### Content

Content encompasses the more formal manifestations of classroom life. It has been defined by Shulman (1986) as the "substance" of teaching and of learning, the specific curricular content and subject matter studied. From his perspective, it is at the "very heart of teaching-learning processes" (p. 8), for teachers and students interact in and through content. It is subject matter and related skills, strategies, and processes. In terms of instruction, content is usually organized as lessons, units, semesters, or years; within these, it is also conceived of as facts, concepts, principles, cognitive strategies, etc.

Several aspects of content are relevant to multicultural education. First, because cultural pluralism is a fact of life in the United States, curricular content and instructional materials must provide multicultural perspectives that reflect the true nature of society and the subcultures that constitute it. These include but are not limited to groups defined by ethnicity, gender, age, handicap, socioeconomic status, and religion. Teachers must examine materials they use with respect to the treatment of groups and topics. Likewise, they need to help students develop skills in analyzing what they read, hear, and see in instructional materials and the media. Finally, teachers must also recognize the connections between local neighborhoods and communities, and the subject areas under study.

Second, if diversity is also the hallmark of our global community, then curricular content and instructional materials must assist students in communicating and interacting with people from different cultures. Teachers today are responsible for teaching students about (a) their own cultural heritage and that of other groups; (b) the ways in which culture influences the sum total of each individual's way of life and that of others; (c) similarities and differences among individuals, within and across groups; and (d) attitudes and modes of behavior that can facilitate or impede cross-cultural understanding. To do this effectively, teachers must have specific knowledge about multiple cultures; more importantly, they must have the desire and skills to interact and communicate in different cultural settings and with individuals from diverse cultural backgrounds (Gibson, 1984).

Third, to teach a diverse group of students, teachers must know how to and be willing to adapt to meet the needs of individual students. Adaptations may be necessary because of students' language, exceptionality, learning style preferences, or other characteristics and may affect content, classroom setting, and instructional strategies. Teachers need to know when accommodation is indicated and what form it should take.

## Process

Process encompasses the less formal and visible aspects of classroom life, the context in which curricular content is transmitted and the processes involved in doing so. Shulman (1986) identifies several contexts in which teaching occurs: individual, group, class, school, family, and community. Every context, he notes, is embedded within a larger context: individuals within groups, groups within classrooms, classrooms within schools, and so on. For this reason, to understand life in classrooms, one needs to know more than just the unique dynamics experienced by a particular group of students and their teacher. Also needed are insights about how the students and teacher are "influenced by the larger contexts in which the class is embedded—the school, the community, the society, the culture" (Shulman, 1986, p. 20).

Awareness of these contexts helps explain why individual students experience classroom life differently. Some events are shared by everyone, while others are interpreted differently according to the particular social, linguistic, and cultural background of the individual. Teachers need to be able to identify how learner preferences, beliefs, attitudes, and behaviors are influenced by culture and how this relationship affects performance. They must also become more aware of how their own preferences, beliefs, attitudes, and behaviors are strongly influenced by their own cultural background and how these in turn affect the way they teach, behave, and interact with students.

Classroom processes are those facets of teaching and learning that involve *interaction, organization, social aspects,* and *management* (Shulman, 1986). In the classroom, transactions occur between teachers and students; as Shulman observes, these are social and organizational, academic and intellectual. Processes are

Multicultural education must embody both content and process.

important avenues through which sociocultural factors influence students' academic achievement and social development. The creation of learning environments responsive to diversity requires consideration of these four process dimensions.

First, there needs to be greater awareness of how social and cultural factors affect interactional patterns in the classroom and in students' homes and communities. To what extent do students experience equality of opportunity to participate? To what degree is classroom participation a function of ethnicity, gender, socioeconomic status, or academic achievement? What differences in language use exist between the home and the classroom, and in what ways do these relate to instruction?

Second, it is essential that teachers recognize how social aspects such as language attitudes and grouping influence performance and perceptions. How do attitudes toward different varieties of English affect teachers and students? What does research reveal about the advantages and disadvantages of grouping? Who wins, who loses, and why?

Third, accommodating the diversity of needs and abilities students bring to the classroom also requires complementary use of instructional and behavioral techniques. How do content, student behaviors, and instructional strategies and settings relate to the management process? What kinds of strategies have been used in adapting curriculum to meet student needs, particularly those of minority and handicapped learners?

Fourth, in organizing students for instruction, teachers need to be attentive to the ways in which they structure learning activities. How does organization affect student learning? What kinds of strategies have been used to adapt classroom structure and organization to individual needs?

## Assumptions, Goals, and Competencies

### Basic Assumptions

The concept of multicultural education presented in this book is based on a set of related assumptions. These will now be made explicit.

**Premise 1** *It is increasingly important for political, social, educational, and economic reasons to recognize that the United States is a culturally diverse society.* The development of skills for living in such a dynamic society is a continuous, legitimate, and necessary part of the formal and informal educational process. Thus, multicultural education can help prepare students for life in the "real world" beyond the school setting, a world inhabited by individuals and groups with cultures distinct from their own (Gollnick & Chinn, 1986). It is preparation for life in a society in which there is "no one model American"; a society in which no group lives in a vacuum but rather exists as part of an interrelated whole (American Association of Colleges for Teacher Education, 1973).

**Premise 2** *Multicultural education is for all students.* A popular misconception regarding multicultural education is that it is intended primarily or exclusively for minority students. Educational policy in some states has helped to promote such a perception by requiring multicultural education only in districts having at least one school with a 25% minority student population (Baker, 1979). Such policies fail to recognize that developing appropriate skills and attitudes for living in a multicultural society is as critical for the nonminority student as it is for the minority student. Because all students ultimately will need to function in our culturally diverse society, all should be exposed to educational experiences that foster the necessary competencies for doing so.

**Premise 3** *Multicultural education is synonymous with effective teaching.* Payne (1983) describes multicultural education as "good teaching and good education"; in essence, it is the "natural way to teach" (pp. 98–99). Theory and practice related to multicultural education reflect the tenets of sound, current educational research and methods. Teachers are encouraged to acquire a deeper and broader understanding of students as learners and to develop an expanded repertoire of strategies and techniques. Multicultural education emphasizes high expectations, adaptation to accommodate individual learner differences, and presentation of all subjects to all students. A multicultural perspective is a legitimate and necessary part of teaching in all classrooms. Indeed, consideration of sociocultural dimensions in the teaching and learning process is central—not peripheral—to issues of school effectiveness and educational reform.

**Premise 4** *Teaching is a cross-cultural encounter.* These few words capture the essence of the connection between culture and the teaching-learning process (Hilliard, cited in James, 1978). Every teacher and every student is a unique cultural being. Each brings to the classroom a distinct combination of beliefs, values, and experiences. These, in turn, influence behavior, perceptions, attitudes, and performance.

The classroom is also a setting in which culture is transmitted and individuals are socialized into a well-established, but often invisible, system of behaviors, values, and beliefs. Powerful and dynamic relationships exist between social and cultural factors (e.g., socioeconomic status, ethnicity, gender, language) and schooling. As pointed out by Smith, Cohen, and Pearl (cited in Baker, 1983), teachers must be able to provide an instructional environment appropriate for learners from diverse backgrounds:

> The school is the only institution through which all children of all cultures can share in the heritage and life of this nation. The teacher who can work only with children from one socioeconomic or cultural group is inadequately prepared to teach in the common school. (p. 46)

**Premise 5** *The educational system has not served all students equally well.* Deficiencies in the educational system have had a disproportionate effect on students who are poor, members of certain minority groups, and those who are culturally, linguistically, and/or socially different from the mainstream student population. The substantial differences in educational achievement among groups of students with different backgrounds constitute a complex problem for which no simple, single-factor solutions exist.

Continuation of this "achievement gap"—as Brown and Haycock (1984) have asserted—does not make educational, economic, or political sense. "All [students], regardless of race, class or economic status, are entitled to a fair chance and the tools for developing powers of mind and spirit to the utmost" (National Commission on Excellence in Education, cited in Gollnick & Chinn, 1986, p. 2). To accomplish this objective, teachers must believe in their ability to reach all of their students, to create learning environments in which all students feel that the acquisition of knowledge is an "equal opportunity process" (Webb, 1983, p. 94).

**Premise 6** *Multicultural education is synonymous with educational innovation and reform.* Although the aims of the numerous recent initiatives promoting school reform are laudable, many offer less than adequate responses to the challenges facing education today. McGroarty (1986) stated that many such calls for reform systematically overlook the sociocultural dimension:

> They neglect the sociocultural influences that, along with traditional matters of curricular offerings and time available for instruction, affect educational outcomes for students. . . .Their potential impact. . .is mediated by the local circumstances in which they are applied; these circumstances are shaped in fundamental ways by the sociocultural influences that permeate the educational process. (pp. 299–300)

Sociocultural factors cannot be neglected if meaningful educational reforms are to be implemented effectively. The problems to be addressed are not simple, and solutions that are not responsive to social and cultural differences will have little significant effect.

**Premise 7** *Next to parents, teachers are the single most important factor in the lives of children* (Baker, 1983). Individual teachers can and do make a difference in student learning (Good, cited in Gollnick & Chinn, 1986), and to a great extent, they determine the degree to which education is truly multicultural (Frazier, 1977). A noted philosopher of education suggests that the three primary functions of schooling are socialization, cultural transmission, and development of self-identity (Green, cited in Pacheco, 1977). Few would argue that teachers play anything less than a central role in all three of these cultural processes.

**Premise 8** *Classroom interaction between teachers and students constitutes the major part of the educational process for most students* (Stubbs, 1976). Increasingly, the quantity and quality of interaction between teacher(s) and student(s) are regarded as critical dimensions of classroom life. The importance of these dimensions to the instructional process was emphasized in a U.S. Commission on Civil Rights Report (1973), which stated that through student-teacher interaction, "the school system makes its major impact upon the child. The way the teacher

In the final analysis, multicultural education is for all teachers and students.

interacts with the student is a major determinant of the quality of education he receives" (p. 3).

## Goals and Competencies

There are two all-encompassing goals related to process and content in multicultural education. The first is to help students acquire knowledge about a range of cultural groups and develop the attitudes, skills, and abilities needed to function at some level of competency within many different cultural environments (Banks, 1979; Gibson, 1984). The second is to apply knowledge of sociocultural factors related to the teaching and learning process to maximize the academic, personal, and social development of all students. These are ambitious, but not unattainable, objectives.

The major purpose of this book is to provide teachers with the knowledge and competencies necessary to implement multicultural education effectively— that is, to achieve the two major goals just stated. Specifically, this book is intended

In the final analysis, multicultural education is for all teachers and students.

to assist teachers in their efforts to develop the following (based in part on Baptiste and Baptiste, 1980; Suzuki, 1984):

- A rationale for multicultural education that will provide the basis for its implementation in the classroom.
- An understanding of the interrelationship of process and content in multicultural education.
- An appreciation of the influence of sociocultural factors on learning and teaching and the ability to apply these insights to maximizing students' academic and social development.
- A recognition of interactional, social, management, and organizational dimensions of culturally pluralistic classrooms and their influence on academic outcomes.
- An understanding of bilingualism and its implications for the education of students with limited English proficiency.
- The ability to incorporate instructional methods and practices that are culturally appropriate for diverse student populations.

- Skills in adapting teaching to meet the needs of individual learners from different backgrounds and with diverse ability levels.
- The ability to evaluate, develop, and modify curricular materials with special attention to the treatment of sociocultural content.
- Skill in developing a curriculum that integrates (a) multicultural perspectives (e.g., ethnicity, gender, socioeconomic status, age, religion, exceptionality), (b) content addressing issues of intercultural and interracial understanding (e.g., cultural awareness, intergroup relations, discrimination and racism), and (c) resources outside the classroom (i.e., home and community).

In discussing the teaching of culturally diverse populations, Etlin (1988) remarked that "to teach them all is to know them all" (pp. 10–11). A good first step in learning how "to teach them all" is to reflect on one's own perspectives. The following self-test on cultural sensitivities, which is adapted from Lockart (cited in Etlin, 1988), highlights teacher attitudes and behaviors most relevant to multicultural education.

CULTURAL SENSITIVITY SELF-TEST

1. Am I knowledgeable about and sensitive to students' cultural backgrounds, values, and traditions?
2. Do I demonstrate respect for cultures and backgrounds different from my own?
3. Do I provide a classroom atmosphere in which students' cultures are recognized, shared, and respected?
4. Do I use culturally appropriate curricular materials to supplement those whose treatment of different groups is limited or biased?
5. Do I give students an opportunity to teach me what I don't know or understand about their cultures? Do learning and teaching operate in both directions in my classroom?
6. Have I discarded stereotypes that interfere with my support of students' academic and personal growth as individuals?
7. Do I involve parents and other community members in classroom activities?

## Did You Know That. . .?

By the year 2000, five billion of the six billion people on earth will be non-White (Baker, 1977). In the United States, projections based on current demographic trends and immigration indicate that the Hispanic population is expected to more than double, from 14.5 million in the mid-1980s to 37 million in 2030, nearly equal to the Black population. The Asian population will more than quadruple during this same period, from 3.5 to 17 million. Overall, non-Hispanic Whites will constitute 69% of the total U.S. population in 2030 (Bouvier, cited in Select Committee, 1985).

About half of all immigrants to the United States since 1930 have been women; two thirds have been women and children (Department of Labor, cited in Select Committee, 1985). In the United States, the average age is 31 for Whites, 25 for Blacks, and 22 for Hispanics (Jacobson, 1986).

In the United States, there are two times as many White poor as non-White poor. In the mid-1970s, almost 5 million poor Whites lived in America's central cities (Selakovich, 1978). Based upon government guidelines for income level needed to maintain an adequate standard of living, the poverty rates for minority children were as follows in 1980: 46.2% for Black children; 38.7% for Hispanic children; and 33% for Native American children (Bureau of the Census, cited in Select Committee, 1985).

Data from the Bureau of Labor Statistics indicates that in the late 1980s, 25% of U.S. workers were college graduates. Among White workers, 26% are college graduates; among Blacks, 15%; and among Hispanics, 13%. For about 40% of the workforce, formal education ended with graduation from high school. High school dropout rates are estimated to be 40% among Hispanics, 23% among Blacks, and 8% among Whites (cited in Yancey, 1988).

In the mid-1980s, 22 of the 26 largest U.S. school systems had enrollments that were at least 50% minority (Fernández, cited in Select Committee, 1985). More than 25% of Hispanic students attend schools with minority enrollments of 90 to 100% (National Council of La Raza, cited in Select Committee, 1985).

## Summary

Multicultural education—an essential part of schooling in a culturally diverse society—aims to prepare students for dealing with the realities of life in a pluralistic nation. It involves recognition of the role of societal, school, social, and cultural elements in the instructional process, as well as the creation of educational environments sensitive to the academic, social, and learning needs of all students. Integrative and interdisciplinary, multicultural education fosters the students' academic, social, and personal development.

This concept of multicultural education emphasizes the interrelationship of process and content. The one represents the substance of curriculum and instruction; the other, the contexts and processes involved in its transmission. Without addressing both dimensions, any specific approach teachers select is incomplete and inadequate. To deal with content alone ignores the "hidden curriculum" enacted in classrooms on a daily basis; to overlook the "intended curriculum" denies the subject matter that is the focal point of classroom life.

This view of multicultural education is based upon several assumptions. It presumes the cultural diversity of our society and the need to serve all students in the schools equally. It recognizes that multicultural education is for all students, that it is synonymous with effective teaching and educational reform. Finally, it recognizes the influence of social and cultural factors on teaching and learning, and the importance of teachers and their classroom interaction with students.

Multicultural education has two primary goals: (a) development of students' knowledge, skills, and attitudes necessary for living in culturally diverse environments and (b) the application by educators of insights regarding the impact of sociocultural factors on teaching and learning to maximize the academic achievement and personal and social development of students. Required teacher competencies are related to classroom processes, curriculum development, instructional materials, bilingualism, adaptation, and home and community involvement.

Finally, multicultural education is relevant for all teachers and all students. To implement its concepts and perspectives with just a few overlooks the essential relationship between multicultural education and effective educational practice in all classrooms, regardless of how homogeneous or heterogeneous they may seem.

# References

American Association of Colleges for Teacher Education. (1973). No one model American. *The Journal of Teacher Education, XXIV*(4), 264–265.

Baker, G. C. (1977). Multicultural imperatives for curriculum development in teacher education. *Journal of Research and Development in Education, 11*(1), 70–83.

Baker, G. C. (1979). Policy issues in multicultural education in the United States. *Journal of Negro Education, XLVIII*(3), 253–266.

Baker, G. C. (1983). *Planning and organizing for multicultural instruction.* Reading, MA: Addison-Wesley Publishing Co.

Banks, J. A. (1979). Shaping the future of multicultural education. *Journal of Negro Education, XLVIII*(3), 237–252.

Baptiste, M. L., & Baptiste, H. P., Jr. (1980). Competencies toward multiculturalism. In H. P. Baptiste, Jr. & M. L. Baptiste (Eds.), *Multicultural teacher education: Preparing educators to provide educational equity* (pp. 44–72). Washington, DC: American Association of Colleges for Teacher Education.

Brown, P. R., & Haycock, K. (1984). *Excellence for whom?* Oakland, CA: The Achievement Council.

Etlin, M. (1988). To teach them all is to know them all. *NEA Today, 6*(10), 10–11.

Frazier, L. (1977). The multicultural facet of education. *Journal of Research and Development in Education, 11*(1), 10–16.

Gibson, M. A. (1984). Approaches to multicultural education in the United States: Some concepts and assumptions. *Anthropology and Education Quarterly, 15*, 94–119.

Gollnick, D. M., & Chinn, P. C. (1986). *Multicultural education in a pluralistic society* (2nd ed.). Columbus, OH: Merrill.

Grant, C. A. (1977). The mediator of culture: A teacher role revisited. *Journal of Research and Development in Education, 11*(1), 102–117.

Grant C. A. (1978). Education that is multicultural—Isn't that what we mean? *Journal of Teacher Education, XXIX*(5), 45–48.

Higgins, P. J., & Moses, Y. T. (1981). Introduction. In Y. T. Moses & P. J. Higgins (Eds.), *Anthropology and multicultural education: Classroom applications* (pp. iii–xiii). (Publication 83-1). Athens, GA: The University of Georgia.

Jacobson, R. L. (1986, March 19). PCB's and other thoughts: A Hodgkinson potpourri. *The Chronicle of Higher Education, XXXII*(3), 29.

James, R. L. (1978). Multicultural education: NCATE standard rationale. *Journal of Teacher Education, XXIX*(1), 13–20.

Lee, M. K. (1983). Multiculturalism: Educational perspectives for the 1980's. *Education, 103*(4), 405–409.

McGroarty, M. (1986). Educator's response to sociocultural diversity: Implications for practice. *Beyond language: Social and cultural factors in schooling language minority students* (pp. 299–334). Los Angeles: Evaluation, Dissemination and Assessment Center, California State University—Los Angeles.

National Council for Accreditation of Teacher Education. (1986). *Standards, procedures, policies for the accreditation of professional teacher education units.* Washington, DC: Author.

Pacheco, A. (1977). Cultural pluralism: A philosophical analysis. *Journal of Teacher Education, XXVIII*(3), 16–20.

Payne, C. (1983). Multicultural education: A natural way to teach. *Contemporary Education, 54*(2), 98–104.

*Planning for multicultural education as a part of school improvement.* Sacramento: California State Department of Education.

Selakovich, D. (1978). The learning style of poor whites. In L. Morris (Ed.), *Extracting learning styles from social/cultural diversity: Studies of five American minorities* (pp. 55–68). Norman, OK: Southwest Teacher Corps Network.

Select Committee on Children, Youth, and Families. (1985). *Melting pot: Fact or fiction? A fact sheet.* Washington, DC: U.S. House of Representatives.

Shulman, L. (1986). Paradigms and research programs in the study of teaching: A contemporary perspective. In M. C. Wittrock (Ed.), *Handbook of research on teaching, 3rd ed.* (pp. 3–36). New York: Macmillan.

Sleeter, C. E., & Grant, C. A. (1988). *Making choices for multicultural education.* Columbus, OH: Merrill.

Stubbs, M. (1976). *Language, schools and classrooms.* London: Methuen.

Suzuki, R. H. (1984). Curriculum transformation for multicultural education. *Education and Urban Society, 16*(3), 294–322.

U.S. Commission on Civil Rights. (1973). *Teachers and students. Report V: Mexican-American education study.* Washington, DC: U.S. Government Printing Office.

Webb, K. S. (1983). On multicultural education—how to begin: A practical response to the NCATE guidelines. *Contemporary Education, 54*(2), 93–97.

Yancey, M. (1988, September 3). One in four U.S. workers graduated from college. *Enterprise-Record* (Chico, CA), p. 5C.

# 2

# Culture: The Classroom Connection

*Culture is a double-ended nexus with an individual at one end and the social group at the other.*

*Nelson Brooks (1979, p. 43)*

French politician Edouard Herriot once observed that "culture is what remains when one has forgotten everything else." In many respects he was right, for much of what is culture influences our lives in ways beyond our awareness at a conscious level. In his classic works on the subject, Hall (1959, 1969) used terms such as "silent language" and "hidden dimension" to describe various aspects of culture. Cultural influences are pervasive, and their impact on the educational process is significant.

In this chapter, the concept of culture is examined from various perspectives. Key concepts such as ethnicity, race, racism, prejudice, assimilation, and cultural pluralism also are explored. Finally, the connection between culture and the classroom is discussed. Sociocultural factors are manifested overtly and covertly through perceptions, attitudes, language, communication styles, and patterns of thinking, teaching, and learning. In combination with school and societal factors, they exert powerful influences upon the academic performance of students.

After completing this chapter, you will be able to

1. Define *culture* and describe its characteristics.
2. Define key concepts necessary for basic cultural understanding.
3. Explore different views on cultural diversity in the United States.
4. Recognize the influence of sociocultural factors on the teaching and learning process.
5. Assess explanations used to account for group variations in school achievement.

## Nature and Components of Culture

To anthropologists, the term *culture* refers to the complex processes of human social interaction and symbolic communication. It is "a *dynamic, creative,* and *continuous process* including behaviors, values, and substance *learned* and *shared* by people that guides them in their *struggle for survival* and gives meaning to their lives" (Arvizu, Snyder, & Espinosa, 1980, p. 5). Culture provides security to group members, but it also can adapt to change. Cultural influences sometimes are obvious and visible, as in certain actions and speech patterns; in other cases, they are almost "invisible," as in patterns of thinking, feeling, and perceiving.

Although definitions of culture are as diverse as they are numerous, anthropologists agree on certain basic points (Mukhopadhyay, 1985). First, they share the view that culture is created collectively by humans and consists of interrelated components: material artifacts (e.g., technology, shelter, transportation); social and behavioral patterns (e.g., social, economic and political organization); and mental products (e.g., conceptual systems, rules for action, values and goals). Second, they agree that culture is a universal, human phenomenon that is cumulative, integrated, pervasive, and psychologically real. As Mukhopadhyay (1985) observes, "It structures how we actually *experience* reality" (p. 19).

Many common perceptions of culture capture only pieces of the concept, such as arts and artifacts, behaviors, social structure, language, history, technology, and symbols. Culture is more than mere objects or material goods, items that can be bought, sold, and exchanged. It defies compilation in a "laundry list" of traits and facts. Because it is shared and learned, culture goes beyond an individual's genetic heritage. Nor would it suffice to limit the concept of culture to the ideal and romantic heritage of a people (as expressed in music, dance, and celebrations) or to the "cultured" class associated with knowledge of the arts, literature, and manners (Arvizu et al., 1980; Cross Cultural Resource Center, 1979).

### The Different Faces of Culture

Culture has different faces, some highly visible, others hidden from view. In anthropology, important distinctions are made between ideal and real culture, implicit and explicit culture (Arvizu et al., 1980). *Ideal* culture refers to what people say they believe or how they think they should behave. Aspects of ideal culture frequently are expressed in proverbs, stories, myths, sayings, and jokes. These may contrast sharply with the *real* culture, which is how individuals actually behave in specific situations. This is one reason descriptions of group "cultural traits" often seem idealized or stereotypic. Not surprisingly, knowledge of actual cultural patterns within a local community often provides greater insight about how individuals behave in real situations than do idealized cultural descriptions.

It is equally important to realize that some elements of culture operate at a conscious level of awareness, whereas others do not. *Implicit* (covert) culture includes elements hidden or taken for granted to the extent that they are not easily observable or consciously recognized by individuals. Values, attitudes, fears, assumptions, and religious beliefs are common elements of implicit culture. *Explicit* (overt) culture, on the other hand, is visible and can be described verbally. It includes styles of dress and housing, speech, tools, and concrete behaviors. In the classroom, teachers are aware of differences in how students dress for school and whether they speak with an "accent." They are much less likely to be aware of values and attitudes students hold, and in some instances, they may not be cognizant of their own.

Anthropologists also distinguish insider (emic) and outsider (etic) views of culture (Arvizu et al., 1980). The *insider* view is the perspective individuals have of their own culture. Members of a cultural group possess in-depth knowledge, common understandings of what is significant, and perceptions based upon a shared conceptual foundation. A group's history and literary heritage provide insider views of the culture in which they were created. In approaching other cultures, however, individuals take an *outsider* view, a comparative perspective grounded in familiar knowledge, attitudes, and perceptions.

How do various cultural elements appear to an outsider? The following passage by Miner (1979) describes in a tongue-in-cheek way how Nacirema concern with dental hygiene might be interpreted by an outsider:

> The Nacirema have an almost pathological horror of and fascination with the mouth, the condition of which is believed to have a supernatural influence on all social relationships. Were it not for the rituals of the mouth, they believe that their teeth would fall out, their gums bleed, their jaws shrink, their friends desert them, and their lovers reject them. They also believe that a strong relationship exists between oral and moral characteristics. For example, there is a ritual ablution of the mouth for children which is supposed to improve their moral fiber. (p. 175)

In reading this passage, did you recognize that Nacirema stands for Americans? If not, you are a "true insider" of American culture.

## Cultural Identity

As Adler (1977) observes, every culture has its own internal coherence, integrity, and logic. Each is an intertwined system of values, attitudes, beliefs, and norms that give meaning and significance to both individual and collective identity. To varying degrees, all persons are culturally bound and conditioned. Within a particular culture, they derive a sense of identity and belonging, a guide for behavior.

An individual's cultural identity is based upon a number of traits and values related to national or ethnic origin, family, religion, gender, age, occupation, socioeconomic level, language, geographical region, residence (e.g., rural, suburban, or urban), and exceptionality (Gollnick & Chinn, 1986). It is determined in large part by the interaction of these primary elements and the degree to which individuals identify with different subcultures. *Subcultures* are cultural groups whose members share some political and social institutions, as well as certain distinctive cultural patterns, that are not generally a part of the culture common to the larger society. Figure 2–1 illustrates how different elements contribute to an individual's cultural identity and how individuals differ in the emphasis they place on the subcultures to which they belong. For example, even though both persons represented in Figure 2–1 are middle-class, Catholic, Italian-American women who live in New York City, one identifies strongly with her ethnic and religious subcultures, whereas the other identifies most strongly with the female subculture.

According to Garza and Lipton (1982), an individual's cultural environment affects the range of stimuli and experiences to which the person is exposed. It also influences the repertoire of responses available in a given situation and the likelihood that the individual will act or behave in a particular way. Chicanos, for example, experience multiple cultural influences. Some influences certainly exert a greater effect than others, but all contribute to the Chicano "cultural equation":

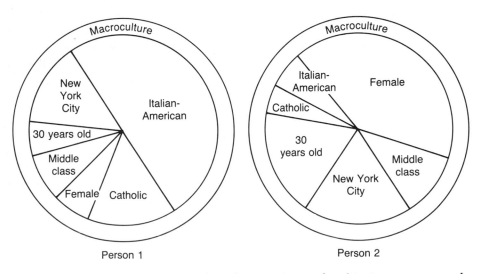

**Figure 2–1** Cultural identity is based on one's membership in numerous subcultures.

**Source:** D. M. Gollnick and P. C. Chinn, *Multicultural Education in a Pluralistic Society* (2nd ed.) © 1986 by Merrill. Reprinted with permission.

Everyone is multicultural to varying degrees, yet unique in terms of specific cultural characteristics.

Everyone is multicultural to varying degrees, yet unique in terms of specific cultural characteristics.

Chicano = Mexican influence + Anglo influence + unique Chicano influence + influences from other cultures (Garza & Lipton, p. 422).

Whenever different cultures are in contact, ongoing processes such as acculturation and change are likely to operate. In addition, variations within subcultural groups (e.g., socioeconomic status, gender, age, region, religion), and the interactions between them, further fragment the cultural environment individuals experience (Laosa, 1977). Such variation at the individual level helps to explain why many of the issues that confront educators in culturally diverse societies are so complex and multifaceted: "Everyone is multicultural to varying degrees with [the] specific cultural characteristics of each individual being unique" (Garza & Lipton, 1982, p. 422).

## Cross-Cultural Awareness

Piaget and Weil are credited with being among the first to study children's development of concepts related to foreign people and countries (Saunders, 1982). Working with children 5 to 10 years of age, they concluded that such concepts are developed early in life and become increasingly sophisticated as children pass through various stages of development. In Stage 1 (egocentric stage), the focus is on oneself as the center of the world. In Stage 2 (sociocentric stage), the focus is on one's own group as the center of attention. Stage 3 is marked by reciprocity and the realization that "one's people are foreigners in other countries, foreigners are not foreign at home and that they too have feelings about belonging to their homeland" (Saunders, p. 114).

Cross-cultural awareness is a primary objective of education that is multicultural, but it is a difficult goal to attain. As Hanvey (1979) observes, it is relatively simple to gain some knowledge of other cultures; it is considerably more difficult to comprehend and appreciate the human capacity for creating cultures and the profound differences in perspective and experience that result. When such differences are identified at a superficial level only, neither understanding nor true acceptance is likely.

Cross-cultural awareness has been described as operating at several levels, which are broadly defined according to competency in recognizing and interpreting cultural elements that contrast with one's own behaviors, values, and beliefs. The four levels defined by Hanvey (1979) are summarized in Table 2-1.

Observations at Levels I and II are likely to be characterized by varying degrees of ethnocentrism and stereotyping. *Ethnocentrism* is the belief that one's cultural ways are not only valid and superior to those of others but also universally applicable in evaluating and judging human behavior. All human beings have a natural tendency to be ethnocentric. For example, in many languages, speakers of the language are referred to as "the people"; all others are denoted as strangers, foreigners or outsiders (Alameda County School Department, 1969; Hanvey, 1979). Persons with strong ethnocentric attitudes and beliefs, especially when these are unconscious, may have considerable difficulty in appreciating and accepting the range of cultural differences that exists in human societies (Arvizu et al., 1980).

**Table 2-1**  Cross-Cultural Awareness

| Level | Information | Mode | Interpretation |
|-------|-------------|------|----------------|
| I | Awareness of superficial or very visible cultural traits; stereotypes | Tourism, textbooks, *National Geographic* | Unbelievable (i.e., exotic, bizarre) |
| II | Awareness of significant and subtle cultural traits that contrast markedly with one's own | Culture conflict situations | Unbelievable (i.e., frustrating, irrational) |
| III | Awareness of significant and subtle cultural traits that contrast markedly with one's own | Intellectual analysis | Believable cognitively |
| IV | Awareness of how another culture feels from the standpoint of the insider | Cultural immersion; living the culture | Believable because of subjective familiarity |

**Source:** R. G. Hanvey, *An attainable global perspective.* Copyright © 1976 by Center for Global Perspectives. Reprinted by permission of author.

*Stereotypes* can be defined as predispositions and general attitudes toward particular groups. They influence perceptions of and behaviors toward different groups and often reflect the information to which individuals have been exposed (Smith & Otero, 1982). Stereotypes, which can be positive or negative, affect how members regard their own group(s) as well as other groups.

When individuals' cross-cultural awareness reaches Level III and higher, they begin to develop a sense of cultural relativity. Striving to understand another people in terms of their own outlook and situation is at the heart of *cultural relativism*. It is an attitude that can best be described in the words of the Native American proverb, "Never judge another man until you have walked a mile in his moccasins" (Gollnick & Chinn, 1986, p. 13).

The process of acculturation is central to what happens at Level IV. In general terms, *acculturation* occurs when intercultural contact between different cultural groups influences the cultural patterns of one or both groups. At the individual level, the critical element is a person's acceptance and adoption of behaviors and values from the new culture. As Johnson (1977) explains, "To 'learn' a culture means to internalize often unstated assumptions and rules for appropriate behavior [and]. . .to interpret and predict the behavior of others as well as to appropriately respond" (p. 13).

Within the classroom environment, teachers may exhibit these various levels of cultural awareness. For example, teachers may observe that students from different cultural, ethnic, or social groups exhibit cultural traits that differ significantly from their own. If teachers' understanding of other cultural, ethnic, and social groups is limited, however, such behaviors and contexts will seem unrelated, and students' actions will be evaluated only from the teachers' cultural perspective (Levels I and II). On the other hand, teachers at Levels III and IV of cultural awareness know that culture affects how individuals act in virtually all aspects of their life, and that its influence is reflected in language, nonverbal communication, behavior, and values. Such teachers recognize, for example, that nonverbal behaviors are not identical across cultures; that children from many Mexican-American, Native American, Punjabi, and Afro-American homes are taught different rules governing eye contact. They realize that such behaviors are cultural traits, and understand how to interpret the meaning of what they observe.

Level III teachers cognitively accept that many behaviors learned in one's own culture are arbitrary and not universally shared. Level IV individuals have moved one step further and begun to acculturate to other cultures; for them, strangeness gives way to greater insight and familiarity. Teachers should strive to develop their cultural awareness to Levels III and IV. For most, Level III is a practical and attainable goal, conducive to implementing an educational program that is multicultural. Ideally, most teachers will also achieve some aspects of Level IV awareness.

## Cultural Diversity in the Classroom

Depending in part on their background, preparation, and personality, teachers approach cultural diversity in the classroom with a wide range of emotions and attitudes. That the potential for cultural conflict exists when teachers and students do not share the same beliefs, values, and behaviors is a reality in all classrooms. Gay (1981) has identified two other realities of human interaction that are relevant to cultural diversity in the classroom:

1. *Classroom conflict cannot be entirely eliminated.* This holds true whether the students are culturally, ethnically, or socially homogeneous or heterogeneous. What is essential is knowing how to minimize and redirect conflict when it occurs.

2. *Points of potential conflict can be identified.* With knowledge of cultural differences and satisfactory observation skills, teachers can recognize at least some of the values, attitudes, and behavioral patterns that may give rise to classroom conflict. Once identified, these can be addressed in such a way as to enhance rather than impede the instructional process.

What, then, can teachers do to enhance their effectiveness in culturally pluralistic settings? First, they need to develop an awareness of culture in themselves, both as individuals and as teachers. This usually is a prerequisite to acceptance of the reality and validity of cultural differences, a first step in dealing with diversity in the classroom (Arvizu et al., 1980; McGroarty, 1986; Saville-Troike, 1978). Second, teachers need to develop an awareness of culture as it is manifested in their students, both as individuals and members of different cultural groups. To understand how culture influences what happens in their classrooms, teachers must have "local cultural knowledge about a group's history, economic circumstances, religions and social organizations, socialization practices, conceptualization of social competence and language uses" (McGroarty, 1986, p. 315). Third, teachers need to know which sociocultural factors influence the teaching and learning process and how they do so. Teachers who develop their cultural knowledge and insights will be prepared to devise effective strategies for working with all students, whatever their backgrounds and capabilities.

## Key Cultural Concepts

Because certain cultural concepts have important implications for multicultural education, teachers should clearly understand and be able to critically evaluate these concepts. In this section, attention is focused on the nature and characteristics of several concepts teachers are likely to encounter. Related research useful in programmatic assessment and curriculum development also is discussed.

### Ethnicity

*Ethnicity*, a dynamic and complex concept, refers to how members of a group perceive themselves and how, in turn, they are perceived by others. Ethnicity is defined on the basis of national origin, religion, and/or race (Gordon, 1964). Attributes associated with ethnicity include (a) a group image and sense of identity derived from contemporary cultural patterns (e.g., values, behaviors, beliefs, language) and a sense of history; (b) shared political and economic interests; and (c) membership that is involuntary, although individual identification with the group may be optional (Appleton, 1983; Banks, 1981). The extent to which individuals identify with a particular ethnic group varies considerably; many have two or more ethnic identities. When ethnic identification is strong, individuals maintain and manifest ethnic group values, beliefs, behaviors, perspectives, language, culture, and ways of thinking.

Many Americans strongly identify with specific ethnic groups (e.g., Afro-Americans, Spanish Americans, Vietnamese-Americans), whereas for others, identification with any single ethnic group is not especially significant. Such individuals may think of themselves as "strictly" American. Nationwide, when people are asked to indicate ethnic or ancestry group, the most frequently reported groups (single and multiple combined) are as follows: English (50 million), German (49 million), Irish (40 million), Afro-American (21 million), French (13 million), Italian (12 million), Scottish (10 million), Polish (8 million), Mexican (8 million), Native American (7 million), and Dutch (6 million). Next in rank order (from 4 to 1 million) are Swedish, Norwegian, Russian, Spanish/Hispanic, Czech, Hungarian, Welsh, Danish, Puerto Rican, and Portuguese (Bureau of the Census, 1983).

Gordon (1964) suggests that ethnicity—based on race, religion, and national origin—interacts with social class to produce differential patterns of identification and behavior. He illustrates this relationship as follows:

> With a person of the same social class but of a different ethnic group, one shares behavioral similarities but not a sense of peoplehood. With those of the same ethnic group but a different social class, one shares the sense of peoplehood but not behavioral similarities. The only group which meets both of these criteria are people of the same ethnic *and* same social class. (Gordon, 1964, p. 53)

It follows that students from the same ethnic group at various socioeconomic levels would be expected to differ in ways that are significant, as would those from different ethnic groups within the same socioeconomic level. Gender similarly interacts with ethnicity and social class.

Each individual simultaneously belongs to an ethnic group(s), socioeconomic class, and gender. Each also constructs a personal reality, which may be influenced and constrained by a person's ethnicity, class, or gender (Grant & Sleeter, 1986). Teachers must understand that each student brings to the classroom a personal reality that represents a complex, dynamic, and unique blend resulting from the interaction of many characteristics.

## Race

*Race* refers to the way a group of people defines itself or is defined by others as being different from other human groups because of assumed innate physical characteristics (Ogbu, 1978). It was originally an anthropological concept used to classify people according to physical characteristics such as skin and eye color and the size and shape of the head, eyes, ears, lips, and nose (Bennett, 1986). Historically, several arbitrary racial classification systems have been developed; these vary in the number and definition of major racial types. Moreover, the view of race that prevails in the United States, although shared by some other societies, is not universal. In many countries, those in Latin America, for example, social characteristics (e.g., status, income, education) rather than physical attributes are often emphasized in establishing racial identity. As Cortes and Campbell (1979) stated, "Racial categorization in the U.S. essentially reflects biological heritage and physical appearance, [whereas] racial categorization in Latin America reflects a broad spectrum of influencing factors" (p.8). Because the Latin American concept of race is based upon a wide range of social factors, changes in individual's wealth, language, residency, occupation, and education can influence their racial classification.

In their discussion of race, Gollnick and Chinn (1986) make several important points. First, despite the movement of large numbers of people from one geographical region to another and the incidence of intermarriage across groups, the concept of race today still has a powerful social meaning. Second, as a concept, race contributes few insights to cultural understanding. Cultural groups defined by nationality, geography, language, and religion seldom correspond with racial categories—at least not to the extent necessary to provide culturally relevant information. Hence, racial identity, in and of itself, does not reveal an individual's nationality, language, or religion. In most countries, for example, many religious and linguistic groups are comprised of members from diverse racial groups. Third, efforts to characterize the population of the United States in government and institutional documents and reports based on combinations of major racial, ethnic, and/or linguistic categories tend to perpetuate existing confusion regarding race and ethnicity. The proverbial apples and oranges are mixed when individuals are asked to define themselves in terms of categories that are not mutually exclusive (e.g., White, Hispanic, or Jewish; an individual could belong to all three of these categories).

## Racism

Two key beliefs undergird the concept of *racism*. One is the belief that the inherited physical attributes of a racial group strongly influence social behavior as well as psychological and intellectual characteristics; in other words, that these latter characteristics are genetic *and* distributed differently among racial groups. The other essential belief is that some racial groups are inherently superior and others are inherently inferior (Bennett, 1986; Banton, 1982). Behaviors and actions based upon these two beliefs are referred to as racism.

A crucial condition contributing to racism is an unequal power relationship between majority and minority groups in society (Gollnick & Chinn, 1986). Racism is practiced when this differential power structure is perpetuated through a society's public and private institutions. Its manifestations can be overt and subtle. In the United States, historically, racism in the form of social prejudice and discrimination has been directed toward Afro-Americans, Mexican-Americans, Puerto Ricans, Asian-Americans, Native Americans, and others. At one time, attempts were made to "prove" that immigrants from eastern and southern Europe were racially and intellectually inferior to those from northern and western Europe. In a study on "American intelligence" conducted in 1923, the researcher identified what he considered to be "conclusive proof that 'representatives of the Alpine and Mediterranean races are intellectually inferior to the representatives of the Nordic race' " (Tyack, 1974, p. 205). This interpretation was later disavowed by the researcher himself.

## Prejudice

In the dictionary, *prejudice* is defined as a negative opinion based upon inadequate knowledge; one type of prejudice is "hatred or dislike directed against a racial, religious, or national group" (Flexner, 1983, p. 714). Kehoe (1984) has synthesized research findings related to prejudice that he believes to be of special interest to teachers. Understanding what is known about prejudice can help teachers respond to many issues in today's classrooms. How can teachers deal with group differences without promoting negative attitudes, stereotypes, and ethnocentrism? How can they respond to differences in prevailing attitudes toward different ethnic groups, attitudes that are positive toward some groups and negative toward others?

The findings Kehoe (1984) has compiled indicate the following:

- There appear to be no inherent racial differences in temperament.
- Prejudice and stereotypes are learned, generally within family and school settings, and frequently without conscious intent. They are not innate.
- Individuals generally do not realize how prejudiced they actually are.
- Individuals prejudiced against members of one ethnic group are likely to be prejudiced against others.
- Prejudice is a poor predictor of discriminatory behavior.
- There is considerable agreement within a society about specific stereotypes assigned to particular groups.
- As a group becomes more distinctive in character, a consensus develops regarding stereotypes associated with that group.
- Individuals expressing antagonistic attitudes toward an ethnic group believe that it has many objectionable qualities.
- The more limited individuals' contact and experience with an ethnic group, the less strongly held and important are their stereotypes about that group. However, stereotypes are not always the result of direct contact; they are also strongly influenced by the social climate in general.
- Individuals not in direct competition with minority group members tend to be less prejudiced toward them.
- Stereotypes resist change. Over extended periods of time, however, changes in established social and economic conditions—especially those that modify relations among groups—can alter stereotypes.
- The beliefs of individuals about their own ethnic group tend to be similar to but more positive than the beliefs of those outside the group.

## Ethnicity and American Pluralism

Many theories have been developed to explain the dynamics of ethnic groups and their place in American society. Educators' beliefs about the place of ethnic groups and the role of schooling in society directly influence their views on curriculum, methods, classroom organization, and other aspects of the educational system. Positions taken on issues related to cultural diversity and pluralism often reflect the assumptions embodied in these theories. For example, opinions about the role of languages other than English in the public schools, the use of ethnic content in the curriculum, and the role of parents in educational decision making often are unconsciously grounded in underlying beliefs about the nature of American society.

Each of the theories described in this section provides only a partial explanation of the social processes observed in American society. To date, no single theory has been proposed that can fully explain the complexity of group interactions and their outcomes in this society. The intent here is to summarize critical elements in the most popular theories and to provide examples of their relationship to educational policy and practice.

## Assimilation Theory

The *assimilation* theory has been described as a "theory of conformity to the majority" (Appleton, 1983, p. 29). It assumes that ethnic minority groups will increasingly adapt to the dominant culture. Over time, according to this theory, ethnic groups will cease to exist as separate entities as their distinctive values, attitudes, and behaviors are replaced by those of the dominant culture (Gordon, 1964).

For assimilation to occur in the fullest sense, it must be both cultural and structural (Appleton, 1983; Gordon, 1964). At the cultural level, minority individuals must adopt the behaviors, values, beliefs, and lifestyle of the dominant culture. A transition is made from one culture to another, with acquisition of the cultural accoutrements that accompany membership in the dominant group. To be fully assimilated, however, individuals must be able to participate fully in the social, political, and economic institutions and organizations of mainstream society. For members of some groups, participation and incorporation into these social systems comes easily; for others, social barriers such as discrimination and racism limit access. As a result, achieving cultural assimilation does not necessarily guarantee structural assimilation. The latter is contingent upon the dominant group's acceptance of members of the minority group's desire to assimilate (Appleton, 1983).

In the United States, assimilation has been synonymous with conformity to a cultural tradition in which English institutions, language, and cultural patterns are viewed as the standard (Gordon, 1964). This is not a recent development. In 1909, a prominent educator referred to immigrants from southern and eastern Europe as follows:

> Everywhere these people tend to settle in groups or settlements, and to set up here their national manners, customs, and observances. Our task is to break up these groups or settlements, to assimilate and amalgamate these people as a part of our American race, and to implant in their children, so far as can be done, the Anglo-Saxon conception of righteousness, law and order, and popular government, and to awaken in them a reverence for our democratic institutions and for those things in our national life which we as a people hold to be of abiding worth. (Cubberly, cited in Gordon, 1964, p. 98)

To those who espouse assimilation in matters of educational policy and practice, "linguistic and cultural diversity are seen as a threat to social cohesion" (Cummins, 1981, p. 21). For assimilation to take place and unity to be maintained, the argument goes, cultural diversity must give way to the primacy of the dominant culture. Appleton (1983) describes how this is translated into school policy. First, conformity to a single cultural orientation is reflected in and promoted by the curricular content, instructional processes, and organizational structures of schools. Second, different ethnic perspectives, languages, and cultures are devalued; they are not considered conducive to attaining educational goals. Programs such as ethnic studies and bilingual education generally are not endorsed and supported by proponents of an assimilationist position.

As a theory, assimilation has been found wanting in its capacity to account for ethnic group experiences in American society (Appleton, 1983). Although many groups have moved toward conformity, others have retained varying degrees of ethnic identity and cohesiveness. For some, cultural assimilation has not automatically resulted in structural assimilation. Hence, the patterns of acceptance and integration at various levels within the social structure have not been comparable for all ethnic groups. Nor has the desire to assimilate been equally strong among all groups. Individual and group reactions to the loss of cultural elements associated with the assimilation process vary, as do perceptions about whether assimilation will bring political, social, and economic benefits for group members.

## Amalgamation (Melting Pot Theory)

The *amalgamation* theory—better known as the melting pot theory—posits the emergence of a unique new culture from an amalgam of cultures in contact with each other (Appleton, 1983). Ideally, this new culture incorporates only the "best," the most desirable, features of each component culture. Early proponents of amalgamation envisioned an emerging American culture that combined European influences and, in time, elements from other ethnic groups (e.g., Afro-Americans, Native Americans).

The problem with this theory is that American society is more analogous to a mosaic, in which individual elements remain distinct, than to a melting pot, in which they lose their individual identity. Although there has been a superficial blending of diverse cultural influences in architectural styles, food, and celebrations, cultural blending of more substantial elements is difficult to identify (Appleton, 1983). In addition, for amalgamation to occur, cultural groups—majority and minority alike—must be willing to relinquish elements of their own culture while adopting those of others, and to fully share power and status within the society. To the extent predicted by the amalgamation theory, this has not been the case in the United States.

As Appleton (1983) observes, if amalgamation had taken place, educational policy and practice would view the role of schooling as one of inculcating the new culture, drawing attention to the composite whole as the sum total of the desirable attributes of all contributory groups. In reality, however, schooling in the United States has placed relatively little emphasis upon valuing the qualities and unique contributions of different groups; by and large, schooling has promoted acculturation into and conformity with the dominant culture. In addition, the United States has not experienced the conditions characteristic of societies in which amalgamation has actually occurred: geographic isolation of the society from other societies; extended contact among groups within the society over time; and limited numbers of diverse groups. Thus, although some amalgamation does take place in pluralistic societies like the United States, "manifestations of assimilation and cultural pluralism are much more common" (Appleton, 1983, p. 32).

## Cultural Pluralism Theory

According to the theory of *cultural pluralism*, each of the diverse groups that coexist within American society maintains a culturally distinct identity. Appleton (1983) describes two basic forms of this theory. In the classical version, group autonomy depends upon maintenance of rigid group boundaries. This separation minimizes the influence of society at large over group members, especially for relatively small and geographically isolated groups (e.g., Amish, Hutterites, Hasidic Jews, and some Native-American groups). In the modified version of the cultural pluralism theory, groups continue to retain elements of their own culture as members take on aspects of the majority culture (making very modest contributions to its changing character in the process). Individuals interact with and adapt to the majority culture but also maintain a separate identity. What emerges has often been described as "hyphenated" Americans (e.g., Cuban-Americans, Chinese-Americans).

The implications of the classical theory of cultural pluralism for schools are significantly different from those of the modified theory. When group maintenance and support are of primary concern, communities respond with schools comprised primarily of students and staff from the same ethnic group. Emphasis is on community control, native language instruction, and a curriculum strong in ethnic studies. When, on the other hand, the goal is to achieve more of a "balance" between the common culture and ethnic attachments, similarities as well as differences are integrated and highlighted. The curriculum focuses upon the national identity and interests while at the same time valuing cultural diversity and pluralistic perspectives (i.e., multicultural education). This approach tends to emphasize integration of students and staff, equal educational opportunity, and a curriculum sensitive to individual and group needs.

According to Appleton (1983), the modified cultural pluralism theory is the most popular cultural theory in the United States today and, of those presented here, best represents what has transpired in American society. It recognizes assimilation and pluralism as ongoing processes, provides for accommodation of cultural diversity in public education, and regards interaction among individuals from different groups as positive. Even within the context of this theory, however, conflicts regarding the goals of cultural pluralism and the nature of government policy with respect to ethnic diversity are not resolved.

## Culture-Education Interrelationship

The influence of social and cultural factors on education has been investigated in recent years, particularly as it relates to (a) variations in the educational achievement of students with similar linguistic, ethnic, and socioeconomic backgrounds and (b) the conditions under which students from different groups experience success or failure in school settings.

### School and Societal Contexts

In his analysis of scholarship on minority education, Cortes (1986) described societal and school factors that influence the education of minority students. *Societal factors* include those forces from the world outside the school that affect areas such as school priorities, student self-concept, teacher perceptions, and educational reform. *School factors* focus on internal dynamics and include teacher expectations and behavior, curriculum, school organization, counseling, assessment, and similar elements. Cortes (1986) developed the model presented in Table 2–2 to summarize how these factors relate to the educational process as a whole. Societal and school contexts are represented as highly complex, interrelated, and interactive entities.

As institutions, schools operate within a larger society, which has powerful and dynamic forces that affect teachers and students directly and indirectly. This "societal curriculum" consists of nonschool elements (e.g., family; community, religious, and social institutions; mass media; ethnicity; socioeconomic status; attitudes) that greatly influence components of the educational process at the school level—specifically, input, instruction, and student characteristics. Within the school context, these societal elements create the setting in which students are to learn, define the process by which they will be taught, and determine the content they are supposed to master. They also influence the attitudes, expectations, skills, perceptions, and motivation students bring to the task, as well as those of the educators who interact with them. In the final analysis, academic achievement, language proficiency, and other educational outcomes reflect the influence of a multiplicity of societal and school factors and their interaction over time. (See Chapter 8 for additional discussion of the societal curriculum and its impact on education.)

The interaction of culture and context is an important concept for educators dealing with sociocultural diversity. As McGroarty (1986) notes, "The notion that culture and context, both of them dynamic and subject to change over time, affect educational outcomes is a powerful one" (p. 301). From this perspective, two points become self-evident. First, attempts to understand the relationship of sociocultural factors to the educational process must take into account specific school and societal contexts. Second, in the search for explanations of differential academic outcomes and educational experiences, it is necessary to look beyond single factors such as language, class, racism, prejudice, or cultural conflict (Cor-

**Table 2–2**  School and Society

| *Societal Context: The Societal Curriculum* | |
|---|---|
| Family | Community |
| Institutions | Mass media |
| Heritage | Culture/ethnicity |
| Language | Educational level |
| Attitudes | Perceptions |
| Socioeconomic status | |
| Other sociocultural factors | |

| *School Context: The School Educational Process* | | |
|---|---|---|
| *Educational Factors* | *Instructional Elements* | *Student Qualities* |
| Theoretical rationale | Goals | Academic skill and knowledge |
| Underlying assumptions | Objectives | Language proficiency and attitudes |
| Administrative knowledge | Curriculum design | Prosocial skills |
| Fiscal/material/ district policies | Staff development | Life goals |
| Teacher knowledge skills attitudes expectations | Parental involvement | Health/nutrition |
| | Evaluation plan | Motivation |
| | Placement | Sociocultural attributes |
| | Counseling | Self-image |
| | Methodology | |
| | Textbooks/materials | |

| *Outcomes* |
|---|
| Academic achievement |
| Language proficiency |
| Prosocial skills |
| Self-image |
| Other cognitive/affective skills |

**Source:** C. E. Cortes, "The Education of Language Minority Students: A Contextual Interaction Model." In *Beyond Language: Social and Cultural Factors in Schooling Language Minority Students.* Copyright © 1986 by California State Department of Education [Evaluation, Dissemination and Assessment Center]. Reprinted by permission.

tes, 1986). At present, no single factor appears to adequately explain differences in educational outcomes among groups.

## Differential Academic Achievement

In the United States, as in many other countries, cultural groups differ in terms of overall educational achievement. Explaining the influence of cultural differences on educational achievement and experiences is not a trivial matter because the solutions proposed to address the situation are clearly contingent upon assumptions made in accounting for the observed variance. Sue and Padilla (1986) have examined four common explanations for the academic underachievement of some minority groups. These are presented in Table 2–3.

For obvious reasons, the *genetic inferiority* explanation is the most destructive and negative. It denies the potential of those identified as "genetically inferior," a list that over the years has included Afro-Americans, Chinese, Hispanics, Native Americans, Jews, Italians, Greeks, Yugoslavs, and others (Sue & Padilla, 1986). Equally detrimental is the notion that nothing can be done to significantly alter the situation because the variations are attributable to heredity.

Those who adopt a *cultural deficit* interpretation ascribe deficiencies to the minority culture itself and to the consequences of racism and discrimination. From an educational perspective, what is perhaps most critical about this explanation is the perception that minority group members are "lacking the cultural competence necessary for dealing with academic and social challenges" (Sue & Padilla, 1986, p. 44). Hence, programs developed from this point of view are compensatory in

**Table 2–3**  Perspectives On Differential Academic Achievement Among Cultural Groups

| Perspective | Attribution of Blame | Primary Solutions |
|---|---|---|
| *Genetic Inferiority* (minorities fail to do well because they are genetically inferior) | The groups themselves, not society | No solutions are possible because little can be done to change heredity |
| *Cultural Deficit* (minorities fail to do well because their culture is viewed as deficient) | The groups themselves, as well as social prejudice and discrimination | Train minorities to be less deficient and eliminate prejudice and discrimination |
| *Cultural Mismatch* (minorities fail to achieve because their cultural traits are incompatible with those in the U.S. mainstream) | No one; cultures just happen to be different | Change groups so that they can participate in the mainstream, but also change schools in order to better accommodate and ameliorate the mismatch |
| *Contextual Interaction* (minorities fail to achieve because of unfortunate interaction of many factors) | No one factor, group, or institution; outcomes produced through the interaction of many factors such as circumstances, cultural values, etc. | Change one or more of the factors or the context to alter interactions and thereby change the outcomes |

**Source:** Adapted from S. Sue and A. Padilla, "Ethnic Minority Issues in the United States: Challenges for the Educational System." In *Beyond Language: Social and Cultural Factors in Schooling Language Minority Students.* Copyright © 1986 by California State Department of Education [Evaluation, Dissemination and Assessment Center]. Reprinted by permission.

approach, making it incumbent upon members of the target group to change in order to improve their status.

In contrast to the cultural deficit view, the *cultural mismatch* explanation assumes that cultures are inherently different but not necessarily superior or inferior to each other. Educational underachievement in some minority groups is thought to occur because their cultural traits do not match those of the dominant culture as reflected in schools. Thus, the educational performance of minority groups is related to the degree of congruence between group values and traits and those of the educational system: the better the match, the greater the likelihood that the level of academic achievement will be high. Efforts to improve the performance of minority students are aimed at increasing the congruence between schools and ethnic cultures; changes in both usually are necessary.

According to the *contextual interaction* explanation, educational achievement is a function of the interaction between two cultural orientations—the cultural values of the larger society and those of the ethnic minority group. The behaviors, beliefs, and perceptions of individuals within specific minority groups are influenced by the more-or-less fortuitous social, economic, and political circumstances they experience. Over time, the changes in beliefs and behaviors that result from cross-cultural interaction may enhance or impede achievement: "The key to understanding achievement is the change that occurs because of the interaction between different cultures" (Sue & Padilla, 1986, p.49). For example, a group's experiences with discriminatory occupational patterns can enhance or devalue the importance of education depending on how the group responds.

This focus on interaction provides a more holistic, comprehensive, and dynamic view than do other explanations of differential academic achievement. Sue and Padilla point out that within this framework, solutions to educational problems require changes in the larger society as well as in the schools, ethnic groups, and communities. At the societal level, dealing with differential achievement patterns requires the elimination of discrimination and prejudice and greater appreciation for cultural diversity. At the local level, significant improvement in educational outcomes for minority-group students depends on school reform (e.g., changes in teacher attitudes toward minority students; adaptations in curriculum and instruction; use of culturally unbiased testing procedures) *and* the adaptation by ethnic minority students and groups to the institutions of American society.

In the final analysis, explanations of differences in academic achievement patterns among cultural groups are not easily separated from sociocultural considerations. Recent scholarship rejects a single cause approach in explaining group differences. The need to examine relationships between sociocultural factors (e.g., language, socioeconomic status, racism, prejudice, cultural conflict) and the societal and school contexts in which they appear is becoming increasingly evident (Cortes, 1986; Sue & Padilla, 1986). The reason is simple: Factors that explain differences in one setting have often been found to lack explanatory power in another. Take language as an example. The performance of students with limited English proficiency is influenced by learner variables such as socioeconomic status, language attitudes, and school orientation. The mere presence of a native language other than English does not explain the observed variability in school performance within and across different language-minority groups.

## Did You Know That. . .?

In the 1980 U.S. census, about 83% of the population reported identification with at least one ethnic group; 6% reported "American" or "United States"; and 10% did not report any ancestry. Nationwide, 52% identified a single specific ethnic origin; 31% reported multiple ethnic attachments. Regionally, multiple ethnic attachments were most common in the north-central and western states and least common in the South (Bureau of Census, 1983).

At the national level, the United States is becoming increasingly multiethnic. Between 1970 and 1980, the census indicated that the population as a whole increased by 11.4%. During this period, however, the number of Asian-Americans doubled; the number of Afro-Americans increased by 17%; Hispanic-Americans, by 61%; and Native Americans, by 71% (Cortes, 1982).

Among Americans generally categorized as "Anglo" (White, non-Hispanic), English-origin is not the most common ancestry. About 29% of all Americans claim some German ancestry; 24% are at least part Irish; and 22% are of English ancestry. Statistically, individuals of "British" origin outnumber other ethnic groups only when those with Scottish or Welsh ancestry are included (Cortes, 1982).

Schools have not been as successful in furthering upward socioeconomic mobility as they were once thought to be. As late as 1950, more than 80% of New York and New Jersey workers of Italian, Irish, and Slavic ancestry were employed in unskilled or semiskilled occupations. In 1973, less than 3% of the corporation directors in Chicago were Polish, Italian, Latin, or Afro-Americans, although these ethnic groups represented 34% of the metropolitan population (Appleton, 1983).

By the year 2000, one out of every three Americans will be non-White. As a group, they will represent a wider range of socioeconomic levels than ever before (Hodgkinson, cited in Polen, 1987). In the mid-1980s, minority students accounted for 30% of the student population in U.S. public schools; children come to school speaking over 100 languages and dialects. Many also come to school poor: 40% of the poor in the United States are children, and 24% of U.S. children live below the poverty line. By age 18, 60% live with only one parent, and 90% of those live in households headed by women ("And justice for all," 1987).

## Summary

All human beings are part of a cultural process so dynamic, complex, and pervasive that much of its impact on individual lives operates below the level of conscious awareness. Culture has been described as creative and continuous, learned and shared. It is at the same time real and ideal, implicit and explicit. Culture influences what individuals think, believe, and value as well as how they behave, communicate, and perceive themselves and others. As members of diverse subcultures, individuals create a cultural identity uniquely their own.

To deal most effectively with cultural diversity, teachers must develop an understanding of the ways various cultural elements affect the teaching and learning process. This requires cultural awareness and knowledge both of one's own culture and that of one's students. It also requires a thorough grasp of the multifaceted connection between culture and the classroom. Key concepts associated with cultural awareness include ethnocentrism, stereotyping, cultural relativism, and acculturation.

Teachers also need to understand the dynamics of ethnicity in American society. Educational policy and practice are influenced by views on social processes. Popular theories used to explain the outcomes of group interaction focus upon assimilation, amalgamation, and cultural pluralism.

Over the years, several explanations have been proposed to account for observed differences in academic performance among ethnic minority groups. The four most common explanations account for differential performance as the result of genetic inferiority, cultural deficiencies, cultural incongruities, or the dynamics of interaction between culture and context. The latter—the contextual interaction model—provides a vision of the school context embedded within the larger context of society as a whole. The interaction of sociocultural factors in these settings influences the educational process and sets the stage for what transpires in the classroom.

## References

Adler, P. S. (1977). Beyond cultural identity: Reflections upon cultural and multicultural man. In R. W. Brislin (Ed.), *Culture learning* (pp. 24–41). Honolulu: University of Hawaii Press.

Alameda County School Department. (1969). *Cultural understanding.* Hayward, CA: Author.

Appleton, N. (1983). *Cultural pluralism in education.* New York: Longman.

Arvizu, S. F., Snyder, W. A., & Espinosa, P. T. (1980, June). *Demystifying the concept of culture: Theoretical and conceptual tools.* Bilingual Education Paper Series, *3*(11). Los Angeles: Evaluation, Dissemination and Assessment Center, California State University—Los Angeles.

Banks, J.A. (1981). *Multiethnic education: Theory and practice.* Boston: Allyn and Bacon.

Banton, M. (1982). Racism: Institutional dimensions. In G. R. Smith & G. Otero, *Teaching about cultural awareness.* Denver: University of Denver, Center for Teaching International Relations.

Bennett, C. I. (1986). *Comprehensive multicultural education.* Boston: Allyn and Bacon.

Brooks, N. (1979). Parameters of culture. In H. P. Baptiste, Jr. and M. L. Baptiste (Eds.), *Developing the multicultural process in classroom instruction* (pp. 42–47). Washington, DC: University Press of America.

Bureau of Census. (1983, April). *1980 census of the population: Ancestry of the population by state* (1980 Supplementary Report). Washington, DC: U.S. Department of Commerce.

Cortes, C. E. (1982). Ethnic groups and the American dream(s). *Social Education, 46*(6), 401–403.

Cortes, C. E. (1986). The education of language minority students: A contextual interaction model. *Beyond language: Social and cultural factors in schooling language minority students* (pp. 3–33). Los Angeles: Evaluation, Dissemination and Assessment Center, California State University—Los Angeles.

Cortes, C. E., & Campbell, L. G. (1979). *Race and ethnicity in the history of the Americas: A filmic approach.* Latin American Studies Program, Film Series No. 4. Riverside: University of California.

Cross Cultural Resource Center (1979). Culture posters. Sacramento: California State University, Department of Anthropology.

Cummins, J. (1981). The role of primary language development in promoting educational success for language minority students. *Schooling and language minority students: A theoretical framework* (pp. 51–79). Los Angeles: Evaluation, Dissemination and Assessment Center, California State University—Los Angeles.

Flexner, S. B. (Ed.). (1983). *The Random House dictionary.* New York: Random House.

Garza, R. T., & Lipton, J. P. (1982). Theoretical perspectives on Chicano personality development. *Hispanic Journal of Behavioral Sciences, 4*(4), 407–432.

Gay, G. (1981). Interactions in culturally pluralistic classrooms. In J. A. Banks (Ed.), *Education in the 80's: Multiethnic education* (pp. 42–52). Washington, DC: National Education Association.

Gollnick, D. M., & Chinn, P. C. (1986). *Multicultural education in a pluralistic society* (2nd ed.). Columbus, OH: Merrill.

Gordon, M. M. (1964). *Assimilation in American life.* New York: Oxford University Press.

Grant, C. A., & Sleeter, C. E. (1986, April). *Race, class and gender in educational research: An argument for integrative analysis.* Paper presented at the meeting of the American Educational Research Association, San Francisco, CA.

Hall, E. T. (1959). *The silent language.* Greenwich, CT: Fawcett Publications.

Hall, E. T. (1969). *The hidden dimension.* Garden City, NY: Anchor Books, Doubleday & Company, Inc.

Hanvey, R. G. (1979). Cross-cultural awareness. In E. C. Smith, & L. F. Luce (Eds.), *Toward internationalism* (pp. 46–56). Rowley, MA: Newbury House. (Reprinted from *An attainable global perspective*, 1976; New York: Center for Global Perspectives).

Johnson, N. B. (1977). On the relationship of anthropology to multicultural teaching and learning. *Journal of Teacher Education, XXVIII*(3), 10–15.

And justice for all. (1987, June 29). *San Francisco Examiner.* (Article on National Education Association Report).

Kehoe, J. (1984). *Achieving cultural diversity in Canadian schools.* Cornwall, Ontario: Vesta Publications.

Laosa, L. M. (1977). Multicultural education—how psychology can contribute. *Journal of Teacher Education, XXVIII*(3), 26–30.

McGroarty, M. (1986). Educator's response to sociocultural diversity: Implications for practice. *Beyond language: Social and cultural factors in schooling language minority students* (pp. 299–334). Los Angeles: Evaluation, Dissemination and Assessment Center, California State University—Los Angeles.

Miner, H. M. (1979). Body ritual among the Nacirema. In E. C. Smith & L. F. Luce (Eds.), *Toward internationalism* (pp. 173–178). Rowley, MA: Newbury House. (Reprinted from *American Anthropologist,* American Anthropological Association; 1956, *58*(3)).

Mukhopadhyay, C. C. (1985). Teaching cultural awareness through simulations: Bafa Bafa. In H. Hernandez & C. C. Mukhopadhyay, *Integrating multicultural perspectives into teacher education* (pp. 100–104). Chico: California State University.

Ogbu, J. U., (1978). *Minority education and caste.* New York: Academic Press.

Polen, D. (1987). Notes from article by Harold Hodgkinson entitled "All one system: Demographics of education—kindergarten through graduate school." *Phi Delta Kappa Newsletter,* Chico State University Chapter 88.

Saunders, M. (1982). *Multicultural teaching.* London: McGraw-Hill.

Saville-Troike, M. (1978). *A guide to culture in the classroom.* Rosslyn, VA: National Clearinghouse for Bilingual Education.

Smith, G. R., & Otero, G. (1982). *Teaching about cultural awareness.* Denver: University of Denver, Center for Teaching International Relations.

Sue, S., & Padilla, A. (1986). Ethnic minority issues in the United States: Challenges for the educational system. *Beyond language: Social and cultural factors in schooling language minority students* (pp. 35–72). Los Angeles: Evaluation, Dissemination and Assessment Center, California State University—Los Angeles.

Tyack, D. B. (1974). *The one best system.* Cambridge, MA: Harvard University Press.

C H A P T E R

# 3

# Classroom Processes: The Hidden Curriculum

*Classrooms. . .are places in which the formal and informal [social] systems continually intertwine.*

*Frederick Erickson (1986, p. 128)*

Teaching activities occur in a variety of contexts—individual, group, class, school, and community. Within the classroom context, two interrelated curricula are negotiated by teachers and students. The first, to some extent, is invisible, hidden in the interactional, social, management, and organizational aspects of classroom life. The second is visible, transmitted through the formal structure of academic content, planned learning experiences, and instructional materials. Together, these curricula establish "what schools are for, what purposes they are designed to accomplish" (Shulman, 1986, p. 8).

The intent in this chapter is to examine the "hidden" curriculum, that is, the behaviors of teachers and students and the transactions between them. As teachers and students enact the formal curriculum, they must also deal with the informal curriculum, which gives direction and structure to classroom life. Teachers must recognize the effect of the elements of this curriculum, and be able to manipulate them, if they are to create an environment that enhances all students' academic performance and self-concept. This cannot be accomplished by focusing on the formal curriculum of content and materials alone.

After completing this chapter, you will be able to

1. Identify processes that determine what transpires in the classroom.
2. Examine interaction, social context, management, and organization as dimensions of culturally pluralistic classrooms.
3. Consider the sociocultural facet of classroom processes.
4. Recognize the influence of classroom processes on outcomes.
5. Develop instructionally sound and culturally responsive strategies for enhancing student performance and self-esteem.

## Classrooms: A Closer Look

Classrooms are socially and culturally organized learning environments (Erickson, 1986). Teaching in pluralistic classrooms demands heightened awareness of the classroom processes that constitute the hidden or invisible curriculum. The more visible the dynamics of these processes become, the more significant their role in multicultural education.

Descriptions of the hidden curriculum focus on the tacit values, attitudes, and unofficial rules of behavior pupils must learn to participate and succeed in school (Eggleston, 1977; Stubbs, 1976). These central components embody the real knowledge transmitted by the hidden curriculum and reflect the patterns of communication and participation deemed appropriate by both teachers and peers. From a sociological perspective, the initiation of students into this curriculum has been associated with developing skills related to the following (Eggleston, 1977):

- Living in "crowds"
- Using time productively
- Accepting assessment by others (teachers and peers)
- Competing to gain praise, rewards, and esteem from teachers and peers
- Living in a hierarchical society and being differentiated in process
- Collaborating with other students to control the speed and progress of what is presented by the teacher in the official curriculum
- Sharing the norms and meanings for participation in classroom activities

To better understand the interplay of these competencies and others within the instructional environment, teachers need to examine in detail the interactional, social, management, and organizational dimensions of the classroom. They also need to recognize how ethnicity, socioeconomic status, gender, and other aspects of culture influence and interact with classroom processes.

## Interactional Dimension

### Teacher Expectations

The relationship between teachers' perceptions of student academic ability, their expectations about how students will perform, and their interaction with individual students is very complex. Some studies support the view that teacher expectations affect outcomes such as student achievement, class participation, and social competence (Good, 1981; Wilkinson, 1981). However, other research has shown that not all teachers are "equally susceptible to the biasing effects of interpersonal expectations" (Rosenthal & Babad, 1985, p. 39).

According to Good (1981), an important contribution of research on teacher expectations has been the "identification of specific ways in which some teachers treat high and low students differently" (p. 416). These teacher behaviors and communication patterns include the following (Good, 1981):

- Location of student seating
- Amount of attention directed toward students (e.g., smiles, eye contact)
- Opportunities given to students to participate
- Amount of wait-time allowed for student responses
- Frequency of clues, prompts, and follow-up questions in problem situations
- Amount of praise and criticism
- Frequency and detail of teacher feedback
- Amount of effort demanded and expectation of task completion
- Frequency and nature of interruptions

Low achievers are likely to experience more variations in teacher communication patterns than high achievers (Good, 1981). For example, some teachers criticize or disparage low achievers' incorrect responses, whereas others reward answers that are marginal or even wrong. Such wide variation in teacher behaviors tends to make low achievers uncertain and tentative. By junior high school, some less successful students become passive learners, reluctant to ask for clarification and assistance from teachers.

Sociocultural factors seem to be associated with teacher expectations and differential treatment of students. As Gollnick and Chinn (1986) point out, students from lower socioeconomic backgrounds tend to be overrepresented among the ranks of low achievers. They cite research showing that teacher expectations—as evidenced through patterns of ability grouping and classroom interaction—also may be influenced by nonacademic student characteristics such as dress, language, cleanliness, and family stability. Generally, such influences tend to work to the disadvantage of students from lower socioeconomic backgrounds and those speaking minority languages or nonstandard dialects of English. It is also no secret that

The relationship between teacher expectations and student learning outcomes is complex.

disproportionate numbers of students from certain ethnic minority groups are underachievers. These realities underscore the need for teachers to examine their own expectations and whether these affect how they interact with students in the classroom.

In summary, then, teacher expectations and perceptions of students are important facets of classroom interaction. These expectations and perceptions often are influenced by the sociocultural characteristics of students and may be reflected in differential treatment of students by teachers in ways that continue, even promote, inequalities of information and skills that exist when children start school (Cazden, 1986). In addition, cultural differences often affect how students respond to and interact with teachers and other students within schools. The effects of cultural differences on classroom interactions and patterns of differential treatment are discussed further in the next two sections.

## Effects of Cultural Differences

Given the pervasiveness of culture in determining patterns of social behavior in general, the existence of variations among cultural groups in the formal and

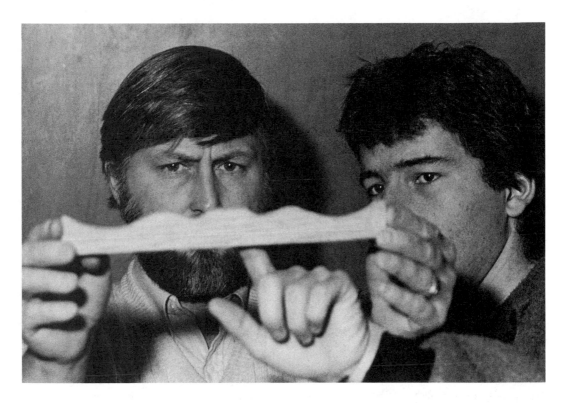

The interaction between teachers and students is at the heart of the educational process in most classrooms.

informal rules governing interaction between individuals should come as no surprise. Such variation may cause problems for students when classroom interactional patterns are not consistent or compatible with those that children experience in their homes and community. In some cases, stylistic variations in what, how, and when something is said may be minor and remain largely unnoticed by teachers and students alike. In other cases, however, cultural variations in interactional patterns can interfere with learning, particularly in the primary grades. Hymes (1981) observed that the differences typically recognized by school and community are the most visible symbols of culture, the most stereotypic of conventions. The less visible aspects of culture associated with everyday etiquette and interaction and with expressions of rights, obligations, values, and aspirations through norms of communication are commonly overlooked. "One can honor cultural pride on the walls of a room yet inhibit learning within them" by overlooking and not accommodating to such cultural differences in communication and interpersonal interactions (Hymes, 1981, p. 59).

In Native-American communities, for example, the classroom learning environment may be structured according to rules not shared by the community to which the students belong. Such discontinuities between school and community can affect teachers and students alike and may be reflected in classroom (a) *tempo* (e.g., how quickly teacher and students interact); (b) *management* (e.g., how teachers control and monitor behavior, what kinds of behaviors are used to intervene, how teachers define what constitutes paying attention, how that attention is focused, how much time is given for students to respond); (c) *organization* of students (e.g., whole class, small groups, group project, one-on-one with the teacher); and (d) *participation* (e.g., frequency of volunteering and responding, willingness to interrupt other speakers) (Mohatt and Erickson, 1981; Philips, 1983).

Especially critical in the Native-American communities observed by researchers were instructional demands that students respond competitively and individualistically. These appeared to violate norms within the culture emphasizing cooperative and group effort. Hence, sensitivity to the culture of Odawan students demands recognition of less obvious aspects of "interactional etiquette," such as avoiding direct commands and refraining from placing students in the "spotlight" (Mohatt & Erickson, 1981). On the Warm Springs Indian Reservation, Philips (1983) found that one-on-one contact between students and teachers or aides and the use of group projects and cooperative learning activities were most compatible with the interactional patterns of the students' culture.

In their interactions with students, teachers should aim to maintain the integrity of the home culture while respecting the demands of the school (Mehan, 1988). Bridges are built to incorporate cultural elements in ways that provide support for students as they learn to deal with the instructional patterns of the classroom. In the Kamehameha Early Education Program (KEEP), for example, classroom practices capitalize on the cognitive and linguistic abilities children bring to the classroom (Au & Jordan, 1981). This program begins with the storytelling approaches that the children experience in their own homes; then a gradual transition is made to the traditional school format of children reading texts and responding to questions posed by the teacher. Similar strategies for establishing links between home and school can work in many settings when teachers are familiar with prevailing cultural patterns.

Heath (1983) described how teachers in the Piedmont Carolinas developed knowledge of communication styles in different communities and used it in adapting the methods and materials related to language and literacy in the classroom. These teachers "constructed curricula from the world of the home to enable students to move to the curricular content of the school" (p. 340). Three strategies used by these teachers were (a) to use knowledge familiar to students to provide a foundation for classroom information; (b) to involve students in identifying and examining familiar ways of knowing and to help them translate these into the labels, concepts, and generalizations used in the school; and (c) to provide opportunities for students to explore how language is used to organize and express information.

As this discussion suggests, the classroom is a complex communicative environment. Classroom interaction has several important elements: communication between teachers and students and among peers; the construction of contexts and meanings; levels of student participation; and evaluation of student ability (Morine-Dershimer, 1985). The cultural background that students bring to the classroom can influence their interpretation of and response to each of these elements.

At the very heart of the educational process in most classrooms is communication between teacher and students. This communication influences students' ability to assimilate curricular content:

> The actual (as opposed to the intended) curriculum consists in the meanings enacted or realized by a particular teacher and class. In order to learn, students must use what they already know so as to give meaning to what the teacher presents to them. Speech makes available to reflection the processes by which they relate new knowledge to old. But this possibility depends on the social system, the communication system, which the teacher sets up. (National Institute of Education, 1974, p. 1)

## Patterns of Differential Treatment

Few would argue that the experiences of students in the same classroom can differ significantly. In one study, the researchers concluded that students "in the same classroom, with the same teacher, studying the same material were experiencing very different educational environments" (Sadker & Sadker, 1986, p. 513). They found, across a range of grade levels, subject areas, classroom settings, and student populations, that about one fourth of the students were silent and did not interact with the teacher at all. The majority of students interacted with the teacher only once during a class period; fewer than 10% of the students had three or more exchanges with the teacher. Such variations in teacher-student interactional patterns have been associated with gender, ethnicity, and achievement level. In many cases, these differences lie beyond the conscious awareness of teachers.

In a summary of research on gender differences in elementary classrooms, Lindow, Marrett, and Wilkinson (1985) reported general, though not universal, agreement that (a) teachers tend to interact more with boys than girls and (b) a significant proportion of the attention focused on boys is negative. The generally observed pattern is that boys are "more active and salient in classrooms" and receive "more of almost any kind of interaction with the teacher that may be measured," including criticism and praise and behavioral, procedural, and academic exchanges (Brophy, 1985, p. 120). This pattern is attributed more to gender role-related differences in student behaviors than to teacher intent, as the pattern is usually observed whether the teacher is male or female. It should also be noted that although boys as a group receive more teacher attention, high-achieving boys tend to receive more positive attention (e.g., approval, questions, detailed instructions, and active teaching attention) than low-achieving boys, who often receive negative feedback such as criticism and reprimands (Brophy & Good, cited in Sadker & Sadker, 1982).

Differential treatment of students by teachers also is related to ethnicity in some classrooms. One of the most frequently cited studies supporting this conclusion involved 429 classrooms in urban, suburban, and rural schools in California, New Mexico, and Texas. Major findings indicated that schools in the Southwest "are failing to involve Mexican American children as active participants in the classroom" (U.S. Commission on Civil Rights, 1973, p. 43). Other studies of interactions in interracial classrooms also have found differences in teachers' treatment of students and variations in student friendship patterns, although the results are less consistent than in the case of gender differences (Schwanke, 1980). In one study of elementary pupils in a multiethnic community, Morine-Dershimer (1985) found that pupils with higher academic status participated more frequently than others in class discussions and their comments were attended to more carefully by peers. In the classes observed, ethnic minority pupils had lower academic status; when they participated, their contributions to discussions received significantly less attention than those of other students.

It is clear that students experience different learning environments in the classroom, although the effects of these differences on educational outcomes and student self-concept have not been fully delineated. Some of the variation is accounted for by student and teacher characteristics. Other variations may result from culturally influenced patterns associated with ethnicity, language, socioeconomic status, and gender. Some differential treatment in classrooms is inevitable; in many situations, it is beneficial. Educators must be willing and able to determine whether differential treatment represents "helpful individualization, or detrimental bias" (Cazden, 1986, p. 447). The best way for individual teachers to do this is to be aware of and to monitor interactional patterns in their own classrooms.

## Monitoring of Interactions

Observations of interactional and discourse patterns in a classroom can clarify how individual students and groups of students respond to different teacher behaviors and how the teacher, in turn, reacts to their behavior. Based upon such observations, teachers can begin to identify behaviors they wish to target for modification and explore alternative strategies for doing so. When there appear to be culturally related differences in the interactional patterns expected in the classroom and those that students experience within their homes and/or community, additional observations in other settings may be appropriate.

Teachers who wish to monitor and examine their own patterns of interaction first need to determine the kind of interaction information they want to collect. They may want to concentrate their attention on one or more aspects of interaction mentioned earlier (e.g., treatment of boys and girls) or focus on other dimensions (e.g., questioning strategies; teacher feedback to student contributions).

Second, they must select an observation technique to help them to describe their interaction with students. Whatever the approach, it should provide useful and accurate information, and within the parameters given, be as simple to use and interpret as possible. Third, they must decide how to collect the information they need. There are a number of options available. Teachers working independently can record activities on audiotape or, with assistance, on videotape. Peer observations also can be used to enhance information obtained through self-monitoring. Colleagues can exchange observation visits as an alternative to the use of recordings.

Numerous approaches to monitoring classroom interactions have been developed. Among those designed for teacher use are approaches for examining interactions directed at boys and girls (Sadker & Sadker, 1982), language choice in bilingual settings (Legarreta-Marcaida, 1981), and verbal and nonverbal aspects of ethnicity (Longstreet, 1978). For more ambitious efforts, some of the ethnographic methods used by researchers are appropriate. Aspects of social relations that can be observed include the norms of interaction in home and school, the contexts in which bilingual children choose to use different languages, and the duration of teacher contacts with individual children and groups (Erickson, 1981; Heath, 1983). For most teachers, monitoring the quantity and quality of their interactions with students is a good place to start; this can be done by counting interactional behaviors and through notetaking.

**Frequency of Interaction**    A very general overview of classroom interaction can be obtained by the simple technique of determining frequencies of student-teacher interactions. Sadker and Sadker (1982) used such frequencies as numerical indicators of teacher attention directed at boys and girls. In this approach, the number of times a teacher elicits a response (e.g., asks a question, issues a directive) from male and female students is counted on several different occasions. The individual counts are adjusted to the same time period and then averaged. In this type of frequency monitoring, no record is kept of the comments themselves nor of the students involved (except for their gender).

Frequency monitoring can also be used to examine teacher interactions with students who differ along other dimensions such as ethnicity and socioeconomic status. It is suitable for monitoring specific teacher communication behaviors (e.g., questioning strategies, overt and covert corrections, praise, criticism, and feedback) and student interaction with peers. It can also be used to examine whether interaction is distributed evenly in different areas of the classroom (e.g., table groupings, front and back, center and sides). One foreign language teacher used this approach to analyze the proportion of Spanish and English spoken in classroom interactions and the functions for each language (e.g., routines, instructions, humor).

**Quality of Interaction**    Verbatim notes of specific facets of interaction can be used to describe the nature of discourse between teachers and students in greater detail. One primary grade teacher used this approach to examine the feedback given to pupils in small reading groups and to assess its influence on their participation. By keeping track of specific comments provided as feedback, he was able to determine which seemed to encourage and discourage pupil contributions and which were neutral. In bilingual classrooms, teachers have kept notes on use of each language for specific cognitive, affective, and management purposes (e.g., explaining, questioning, expressing feelings, disciplining). Such notes can provide a rough indication of the balance achieved in the use of both languages by function.

## Social Context Dimension

### Language Attitudes

Language attitudes—the feelings, beliefs, and values associated with one's own language and/or dialect and those spoken by others—influence perceptions regarding the social identity, status, and ability of the speakers of a given language (Ramirez, 1985). All speakers of English reveal a particular dialect or variety of the language. Chaika (1982) observes that regional dialects traditionally have symbolized allegiance to a region; conveyed positive, shared connotations associated with valued traits; and signaled social bonding within class and ethnic groups. Accents and dialectal variations, however, also can have negative connotations and in many societies are impediments to access to social, educational, and economic opportunity.

Attitudes and values attached to some facets of language (e.g., regional accent) are evident and widely acknowledged. These are often captured in humor and parodies. However, people rarely are aware of the depth of reactions to divergent language styles and the speakers who use them. "The ideal of linguistic democracy, in which the speech of every citizen is regarded with equal respect by all others, is perhaps the most unrealistic of all social ideals. Speech is one of the most effective instruments in existence for maintaining a given social order" (Christian, cited in Peñalosa, 1980, p. 183). *My Fair Lady* illustrates some of the language attitudes and the resulting social consequences to which Christian is alluding.

Sociolinguistic research has provided considerable insights about the nature, incidence, and implications of these attitudes. For example, many adults and children display well-defined evaluational reactions to spoken language (Lambert, Hodgson, Gardner, & Fillenbaum, 1972). In Canadian research, speakers of English and French were asked to evaluate the personality characteristics of individuals speaking both languages. The raters did not know that they were listening to the same individuals speak both languages. Ratings were more favorable when the individual spoke English than French; this was true whether the raters were French or English Canadians. Dialect surveys also have revealed hidden attitudes toward ethnicity, region, and gender—attributes that often are reflected in speech patterns (Chaika, 1982). Those who have grown up in families speaking certain varieties of English or other languages are likely to recall situations in which their ability and competence were equated, perhaps negatively, with features of their speech. In the United States, attitudes toward ethnic languages also appear to be influenced by the number of speakers residing in a given community. According to Kjolseth (1982), "The more locally irrelevant an ethnic language and culture is, the higher its social status, and the more viable it is locally, the lower its social status" (p. 7).

In general, those who achieve the highest degree of success in U.S. society tend to have the least accented speech (Gonzalez, cited in Peñalosa, 1980). The significance of this reality has not gone unnoticed among speakers of different varieties of English. Few television newscasters, for example, speak with a distinctive accent, and some have consciously eliminated certain regional characteristics from their speech. Although existing attitudes may change, achievement-oriented Chicanos have "traditionally made an effort to erase all traces of Spanish influence from their English" (Tovar, cited in Peñalosa, 1980, p. 191).

Language attitudes—both positive and negative—also operate within the classroom and can affect the teaching and learning process. Language plays a major role in establishing the social identity and relationships of teachers and students in the classroom. As Ramirez (1985) observed, the initial impressions teachers form about students are often based upon features of their speech. Once established, these views appear to remain relatively fixed and may influence initial assessments of student ability as well as teacher expectations. Moreover, negative teacher attitudes may reinforce similar student attitudes toward their own or others' nonstandard language use. Thus, students may be subjected to teacher and peer prejudice because of the dialect they speak (Hall & Guthrie, 1981).

Because of the prestige associated with standard English, many teachers accept the premise that equality of opportunity is impossible unless all English speakers can use standard English at the level required for high status jobs or professions. Those who accept this premise are faced with a dilemma, however. As Chaika (1982) observes, the speech of children and adolescents resembles that of the people with whom they identify. Black English, for example, is strongly valued by many Blacks as a symbol of intimacy and solidarity—it represents "intergroup distinctiveness from the white community" (Beebe, 1988, p. 65). Differences between Black English and standard English are constantly reinforced and, according to Beebe, apparently increasing among many Blacks. Students who do not identify with speakers of standard English are not likely to emulate their speech patterns. In addition, students who choose to use standard English must often confront peer pressure and accept corrections they may interpret as insulting to their own speech patterns and self-identity.

One approach reported to be effective with inner-city high school students is sociodrama. This technique can help students develop proficiency in standard English appropriate to various situations without relying on excessive use of grammar and pronunciation exercises (Chaika, 1982). In a typical sociodrama exercise, students are asked to assume roles and act out situations in which they would be using standard forms of the language (e.g., interviewing for a job, complaining to someone in authority, and speaking in a style suitable for the assigned role). A similar technique can be applied to writing (e.g., newspaper articles) and used in combination with group work and peer editing.

## Student Status

Within the social environment of the classroom, the status of students is determined by and manifested in various ways (Cohen, 1986). At the elementary level, for example, academic status is determined largely by competence in reading and mathematics. Furthermore, students ranked high on reading ability in the minds of teachers and fellow students are generally also expected to do well in unrelated school tasks; conversely, those who are regarded as poor readers are not expected to do well. Peer status at all grade levels also is associated with other characteristics: individual traits (e.g., athletic ability, attractiveness, popularity) and societal distinctions related to class, race, ethnicity, exceptionality, and sex.

Cohen (1982) reported that in interracial schools, interactions are dominated by Whites when valued intellectual tasks are involved and that the participation and task engagement of minority students in school activities generally is less than that of Whites. Both patterns reflect and reinforce teacher and student expectations that minority students will be less competent and successful. Similar patterns have been observed for students clearly identifiable as members of minority groups. In the classroom, teachers must deal with multiple status characteristics. In combination, these interact and have a powerful effect on the nature and extent of participation in the classroom and on expectations for competence held by teachers and students. In general, the higher the status of students, the higher the expectations of them, and vice versa.

Teachers can modify expectations in interracial educational settings in several ways (Cohen, 1982). For example, teachers can influence expectations through positive evaluations of student competence. Because of their high status as evaluators, teachers—especially those from the same ethnic group as students—can affect how students see themselves in relation to others. The presence of individuals with different ethnic and cultural characteristics in positions of high status and authority (teachers, administrators) also can alter student perceptions. Finally, use of special norms (e.g., listening to peers, allowing all students to contribute) in cooperative group activities appears to promote equality of interaction.

## Instructional (Ability) Grouping

Several important generalizations have emerged from research on instructional or ability grouping. As defined by Findlay and Bryan (1975), *ability grouping* is the organization of classroom groups in a graded school according to age, grade level, and standing on measures of achievement or capability. It is not synonymous with the accepted and widespread practice of instructional grouping *within* classrooms. The following discussion is based largely on findings summarized by Hallinan (1984) and Findlay and Bryan (1975).

*The most commonly stated basis for instructional grouping is student ability.* The basic motivation is a desire to establish homogeneous groups, which are easier to teach. At the elementary level, pupils usually are placed in ability groups; at the secondary level, tracking into separate classes is the more typical pattern. The dominance of this pattern is such that heterogeneous ability groupings are rare. In actual practice, however, the assignment of students to tracks or ability groups depends, to a considerable extent, on factors other than the ability or academic achievement of students as individuals. Group assignments often are influenced by school and classroom characteristics such as achievement distribution and organizational and management considerations.

*Students in low groups generally have quantitatively fewer and qualitatively inferior opportunities to learn than those in higher levels.* In one study of secondary schools, for example, students in higher tracks spent 80% or more of their time involved in instruction (Oakes, cited in Grant & Sleeter, 1988). Instruction in these tracks was clear, varied, and focused on higher thinking skills and content necessary for college. Those in lower tracks, however, spent less of their time on instruction (67%), and did half as much homework as did students in high tracks. Instruction provided in lower tracks was characterized by considerable rote memorization and routine activities and emphasized basic education skills. As Mehan (1988) observes, education is differentially distributed across groups and tracks. During instruction, student behavior also varies according to track and ability level. In particular, more task-related interactions occur in higher ability groups than in lower groups, in which off-task behaviors are common.

*Significant differences in student social status exist both within and between different tracks and ability levels.* Because academic status contributes to the social status of students among peers, the hierarchy defined by grouping influences the social position of students within the classroom and school. It is not surprising that assignment to low-ability groups "carries a stigma that is generally more debilitating than relatively poor achievement in heterogeneous groups" (Findlay & Bryan, 1975, p. 20). In the United States, both socioeconomic status and ethnicity influence placement in tracks; in general, low-income and minority students are found in disproportionate numbers in lower groups and tracks and middle-income students in average and higher groups (Sleeter & Grant, 1988; Winn & Wilson, 1983). Research suggests that homogeneous grouping increases social-class differences, whereas heterogeneous grouping appears to reduce them (Findlay & Bryan, 1975).

*Instructional grouping usually hinders learning and academic achievement among students assigned to low groups.* This negative effect of grouping is most pronounced for low-ability groups. In these groups, students may be "restrained more by poor-quality instruction or amount of time spent off-task than by any limitations in ability to learn" (Hallinan, 1984, p. 236). Some students—particularly those from lower socioeconomic levels and members of minority groups—also may experience a lowering of self-esteem and changes in attitudes toward school when they are placed in low-ability groups (Winn & Wilson, 1983). Indeed, the only students for whom ability grouping appears to have any beneficial effects in terms of academic achievement are those placed in high-ability groups and tracks.

The potential negative consequences of grouping can be counteracted in several ways. First, teachers must provide constancy in the quality of instruction across levels (Hallinan, 1984). Accounting for the academic performance of individual students requires examination of the mode of instruction and learning climate within levels. To ameliorate many of the negative effects of grouping, students in low-ability groups must have access to quality instruction and "high-status knowledge" (i.e., the academic skills, content, attitudes, and experiences that characterize informed, educated, and productive members of society) (Hallinan, 1984; Nevi, 1987). Teachers also should avoid labeling, allow for mobility across groups, and consider status effects in assigning peer groups (Hallinan, 1984). Use of descriptive labels for groups should be avoided because it serves only to ascribe characteristics that may be inaccurate and damaging. Students should be reassigned to different groups if their learning rates, performance, and motivation change. The negative effects of status expectations on learning by low-ability and low-status students can be reduced by use of strategies such as cooperative learning and tutoring. Students also need to recognize (a) that each group contains students with differing qualities and abilities and (b) that group assignments are relative, subject to achievement distributions within each class. At the school level, alternative procedures for planned heterogeneous grouping can be explored (Findlay & Bryan, 1975).

In summary, tracking and ability grouping can have unintentional negative effects on the educational and career opportunities of students, as well as their social and emotional development. Teachers must recognize and make every effort to minimize the negative academic and social effects of grouping. The grouping of students for instructional purposes must contribute to the goals of helping students reach their full potential, as individuals and members of society, and of providing equality of educational opportunities. If implemented without sufficient concern for its potentially negative effects on some students, however, this widespread practice may result in more harm than good.

## Management Dimension

In today's classrooms, teachers are faced with an ever expanding spectrum of student needs and abilities. To respond effectively to this heterogeneity requires adaptations in how the total curriculum is implemented and the complementary use of teaching and behavior management techniques.

Hoover and Collier (1986) describe one approach used with minority and minority handicapped students that integrates classroom management and curricular adaptation. In this approach, adaptations are based on analysis of four basic elements individually and in relation to one another: (a) *content* (subject-specific knowledge, attitudes, and skills); (b) *instructional strategies* (teacher repertoires of instructional and management methods and techniques); (c) *instructional settings* (teaching contexts or groupings); and (d) *student behaviors* (individual abilities to manage and control learning and comportment in diverse situations, activities, and groups).

According to Hoover and Collier (1986), the interaction of these curricular elements has important consequences for classroom management, as outlined in Figure 3–1. For example, content may directly influence the selection of instructional strategy and setting; it is also influenced by student behaviors. Likewise, the choice of strategy affects setting and student behaviors, which in turn also influence each other. Suppose, for example, that individual students display disruptive behaviors

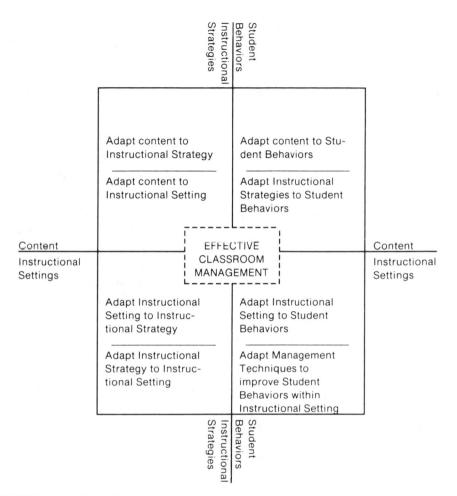

**FIGURE 3-1**  Model of classroom management based on interactions and adaptations of four basic elements: content, instructional strategies, instructional settings, and student behaviors.

**Source:** J. J. Hoover and C. Collier, *Classroom Management Through Curricular Adaptations.* Copyright 1986 © by Hamilton Publications. Reprinted by permission.

in small-group situations; with this type of student behavior, strategies maximizing active involvement for all group members are likely to be more effective than those requiring turn-taking. Because of the reciprocal interactions between curricular elements, learning or behavior problems usually are related to more than one element.

Although Hoover and Collier focus primarily on minority and minority handicapped students, their approach is applicable to other learners. The important point to remember is that adaptations in one element—content, setting, strategies, or student behaviors—are likely to have a reciprocal effect on other elements. Thus, changes in content may require concurrent accommodations in strategies or setting; changes in group size and composition may affect choice of strategy and student behavior.

Hoover and Collier (1986) describe specific teaching and behavior management techniques that are helpful in adapting curriculum to meet student needs. For adapting instructional techniques, they suggest the following:

- Provide alternate modes of response (oral rather than written; visual or graphic rather than verbal).
- Shorten assignments by abbreviating the task given or dividing more complex tasks into segments.
- Ensure that students experience success and develop self-confidence by initially assigning relatively easy tasks or assignments and then gradually increasing the level of difficulty as they progress.
- Incorporate student input in curricular planning in ways that promote students' sense of ownership in the process and decision-making skills.
- Let students choose among alternative activities and assignments.
- Negotiate verbal or written contracts with students to improve motivation and to clarify responsibilities (expectations, assignments, rewards).
- Modify the presentation of abstract concepts by using concrete learning activities, teaching the vocabulary required for cognitive academic tasks, and incorporating visual aids, objects and materials (manipulatives), and student experiences.
- Select written texts with an appropriate reading level in terms of complexity of vocabulary and concepts and/or provide first-language materials for limited-English-proficient students.
- Use clues or prompts to assist students working on assignments.
- Establish academic and behavioral expectations and communicate these clearly and concisely to students.

Hoover and Collier (1986) suggest complementing instructional adaptations with specific behavior management techniques. Of primary importance is positive reinforcement that provides feedback or rewards for appropriate responses and behavior in ways that are culturally and personally relevant. They also suggest using nonverbal signals and cues that do not draw attention to individual students (e.g., flicking lights on and off; ringing a bell) when classroom behavior becomes inappropriate. They caution that proximity (strategic positioning) and touch control, while widely used and often effective, are culturally sensitive forms of nonverbal communication. Teachers must remember that personal space is defined differently across cultures. Standing behind students to monitor behavior or within a certain distance can convey very different messages from those intended. Likewise, a gentle tap on the shoulder or head could violate accepted norms of interpersonal contact for some students. Teachers can decide to ignore certain behaviors to reduce the likelihood of confrontations over minor instances of misbehavior. Finally, student accountability and recognition of their responsibility for performance and actions should be promoted.

Hoover and Collier offer teachers using this approach the following advice: Make only those modifications that are indicated and be flexible, consistent, and persistent in trying different techniques.

# Organizational Dimension

Classroom organization refers to how teachers organize students for instruction— the social structure they create, the social relationships and academic outcomes they produce. Ames and Ames (1984) have described the structure of classrooms as competitive, cooperative and individualistic. Each structure is based on a different value orientation with its own way of evaluating the performance of individual students both in relation to instructional goals and in relation to other students. Within a competitive structure, achieving a goal or reward is related— implicitly or explicitly—to how other students perform, whereas in a cooperative structure students work with each other toward a common goal. By contrast, when the structure is individualistic, students work toward independent goals. Within these varied structures, students learn to interpret how they perform on academic tasks differently and attach different meanings to success and failure on academic tasks. Not surprisingly, how teachers structure the learning environment affects academic achievement, motivation, and instructional behavior.

In this section, competitive, cooperative and individualistic structures provide the framework for a discussion of classroom organization and its interaction with social and cultural factors (especially socioeconomic status and ethnicity). Then attention is focused on two strategies used in adapting organization in heterogeneous classrooms. These are cooperative learning and tutoring.

## Competitive, Cooperative and Individualistic Structures

**Competitive Structures**   Competition is a basic element in American culture: it has been described as the primary method used by Americans to motivate members of groups (Stewart, 1979). Most classrooms in the U.S. have a learning environment with a competitive structure, and given the value placed on individualism and achievement, many students respond well to competition as a motivating force.

There is evidence that within a competitive structure, student perceptions of their own ability and their feelings of personal satisfaction are related to how well they perform as compared to other children (Ames, 1984; Ames & Ames, 1984). When they succeed, children's assessment of their ability is high; when they fail, it is low. On the positive side, competition can enhance the social status and self-esteem of high-achieving learners. On the negative side, most studies suggest that the impact of competitive structures on motivation tends to be negative—

particularly for low-achieving children (Ball, 1984). Children learn to attribute success and failure primarily to ability, rather than effort, the nature of the task, or other factors: "We cannot help but speculate that declines in children's self-perceptions of their ability over the elementary school years, may, in part, be a consequence of the competitive nature of many classrooms and the increased emphasis placed on social comparison as children progress through school" (Ames & Ames, 1984, p. 45). In essence, children's affective reactions to success and failure in the competitively-structured classroom are closely related to perceptions of their own ability, their performance relative to other children, and their feelings of personal satisfaction.

Students whose value orientations differ are not as likely to respond to a competitive structure with the same enthusiasm as members of the dominant culture. Some researchers have even argued that the value orientations of some groups may interact with competitive classroom structures to produce "negative academic and social schooling outcomes" (Kagan, 1986, p. 268). Socioeconomic status and ethnicity are among the social and cultural factors which appear to influence social orientation. In some non-Western cultures, an intense attachment for family and community can preclude the incentive to excel over others (Stewart, 1979). Moreover, although the motivation to achieve varies across settings in different cultures, its relationship to socioeconomic status is strong; in the United States the effect of socioeconomic status on achievement motivation is larger than that attributed to ethnic differences (Ball, 1984; Cooper & Tom, 1984).

**Cooperative Structure**   Ames and Ames (1984) suggest that in a learning environment with a cooperative structure, children focus attention not only on  personal achievement, but also on group performance and individual effort toward the common goal. How high- and low-achieving students evaluate their own performance is considerably influenced—in a positive or negative direction—by the group's overall performance: "Social context is a potent factor in children's affective reactions to success and failure" (p. 45). Kagan (1986) has found that cooperatively oriented students perform better in cooperatively structured classrooms, although competitively oriented students seem to prefer competitively oriented classes.

At an interpersonal level, students appear to minimize perceptions of differences in ability and performance. Group interaction provides a way of challenging and changing expectations for competence based upon status characteristics (i.e, "agreed-upon social rankings") related to academic, peer, and societal characteristics such as race, social class, and sex (Cohen, 1986). These social rankings, which operate to the disadvantage of students assigned low status within the classroom are less likely to be reinforced within cooperative structures than in other organizational settings.

On the plus side, cooperation can have positive effects on academic achievement, intergroup relations, self-esteem, and social skills. Ethnic minority students generally show significantly greater academic gains in cooperative settings than in traditional classrooms; other students show equal or somewhat greater

Cooperation can have a positive influence on academic achievement, intergroup relations, self-esteem, and prosocial development.

gains. Although average and low achievers benefit most in learning environments with a cooperative structure, it is not at the expense of high achievers, whose performance is comparable to that in traditional classrooms (Kagan, 1986). The positive effects of cooperation on student achievement have been reported at elementary and secondary levels, in urban, suburban, and rural schools, among diverse populations, and across subject areas such as mathematics, language arts, social studies, and reading (Slavin, 1981). On the minus side, teachers are advised against using cooperative strategies in situations when group failure can "undermine the potentially positive effects of this noncompetitive structure" (Ames & Ames, 1984, 45).

**Individualistic Structure**   As described by Ames and Ames (1984), a noncompetitive individualistic structure is characterized by continuity of performance over time, self-improvement and task-orientation. Within this type of structure, children's success and failure on academic tasks is independent of others. Each student has an equal opportunity to achieve success when goals are based on their own performance, and progress on tasks is at their own rate. Mastery learning, for example, assumes that all students are capable of attaining acceptable levels of achievement. Proponents of mastery learning argue that this is especially critical for students who are not achieving academically (Bennett, 1986). However, as Ames (1984) points out, elements of an individual perspective (e.g., self-improvement, performance over time) can also be effectively incorporated within nonmastery approaches.

Ideally, an individualized structure creates an orientation in which effort is valued and students are attentive to the learning strategies they use to achieve success. Ames and Ames have found that students in individualistic structures tend to relate success or failure on tasks to their own performance over time. When this happens, students are less likely to view current performance as isolated from the effort they put forth to accomplish a task and their performance on related activities. Teacher perceptions are also affected by a task-oriented, individualistic structure, as teachers place greater emphasis on student performance in relation to specific goals and individual effort.

In summary, interpreting the effects of social structures is a complex aspect of classroom process. Research reveals that how classrooms are organized affects student learning, as individuals respond differently to the various structures teachers create. In essence, the structure of the learning environment—competitive, cooperative or individualistic—provides students with opportunities "to realize certain goals and not others by influencing student motivational processes and achievement patterns" (Ames, 1984, p. 204).

## Adapting Organization

 Although individual teachers may emphasize different structures, most are likely to use all three structures—competitive, cooperative and individualistic—in their classrooms at one time or another (Ball, 1984). Hence, from a practical standpoint, teachers need alternative strategies to adapt organization in heterogeneous classrooms. Cooperative learning and tutoring exemplify two of the many strategies teachers can use.

**Cooperative Learning**   As described by Kagan (1986) and Slavin (1981), cooperative learning methods generally have three features in common:

1.  The class is divided into small teams whose members are "positively interdependent" (i.e., the achievement of each team member contributes to the rewards of all).
2.  Task and reward structures also make individuals accountable for their own learning.
3.  Improvement over past performance contributes to the entire group's reward.

Kagan (1986) and Slavin (1981) described numerous specific cooperative learning approaches. All of them promote student interaction, interdependence, and cooperation. In one common approach, the teacher presents material to the entire class and then students assemble in heterogeneous teams of four or five members. Using worksheets, these *student teams-achievement divisions* (STAD) practice and master the information to be learned. Each student takes a quiz on the material individually. Team scores are determined by the extent to which each student improves over past performance. Individuals and teams demonstrating the greatest improvement are recognized. In the *teams-games-tournaments* (TGT) approach, a variation of the STAD approach, students play academic games with members of other teams whose past performance is similar to their own.

In the *jigsaw* approach, students are individually given information that they must master and "teach" to other team members. Teams have three to seven members (preferably five or six). Students are also given training to promote team building, communication, and leadership. Students are individually tested on their mastery of the material. In some cases, students are given information to be learned by the teacher; in other cases, they obtain it from textbooks, narrative materials, short stories, biographies, or other sources.

The *group investigation approach* requires students to accept considerable responsibility for deciding what they will learn and how they will organize themselves to master the material and communicate what they have learned to other class members. In this approach, students identify the topic to be investigated, organize into research groups, plan the learning task, prepare and present a final report and evaluate their efforts.

*Team-assisted individualization* combines features of cooperative and individualized learning. In this approach, group support is provided to assist students in completing individual learning modules. Another cooperative approach called *Finding out/descubrimiento* is designed specifically for use in bilingual classrooms. This method is organized around 170 mathematics and science activities in multiple-learning centers. Linguistically heterogeneous groups work cooperatively and interact to complete the activities.

**Tutoring**   In recent years, tutoring has gained prominence as a method that helps students—including those at risk of school failure—attain individual, academic goals. From a teacher perspective, it is especially important that the positive cognitive and affective effects of tutoring can be as significant for the tutors as for the tutees. When older students serve as tutors, the process often produces "achievement gains for the tutors as well as for the tutees" (Slavin, 1987, p. 113).

The positive role of tutoring in multicultural education has been well established with students across the spectrum of socioeconomic levels and ethnic backgrounds as well as those with learning disabilities (Bennett, 1986; Saunders, 1982). In a discussion about multicultural teaching in England, Saunders observed that cross-age tutoring enhances the identity and learning of children from minority groups. Advantages accrue to both tutor and tutee as basic skills are practiced and repeated, social interaction skills are fostered, and, in the case of bilingual

Cooperative learning methods are generally characterized by small teams, whose members are interdependent, and a task and reward structure that makes individuals accountable for their own learning.

students, language options are provided. Working in tandem, students can also share teaching responsibilities on a common learning task.

According to Jenkins and Jenkins (1987), research and experience suggest that the successful peer tutoring programs at the elementary and secondary levels are characterized by certain features. These include the following:

- Use of highly structured and carefully prescribed lesson format.

- Definition of objectives in terms of teachers' own classroom curricula and evaluations of student performance based upon those classroom materials.

- Careful selection of tutoring content by teachers and monitoring to ensure that students achieve mastery.

The positive cognitive and affective effects of peer tutoring can be as significant for tutors as tutees.

- Careful consideration of the frequency and duration of tutoring lessons.
- Provision of systematic training for tutors.
- Creation of a positive class climate and provision for active supervision.
- Measurement of student progress on a daily basis.

## From Process to Outcomes

The processes that occur in a school as a whole and in individual classrooms can and do influence educational outcomes significantly. Teachers know this from personal observation, and researchers have demonstrated that it is so (Erickson, 1986; Good & Brophy, 1986). School variables are important determinants of student achievement. Characteristics of student populations such as socioeconomic level and minority-group status are *not* sufficient to predict how students will actually perform. What transpires at the school level must be taken into account because differences among schools, as among teachers, significantly affect students and their achievement. Moreover, since the vast majority of the variation in student achievement—from 70 to 90%—actually occurs *within* schools, overall school effectiveness clearly is contingent upon effective teaching at the classroom level (Cohen, cited in Good & Brophy, 1986, p. 581).

Significant differences in pupil performance across classrooms at the elementary level have been observed among groups historically marked by persistent and disproportionate school failure. Although the probability that children from low-socioeconomic backgrounds and others at risk will underachieve in school is "powerfully influenced" by social processes and individual differences, their school performance also is subject to considerable influence by individual teachers (Erickson, 1986).

Unfortunately, "positive teacher influence on the achievement of children at risk seems to be the exception rather than the rule" (Erickson, 1986, p. 125). Compared to other developed countries, the United States does not fare as well as might be expected. For example, Erickson (1986) reported that the relationship between social class and school achievement is greater in the United States than in Italy, Sweden, Finland, Japan, and Flemish-speaking Belgium. Although teachers can have a significant impact on children at risk, the dramatic possibilities of their "powerful" positive influence are not being realized systematically in U.S. schools.

The situation just described need not continue. Knowledge of classroom processes holds considerable promise for helping teachers to be more effective. This is demonstrated by one study of schools in low-socioeconomic districts with predominantly White and Black student populations identified as high or low achieving on the basis of academic performance (cited in Good & Brophy, 1986). In this study, various classroom elements were assessed and associated with achievement level. In high-achieving schools, whether predominantly White or Black, the following features prevailed:

- Students spent most of their class time productively involved in instructional activities.
- Teachers believed that, with few exceptions, students were capable of mastering the content and expected them to do so.
- Teachers used reinforcement patterns that provided appropriate rewards and encouraged higher levels of achievement.
- Heterogeneous or flexible grouping procedures were implemented.

In contrast, the following characteristics were common in low-achieving schools:

- The quantity and quality of instruction varied considerably among classrooms (e.g., some teachers had managerial problems; in many classrooms, students engaged in limited productive, task-relevant work and academic interaction).
- Students considered to be less capable were "written off."

- Performance expectations were low.
- Teachers' reinforcement practices were variable and sometimes inappropriate.
- Grouping procedures often were used for management rather than instructional purposes and provided for little mobility among groups.

The major findings of this study thus illustrate how various aspects of classroom processes discussed earlier can contribute to educational outcomes, either positively or negatively.

The importance of classroom processes, especially teacher behaviors to student achievement, is further demonstrated by research examined by Brophy (1982). Teachers know that the characteristics and attributes of effective teaching defy easy description. "Effective" teachers are not "ordinary" teachers: they are more dedicated, better organized, and more efficient in classroom management. That students in their classrooms experience more academic success is the "cumulative result of daily planning, thorough preparation, and simple hard work" (Brophy, 1982, p. 529).

Based upon observations of typical teachers and students involved in routine classroom activities in inner-city schools, Brophy (1982) identified a set of teacher behaviors that consistently promotes student learning. These teacher behaviors are common elements in effective basic skills instruction; for many experienced teachers, Brophy's findings validate practices they have found to be successful in their own classrooms. They also attest to the fact that teachers make a difference.

The following questions focus attention on the attitudes and skills underlying the behaviors identified by Brophy. They can serve as an informal guide for teachers to evaluate their own classroom practices, taking into account variations in setting (urban, rural, suburban), class size, composition, group dynamics, and so forth.

SELF-ASSESSMENT OF CLASSROOM PRACTICES

*Teacher expectations, role definitions, and sense of efficacy*

Do you accept responsibility for teaching all students?

Do you believe in students' ability to learn?

Do you believe in your own ability to teach all students?

Do you persevere in finding methods and materials that work?

Do you view student difficulties with a positive attitude, as challenges rather than failures?

*Student opportunity to learn*

Do you allocate most available class time to instruction?

Do classroom organization and management maximize learning time?

Classroom organization and management should maximize learning time and student involvement in academic activities.

*Classroom management and organization*

> Do you establish an efficient classroom learning environment?
>
> Do you involve the students in academic activities?
>
> Do you use effective group management techniques?
>
> Do you instruct students on classroom procedures and routines?
>
> Do you convey expectations clearly and follow through consistently?
>
> Do you hold students accountable?

*Curriculum pacing*

> Do you engage students in meaningful tasks?
>
> Do you match student achievement levels with assigned tasks?
>
> Do you aim for success rates of 90–100% on independent seatwork?
>
> Do you aim for success rates of at least 70–80% on large-group instruction?

*Active teaching*

Do you provide active instruction in large- and small-group settings (e.g., demonstrate skills, explain concepts, conduct activities and reviews)?

*Teaching to mastery*

Do you provide opportunities for practice and application following active instruction?

Do you monitor student progress and provide feedback and remediation?

Do you teach the basic skills thoroughly?

*Supportive learning environment*

Do you maintain a strong academic focus and high standards?

Do you demand that students do their best?

Do you provide a pleasant, friendly, and supportive atmosphere?

## Did You Know That. . .?

In many countries throughout the world (e.g., India, Belgium, Iraq, South America, New Zealand, Great Britain), most classrooms (traditional and nontraditional) are "dominated by teacher talk" (Delamont, 1976, p. 96). In the United States, the most basic pattern of dialogue between teachers and students is the question-answer sequence. This has been the dominant pattern for more than 50 years (Morine-Dershimer, 1985).

Although negative teacher expectations and perceptions based upon students' language usage may influence academic achievement, the use of nonstandard English, in and of itself, "has *not* been demonstrated to be a *causal* factor in school achievement" (Morine-Dershimer, 1985, p. 17).

Gender-related differences in skills development vary across cultures. In the United States, boys encounter more difficulties with reading, whereas in Germany, it is the girls who have reading problems. In Japan, reading problems are not associated with gender (Safran, 1983).

A study of 10,000 students in Toronto revealed that the most important single source of information influencing teacher expectations were certifications of student aptitude derived from ability-group placements (Williams, cited in Winn & Wilson, 1983).

When 421 randomly selected Black junior and senior high school students were reassigned to an ability group one level higher than their previous level, their grades improved, peer attitudes towards them changed, and teacher expectations increased (Tuckman & Bierman, cited in Winn & Wilson, 1983).

## Summary

Classroom processes encompass the behaviors of and interplay between teachers and learners. The most important dimensions of this "hidden curriculum" are interaction, social context, management, and organization. Classroom interaction involves several interrelated components. Teacher expectations—conveyed to students verbally and nonverbally—influence student performance and self-perceptions. Differential communication patterns reflecting teacher expectations can affect student performance. Cultural differences in patterns of interpersonal interaction and communication also can affect students' behavior in the classroom.

As the instructional relevance of discrepancies between community and classroom contexts is recognized by educators, they are beginning to build bridges, that is, developing linkages that respect practices in the home and enable students to make a transition to the instructional demands of the classroom. They also are examining the quantity and quality of teacher-student interaction, particularly as it relates to gender, ethnicity, and social class. At present, it is generally believed that boys receive more of all types of interaction than girls, and there is some evidence that students from certain minority groups and lower socioeconomic backgrounds are not involved as active participants to the same extent as other students.

Language attitudes are an important part of the social context of the classroom. Possibly the most powerful of social markers, language influences social identities, relationships between teachers and students, and academic achievement. Another aspect is the status of students with teachers and peers. Determined by a combination of factors including academic achievement, individual traits, and sociocultural factors, status attributions are related to expectations held by teachers and students as to which students are competent and successful and which are not. Status characteristics can be modified, to some extent, through positive evaluations, the presence of role models, and cooperative learning activities. A third aspect of the classroom social context is instructional grouping. Grouping and tracking of students by ability results in students being exposed to differential learning experiences in terms of the quantity and quality of instruction and of academic content. Grouping also appears to reinforce social distinctions existing outside the classroom and to negatively affect the cognitive and affective development of learners in middle- and low-ability groups and tracks. Ideally, educational practice in individual classrooms and throughout a school would ensure constancy in the quality of instruction across groups, provide all students access to "high-status" knowledge, and allow mobility between groups.

The challenge of addressing the wide range of student abilities and needs in heterogeneous classrooms demands that teachers approach management with an eye to curricular adaptation. This requires consideration of content, instructional strategies and settings, and student behaviors. Individually and in combination these elements are central to the process of accommodating diverse student requirements. After they have been examined, specific techniques can be used to modify instruction and management as necessary.

Traditional classroom organization emphasizes individualistic, competitive values. However, alternative approaches to classroom organization, based on a cooperative orientation, can produce positive academic and social outcomes for nearly all students. Models for cooperative learning feature positively interdependent teams of students, individual accountability, and self-improvement. Particularly effective with average and low achievers, cooperative learning can be used with diverse student populations and is applicable across grade levels and subject areas. Peer tutoring also has been shown to provide significant cognitive and affective benefits for both tutors and tutees.

Schools make a difference and so do individual teachers. Schools and classrooms characterized by high- and low-achieving students differ markedly in terms of the classroom dimensions discussed in this chapter. These include, but are not limited to, teacher expectations, positive interaction, classroom management through curricular adaptations, and appropriate grouping. Finally, demonstration of the effect of teacher behaviors on student achievement substantiates the message central to all that has been said: First, teachers can and do make a difference. Second, by applying what is presently known about teaching and learning, teachers could make an even greater difference.

## References

Ames, C. (1984). Competitive, cooperative and individualistic goal structures: A cognitive-motivational analysis. In R. Ames & C. Ames (Eds.), *Research on motivation in education*, Vol. 1 (pp. 177–207). Orlando, FL: Academic Press Inc.

Ames, C., & Ames, R. (1984). Goal structures and motivation. *The Elementary School Journal*, 85(1), 39–52.

Au, K. Hu-Pei, & Jordan, C. (1981). Teaching reading to Hawaiian children: Finding a culturally appropriate solution. In H. T. Trueba, G. P. Guthrie, & K. Hu-Pei Au (Eds.), *Culture and the bilingual classroom* (pp. 139–152). Rowley, MA: Newbury House.

Ball, S. (1984). Student motivation: Some reflections and projections. In R. Ames & C. Ames (Eds.), *Research on motivation in education*, Vol. 1 (pp. 313–327). Orlando, FL: Academic Press Inc.

Beebe, L. M. (Ed.) (1988). *Issues in second language acquisition*. New York: Newbury House Publishers.

Bennett, C. I. (1986). *Comprehensive multicultural education*. Boston: Allyn and Bacon.

Brophy, J. E. (1982). Successful teaching strategies for the inner-city child. *Phi Delta Kappan*, 63(8), 527–530.

Brophy, J. E. (1985). Interactions of male and female students with male and female teachers. In L. C. Wilkinson & C. B. Marrett (Eds.), *Gender influences in classroom interaction* (pp. 115–142). Orlando, FL: Academic Press.

Cazden, C. B. (1986). *Classroom discourse*. In M. C. Wittrock (Ed.), *Handbook of research on teaching* (3rd ed., pp. 432–463). New York: Macmillan.

Chaika, E. (1982). *Language: The social mirror*. Rowley, MA: Newbury House.

Cohen, E. G. (1982). Expectation states and interracial interaction in school settings. *Annual Review of Sociology*, 8, 209–235.

Cohen, E. G. (1986). *Designing groupwork*. New York: Teachers College Press.

Cooper, H., & Tom, D. Y. H. (1984). Socioeconomic status and ethnic group differences in achievement motivation. In R. Ames & C. Ames (Eds.), *Research in motivation in education*, Vol. 1 (pp. 209–242). Orlando, FL: Academic Press Inc.

Delamont, S. (1976). *Interaction in the classroom*. London: Methuen.

Eggleston, J. (1977). *The sociology of the school curriculum*. London: Routledge & Kegan Paul.

Erickson, F. (1981). Some approaches to inquiry in school-community ethnography. In H. T. Trueba, G. P. Guthrie, & K. Hu-Pei Au (Eds.), *Culture and the bilingual classroom* (pp. 17–35). Rowley, MA: Newbury House.

Erickson, F. (1986). Qualitative methods in research on teaching. In M. C. Wittrock (Ed.), *Handbook of research on teaching* (3rd ed., pp. 119–161). New York: Macmillan.

Findlay, W., & Bryan, M. (1975). *The pros and cons of ability grouping*. Bloomington, IN: Phi Delta Kappa Educational Foundation.

Gollnick, D. M., & Chinn, P. C. (1986). *Multicultural education in a pluralistic society* (2nd ed.). Columbus, OH: Merrill.

Good, T. L. (1981). Teacher expectations and student perceptions: A decade of research. *Educational Leadership*, Vol. 38, No. 5, 415–422.

Good, T. L., & Brophy, J. E. (1986). School effects. In M. C. Wittrock (Ed.), *Handbook of research on teaching* (3rd ed., pp. 570–602). New York: Macmillan.

Grant, C. A., & Sleeter, C. E. (1986, April). *Race, class and gender in educational research: An argument for integrative analysis*. Paper presented at the meeting of the American Educational Research Association, San Francisco, CA.

Hall, W. S., & Guthrie, L. F. (1981). Cultural and situational variation in language function and use—Methods and procedures for research. In J. L. Green & C. Wallat (Eds.), *Ethnography and language in educational settings* (pp. 209–228). Norwood, NJ: Ablex Publishing Co.

Hallinan, M. (1984). Summary and implications. In P. L. Peterson, L. C. Wilkinson, & M. Hallinan (Eds.), *The social context of instruction* (pp. 229–240). Orlando, FL: Academic Press.

Heath, S. B. (1983). *Way with words*. New York: Cambridge University Press.

Hoover, J.J., & Collier, C. (1986). *Classroom management through curricular adaptations*. Lindale, TX: Hamilton Publications.

Hymes, D. (1981). Ethnographic monitoring. In H. T. Trueba, G. P. Guthrie, & K. Hu-Pei Au (Eds.), *Culture and the bilingual classroom* (pp. 56–68). Rowley, MA: Newbury House.

Jenkins, J. R., & Jenkins, L. M. (1987). Making peer tutoring work. *Educational Leadership*, 44(6), 64–68.

Kagan, S. (1986). Cooperative learning and sociocultural factors in schooling. In *Beyond language: Social and cultural factors in schooling language minority students* (pp. 231–298). Los Angeles: Evaluation, Dissemination and Assessment Center, California State University—Los Angeles.

Kjolseth, R. (1982). Bilingual education programs in the United States. In P. R. Turner (Ed.), *Bilingualism in the Southwest* (2nd ed., pp. 3–28). Tucson: University of Arizona Press.

Lambert, W. E., Hodgson, R. C., Gardner, R. C., and Fillenbaum, S. (1972). Attitudinal and cognitive aspects of intensive study of a second language. In R.C. Gardner & W.E. Lambert, *Attitudes and motivation in second-language learning* (pp. 293–305). Rowley, MA: Newbury House.

Legarreta-Marcaida, D. (1981). Effective use of the primary language in the classroom. *Schooling and language minority students: A theoretical framework* (pp. 83–116). Sacramento: Evaluation, Dissemination and Assessment Center, California State University—Los Angeles.

Lindow, J., Marrett, C. B., & Wilkinson, L. C. (1985). Overview. In L. C. Wilkinson & C. B. Marrett (Eds.), *Gender influences in classroom interaction*. Orlando, FL: Academic.

Longstreet, W. S. (1978). *Aspects of ethnicity*. New York: Teachers College Press.

Mehan, H. (1988, April). Teacher education issues session. Linguistic Minority Project Conference, Sacramento, CA.

Mohatt, G., & Erickson, F. (1981). Cultural differences in teaching styles in an Odawa school: A sociolinguistic approach. In H. T. Trueba, G. P. Guthrie, & K. Hu-Pei Au (Eds.), *Culture and the bilingual classroom* (pp. 105–119). Rowley, MA: Newbury House.

Morine-Dershimer, G. (1985). *Talking, listening, and learning in elementary classrooms*. New York: Longman.

National Institute of Education (1974). *Teaching as a linguistic process in a cultural setting: Conference on Studies in Teaching, Panel 5*. Washington, DC: National Institute of Education.

Nevi, C. (1987). In defense of tracking. *Educational Leadership, 44*(6), 24–26.

Peñalosa, F. (1980). *Chicano sociolinguistics*. Rowley, MA: Newbury House.

Philips, S. U. (1983). *The invisible culture*. Research on Teaching Monograph Series. New York: Longman.

Ramirez, A. G. (1985). *Bilingualism through schooling: Cross-cultural education for minority and majority students*. Albany: State University of New York Press.

Rosenthal, R., & Babad, E. (1985). Pygmalion in the gymnasium. *Educational Leadership*, Vol. 43, No. 1, 36–39.

Sadker, M. P., & Sadker, D. M. (1982). *Sex equity handbook for schools*. New York: Longman.

Sadker, M. P., & Sadker, D. M. (1986). Sexism in the classroom: From grade school to graduate school. *Phi Delta Kappan, Vol. 67 (7)*, 512–515.

Safran, C. (1983, October 9). Hidden lessons. *Parade Magazine*, p. 12.

Saunders, M. (1982). *Multicultural teaching*. London: McGraw-Hill.

Schwanke, D. (1980). Interracial classroom interaction: A review of selected literature. *Journal of Classroom Interaction, 15*(2), 11–14.

Shulman, L. (1986). Paradigms and research programs in the study of teaching: A contemporary perspective. In M. C. Wittrock (Ed.), *Handbook of research on teaching* (3rd ed., pp. 3–36). New York: Macmillan.

Slavin, R. E. (1981). Synthesis of research on cooperative learning. *Educational Leadership*, Vol. 38, No. 8, 655–660.

Slavin, R. E. (1987). Making Chapter 1 make a difference. *Phi Delta Kappan, 69*(2), 110–119.

Sleeter, C. E., & Grant, C. (1988). *Making choices for multicultural education*. Columbus, OH: Merrill.

Stewart, E. C. (1979). American assumptions and values: Orientation to action. In E. C.

Smith & L. F. Luce (Eds.), *Toward internationalism* (pp. 1–22). Rowley, MA: Newbury House. (Reprinted from *American Cultural Patterns: A Cross-Cultural Perspective,* 1972; copyright by Edward C. Stewart.)

Stubbs, M. 1976. *Language, schools and classrooms*. London: Methuen.

U.S. Commission on Civil Rights. (1973). *Teachers and students. Report V: Mexican American education study*. Washington, DC: U.S. Government Printing Office.

Wilkinson, L.C. (1981). Analysis of teacher-student interaction: Expectations communicated by conversational structure. In J. L. Green and C. Wallat (Eds.), *Ethnography and language in educational settings* (pp. 253–268). Norwood, NJ: Ablex Publishing Co.

Winn, W., & Wilson, A. P. (1983). The affect and effect of ability grouping. *Contemporary Education, 54*(2), 119–125.

# C H A P T E R

# 4
# Bilingualism in a Multicultural Society

*Trilingual: Speaks three languages*
*Bilingual: Speaks two languages*
*Monolingual: American*

*Russell M. Campbell*
*(1984, p. 114)*

Let's begin this chapter with a story. Once upon a time there was a cat that lived in a large house. Fond of chasing mice, the cat was especially intent on catching a certain mouse that always seemed to just elude him, escaping into the nearest little hole. As the mouse remained in his hideaway, safely out of reach, the cat could do nothing but wait for another chance and hope that next time things would be different. Shortly after another successful escapade, the mouse heard barking outside his hole. Certain that the cat had departed, he ventured confidently out of his hiding place. To his surprise, the mouse immediately found himself in the tight grasp of his old nemesis. In a trembling voice, he asked where the dog was. Pleased with his long-awaited triumph, the cat responded that there really was no dog. He was, you see, bilingual. The moral of this story, at least from the cat's perspective, is that being bilingual definitely can have its advantages.*

The topic of this chapter is bilingualism (i.e., proficiency in two languages) and its relationship to education in American society. Learning a language is a complex and fascinating process, which virtually all people experience. Some also acquire proficiency in a language(s) other than their native one. Although English

*Adapted from *BBC Modern English* (1976), 2(10), 34. Cited in Tiedt and Tiedt (1986).

is the primary language of American culture, usage of languages other than English is common in many homes and communities. Thus, the public schools have always had some students who were bilingual, speaking English and the language of their cultural heritage. In the past, as well as currently, some students also have entered school familiar with only one language, a language other than English. For such students with limited English proficiency, learning a second language—namely, English—is a necessity. In addition, some English-speaking students begin the process of learning a second language while in school.

After completing this chapter, you will be able to

1.  Understand the historical tradition of bilingualism in the United States.
2.  Understand the relationship between first- and second-language acquisition and identify factors that encourage language learning.
3.  Identify federal legal mandates related to the education of language-minority students.
4.  Distinguish between bilingual education, English as a second language, and foreign language education.
5.  Develop strategies for teachers working with language-minority students.

## Educating Language-Minority Students: Past and Present

### Personal Perspectives

Think back to your first day of school. It's an exciting one for many children; a trying one for others. Especially for a child who does not know the language used in the school, the whole experience can be painful. After fifty years, Cardenas' (1986) still vividly recalls his first days in school:

> In the mid-1930s, without an adequate knowledge of the English language, I was placed in an all-English first-grade instructional program. I still remember how I felt. The experience was not merely uncomfortable, unpleasant, or challenging; it was traumatic, disconcerting, and terrorizing. (p. 360)

For older students, moving to a new community and starting classes in a new school can also be a stressful and frightening experience. The first day of school in a *new country* is even more difficult, as this original account from a Southeast Asian student looking back on her first day at school in the United States suggests:

> A very scary experience, long ago when I first came to the United States. My uncle took me to __ High School to enrolled. After we enrolled my uncle took me to the classroom then he go home and let me stayed in the classroom. I was very scare because the teacher was sitting in front the classroom. I looked at him, he was big and tall.

When he came near me and I looked at his mouth and nose, and his mouth were opened and his talking to me but I did [not] know what he talking about and I was very scared and when he looked at me and came near me, I did cries but my tear were came out to my face. After that day I came home and I never go back to school untill one year later. That was a very scary experience for me at that time. (Yang, 1987)

## Historical Perspectives

Distinguishing between myth and reality in debates on educational policy and practice related to language is not always easy. Debates, whether on talk shows, on the editorial page of the local newspaper, or at the kitchen table, often are intense and emotional, to say the least. Regrettably, certain oft-repeated arguments are based on limited or inaccurate perceptions of what the educational experience has been for limited-English-proficient students. Because these beliefs are widely held, they sometimes confound and confuse the real issues in the education of non- and limited-English-speaking students; for this reason, these myths warrant the attention of educators.

**The Submersion Myth**    The first myth relates to the rather pervasive belief that limited-English-proficient students share similar experiences and can make a uniformly smooth transition to English instruction in the public schools (McConnell, 1982; Tyack, 1974). It is often expressed something like this: My parents (grandparents, great-grandparents, etc.) came here from the Old Country in 19__. They spoke no English when they came. In the public school they attended, they were taught only in English, and they never had any problems.

The approach to schooling of language-minority students reflected in this myth is generally known as *submersion*. Submersion, or the "sink-or-swim" model, is the practice of placing limited-English-speaking students in classes designed for native speakers. This is done with no modification in input or content to accommodate second-language learning. Students are expected to acquire English as they deal with content just like other students. As the appellation suggests, those who succeed swim; the others sink. Underlying the submersion approach is the assumption that the more language-minority students are exposed to English, the faster and better they will develop proficiency in the language. Although this notion may appear to have intuitive appeal, it is not supported empirically, for reasons that will become clear in the course of this chapter. In general, research has shown that many language-minority students exposed to this type of situation tend to lose their mother tongue faster than they acquire proficiency in English (Trueba, 1981).

Although many children have done well under these circumstances, many others have not done as well as most Americans would like to believe. Among immigrant groups, the actual documented progress of limited-English-proficient children suggests a very different picture from what is commonly depicted. Immigration to the United States reached its peak between 1900 and 1910. In 1911, the U.S. Immigration Service reported, based on a study of over 2 million children of immigrant families, that 43% of the children whose parents were from non-English-speaking countries were one or more grade levels behind in school, whereas 26.7% of native White children and 29.9% of those from English-speaking countries were below grade level. The percentages (by nationality) of children below grade level were even higher for those not born in the United States: German, 51%; Russian Jews, 59.9%; and Italian, 76.7% (Cohen, cited in Fillmore & Valadez, 1986; McConnell, 1982).

Dropout rates provide a second important indicator of how immigrants fared in schools. Here, too, the percentages of immigrant children not completing their education were considerably higher than those of native-born, English-speaking students. A 1926 study conducted in Hartford, Connecticut, found that 66% of immigrant children from non-English-speaking countries, but only 36% of the native White students, in the high schools dropped out by their junior year (McConnell, 1982).

In the face of such clear-cut data demonstrating the historical underachievement of language-minority students in U.S. schools, why does the popular myth to the contrary persist? One possible explanation lies in certain changes in American society. In the past, dropout rates were high, not only for limited-English-proficient children but also for the student population as a whole. Early in this century, secondary schools were still rather elitist institutions: less than 10% of the high-school-age population was in school; only about 1 in 20 graduated by age 17 (U.S. Commission on Civil Rights, 1975). In California, 18% of immigrant children were not even enrolled in schools in 1913 (Hartmann, cited in U.S. Commission on Civil Rights, 1975). At that time, completing high school was not the economic and social imperative that it is today because the job market provided relatively ample opportunities for those with limited education. Hence, the educational experiences of past generations, although in reality often difficult and limited, are likely to be perceived in a positive light because most immigrant children, even if they did not fare very well in school, did find a place in the workforce. However, the extent to which the limited schooling attained by immigrants and their children limited their access to professions and occupations requiring more education has been largely overlooked.

Many Americans also assume that all language-minority students are immigrant children. In reality, language-minority groups in the United States today are quite diverse. For some groups, recent immigration has indeed provided a major source of vitality and growth (e.g., Asian-Americans). For others, language maintenance has not depended on immigration but rather on continued usage in geographically isolated language communities (e.g., Native Americans). In still other groups, limited English proficiency results from a combination of recent immigration and continued usage of another language by established nonimmigrant populations (e.g., Hispanics).

The historical experiences of immigrants and the diversity among language-minority groups today, thus, belie the common misconception that all limited-English-proficient students face the same linguistic (and cultural) barriers and respond to them in the same way. The demonstrable differences in the school performance of different European immigrant groups in the past, as well as among Asian-Americans, Hispanics, and other language-minority groups at present, have no single, definitive explanation. Some educators believe that variability in school achievement among language-minority students may be related to patterns of intergroup relations within the society as a whole as well as differences within groups (Ogbu & Matute-Bianchi, 1986; Cruz, cited in Schreiner, 1985).

**The English-Only Myth** According to the English-only myth, bilingual education in general and the incorporation of native languages and cultures other than English are recent phenomena (Baca & Cervantes, 1984; McConnell, 1982). The basic argument goes something like this: Today's language-minority populations are making demands that differ markedly from years ago. My parents (grandparents, great-grandparents, etc.) had to learn English as a second language, and they didn't ask that their language be used in the schools.

Those who voice this belief may be ignorant about or denying how their ancestors actually felt. This view also overlooks the integral part that language plays in fostering individual and group identity. The actual experience is that strong attachments to language are commonplace and natural, in the United States and other countries. Immigrant and ethnic language groups alike have often experienced a strong need and desire to preserve their native language, particularly in the first and second generations. To the extent that bilingualism is valued in our society, such loyalty to a native language can be viewed as a positive phenomenon. To the extent that bilingualism is viewed as indicating a less than total commitment to American culture and values, it may be resented and disparaged.

Language loyalty, which encompasses the symbolic attachment individuals feel toward their native language and everything that it represents, is a phenomenon that cuts across linguistic and ethnic groups. In fact, some historians contend that the fear among some English-speaking Puritans who had settled in Holland that their children would stop using English contributed significantly to their decision to leave Holland, join with other Pilgrims, and set sail on the Mayflower! Historically, shifts in language usage among most immigrants to the United States have followed a general pattern: acquisition of English in the first generation, bilingualism in the second, and displacement of the native language by English in the third.

The English-only myth also ignores the fact that the use of languages other than English for instructional purposes has a long tradition in the United States. Historically, native languages were often incorporated into religious instructional programs and private schools before finding their way into public schools. Contrary to popular belief, the use of languages other than English in schools has not been limited to any single national or ethnic group, nor has it been confined to the present period in history, although the languages involved have changed with shifts in immigration and demographic patterns. In the nineteenth century, German, Polish, and Scandanavian languages were at the forefront; today, the emphasis is on Spanish as well as Asian and Native American languages.

Even a cursory glance through the history of American education demonstrates that a bilingual tradition has existed in the public schools for many years. In the nineteenth century, for example, bilingual programs were prevalent in many communities with large German populations (Hernandez, 1982). For decades, Germans constituted the largest non-English-speaking immigrant group in the nation, and between 1820 and 1910, 6 million Germans arrived in the United States (Zeydel, 1961). In 1850, they represented 75% of the foreign-born non-English-speaking population; even in 1880, when 3.4 million non-English-speaking inhabitants were foreign born, 60% were German (Kloss, 1977). Initially, German immigrants tried to establish schools modeled upon those in Germany, and numerous private schools were created and supported in cities with large German populations (e.g., Cincinnati). In 1860, Germans in St. Louis preferred their own schools to the city's by a ratio of four to one. At the time, there were 38 private schools, almost all parochial, and use of German in these institutions was the norm (Troen, 1975). It is worth noting that the German private schools waned in importance only after the public schools improved in quality and yielded to pressure from the German community to make the teaching of German part of the curriculum. By 1900, at least 231,700 students were studying German in public elementary schools in the Midwest (Tyack, 1974). Over the years, the role of German in the schools underwent considerable change: at the outset, serving as a language of instruction; later, as a subject. Many programs existed for years, even decades. Decline of these programs came with changes in immigration patterns and the advent of World War I.

One fundamental tenet of the early bilingual German programs was the goal of language maintenance: "The Germans wanted their children to know English, but they did not want them to lose the German language and the traditions of German culture" (Herrick, 1971, p. 61). The German community was politically active in promoting use of their native language as a means of instruction in the public schools. Efforts were also made to convince English-speaking citizens of the scholarly, economic, and cultural value of learning a second language, and the advantages of initiating the study of a foreign language at an early age (*School Report: Chicago, 1900*).

The point to be made here is that the desire to have instruction provided in the native language, generally *in addition to* but not in lieu of English, has been widely shared among immigrant and ethnic groups. This is not intended to suggest that all groups have been equally successful in achieving their goals. Such is not the case, especially among nonimmigrant groups. In fact, until fairly recently, few language-minority students received special assistance in schools. To ignore the existence of this bilingual tradition in U.S. schools, however, limits current thinking about schooling of today's language-minority students and falsely suggests that a monolithic English-only policy existed in the past.

## Contemporary Perspectives

Recent decades have brought changes in the way schools are required to address the needs of language-minority students. Impetus for many of these changes has come as a direct result of landmark federal education legislation and judicial decisions. Federal mandates now wield considerable influence in elementary and secondary education, an area in which local and state discretion had long been paramount. In this section, several key events in the development of educational policy toward issues related to limited-English-proficient students are discussed.

**Federal Legislation**    The Bilingual Education Act of 1968, under Title VII, first authorized use of federal funds for programs designed to meet the special educational needs of limited-English-proficient students. Reauthorized in 1974, 1978, and 1984, federal policy encourages the establishment of programs using bilingual educational practices, techniques, and methods or of alternative instructional programs in school districts in which bilingual programs are not feasible. The stated objective of federal policy is "to establish equal educational opportunity for all children and to promote educational excellence" (The 1984 Bilingual Education Act, 1985, p. 15). This piece of legislation provides the major source of federal support for bilingual education. At present, federal funding for bilingual education accounts for less than 10% of the total services provided to limited-English-proficient students (Secada, 1987). The federal government also supports several other programs directed at children and adults with limited English proficiency (Table 4-1).

**Definition and Number of Language-Minority Students**    According to the definition provided in the 1984 Bilingual Education Act, individuals who are "limited English proficient" (LEP) are those not born in the United States; those whose native language is not English; those from environments in which English is not the dominant language; and American Indian and Alaskan natives who come from environments in which a non-English language has significantly influenced their proficiency in English.

At the beginning of the 1980s, 4.5 million children in the United States spoke languages other than English at home; almost 2.9 million were classified as having limited English proficiency (Waggoner, 1984a). At that time, almost one in

**Table 4-1**    Federally Supported Programs for Limited-English-Proficient Children and Adults

| Program | Number of Students Served |
|---|---|
| Bilingual Education | 205,000 |
| Emergency Immigrant Education | 422,529 |
| Transitional Program for Refugee Children | 82,000 |
| Chapter 1 | 592,000 |
| Migrant Education | 312,000 |
| Indian Education/Head Start | 70,000 |
| Bilingual Vocational Education | 1,200 |
| Adult Education | 550,000 |

**Source:**    Based on data from U. S. Department of Education, cited in Secada (1987).

every four teachers in the public schools currently had limited-English-proficient students in their classes (Olson, 1984), and another one quarter had taught language-minority students at some time. Language-minority students accounted for 17% of the U.S. school-age population in 1980. They constituted 50% of the school-age population in New Mexico; 33% or more in Arizona, California, Hawaii, and Texas; and 25% in New York (Waggoner, 1984b). Immigration and population trends since the early 1980s have resulted in increases in both the absolute numbers and proportion of language-minority students in many schools.

*Lau v. Nichols*    In 1974, the U.S. Supreme Court decided unanimously, in the case of *Lau v. Nichols*, that the failure of the San Francisco School District to provide English language instruction or other forms of instructional support to approximately 3,000 limited-English-proficient students of Chinese ancestry constituted denial of equal treatment and educational opportunity. Basing their decision on Title VI of the Civil Rights Act of 1964 (prohibiting agencies receiving federal funds from discriminating on the basis of race, color, or national origin), the justices determined that "there is no equality of treatment merely by providing students with the same facilities, textbooks, teachers and curriculum; for students who do not understand English are effectively foreclosed from any meaningful education" (cited in Ochoa, n.d., p. 9).

The justices went on to state that imposing a requirement that children acquire basic language skills before participating in an educational program was to make a mockery of public education. For those with limited proficiency in English, the classroom experience would be neither comprehensible nor meaningful. The decision in *Lau v. Nichols* affirmed the Department of Health, Education, and Welfare memorandum of May 25, 1970, extending the Civil Rights Act of 1964 to national origin-minority group children and mandating school districts to provide instructional programs appropriate to the needs of these students (Ochoa, n.d.). Although the Lau decision influenced the subsequent growth and development of bilingual education, the Supreme Court did not specify the exact approach school districts had to use in order to provide more meaningful education for language-minority students.

**Federal Guidelines for Language-Minority Students**    Federal guidelines for implementing the Lau decision were issued in 1975 by the Office of Education and Office for Civil Rights. School districts that had 20 or more students with a language other than English as their primary or home language were asked to demonstrate that they provided an effective instructional program for linguistically different students (Ochoa, n.d.). Districts were strongly encouraged, but not required, to implement bilingual programs. Failure to comply with federal requirements could result in the loss of federal funds. In the period following promulgation of the Lau remedy guidelines, legislation mandating and authorizing bilingual education has been enacted in many states across the nation. In general, these laws require districts to identify students' primary language; assess skills in English and the primary language; provide services; and reassess language skills (Ochoa, n.d.). By the early 1980s, 60% of the states had enacted statutes permitting or mandating funding for bilingual education; 10% of the states expressly forbade its implementation; the remainder had not enacted any provisions (Center for Applied Linguistics, cited in Baca & Cervantes, 1984).

## Instructional Programs

The next generation's skills for living in a pluralistic society and a multilingual global community are being developed today. Bilingualism is an inextricable part of that future. At present, three instructional programs—bilingual education, English as a second language, and foreign language education—offer students from diverse backgrounds opportunities to develop proficiency in English and other languages.

### Bilingual Education

In the United States, *bilingual education* is essentially "an instructional approach in which students who do not speak the language of school are taught partly in the language of their homes, and partly in the language of the school" (Fillmore

The next generation's skills for living in a pluralistic society and a multilingual global community are being developed today. Bilingualism is an important part of that future.

& Valadez, 1986, p. 648). In bilingual programs, the language of the school serves a dual role: It is used as a medium of instruction and also is learned as a second language. Although bilingual programs in the United States are targeted primarily to meet the needs of language-minority students, they can and do serve children fluent in English. For these children, bilingual education provides a unique enrichment opportunity for academic, linguistic, and cultural development in a second language.

The three basic educational goals of bilingual education for language-minority students are (a) to attain high levels of proficiency in English, (b) to achieve academically in all content areas (including mathematics, science, and reading/language arts) to the best of their ability, and (c) to experience positive personal growth (*Basic Principles for the Education of Language-Minority Students*, 1982). The first goal recognizes the obvious importance of developing language skills in English, which is essential for full participation in our society educationally, economically, and socially. The second and third goals are common to the general education of all students. To take on all three goals at the same time is at the heart of bilingual education.

No one model describes all types of bilingual programs. They differ considerably along a number of dimensions including purpose and language use. *Maintenance* programs are designed to provide continued instruction and language development in both languages, whereas *transitional* programs are intended to help students adjust to English instruction. In the latter, skills in the home language are developed and maintained only until students are able to function exclusively in English. Since the vast majority of bilingual programs are of this type, full bilingualism is an ideal, but rarely a reality. In one survey, only 15% of the bilingual education programs examined identified maintenance of students' first language as a goal (Development Associates, cited in Hakuta & Gould, 1987).

One major reason for use of a native language is the conviction that students' access to knowledge and skills in different content areas should not be contingent upon the initial mastery of English. Most curricular content is not language specific; it can be taught in one language and later transferred into a second language as proficiency develops. This includes literacy-related skills. In fact, as discussed later, development of the first language appears to provide the underlying foundation for development of the second.

A second reason for providing instruction in students' native language is the considerable length of time needed to acquire a second language. It usually takes language-minority students several years to develop proficiency in English. Because language provides the cornerstone for intellectual development, demanding that students learn English first can significantly delay, sometimes permanently, their academic development. In bilingual classrooms, content presented in English can be reinforced in the native language and vice versa.

Finally, affirmation and acceptance of individual students' language and cultural heritage in school promotes academic achievement and development of a positive self-concept. The transition to a second language can be traumatic for students at both elementary and secondary levels. The presence and use of the

Bilingual education promotes academic, linguistic, and cultural development in a second language.

home language can help to ameliorate the feelings of discomfort, fear, and even terror some language-minority students experience, such as those described near the beginning of this chapter.

Educators and policymakers are divided in their views on bilingual education. Some believe that "little or no English is used" in bilingual programs (generally a misconception) and that students must "put aside their native languages if they are to succeed in learning English" (Fillmore & Valadez, 1986, p. 651). Others take the position that bilingual education increases the "social disadvantage" and promotes linguistic and cultural pluralism that is politically and socially divisive. Finally, some critics question the role of the federal government in educational programs promoting maintenance of ethnic languages and cultures. At issue, in part, is whether languages spoken by minority groups in the United States "constitute a national asset which should be developed rather than eradicated" (Fillmore & Valadez, 1986, p. 651).

Those who support bilingual education contend that sufficient research has been conducted to establish its effectiveness (Dolson, 1985; Willig, 1987). In fact, much of the work on second-language development discussed in this chapter has emerged from bilingual classrooms. To date, however, this research, although significant, has not been generally accepted as conclusive evidence that bilingual education programs are beneficial and effective (Fillmore & Valadez, 1986). At present, public discussion about bilingual education sometimes is dominated by political agendas and emotional reactions that preclude consideration of basic instructional issues. In dealing with bilingual education, teachers are advised to keep the following in mind: Is it the concept or its implementation that is in question? What are the educational needs of the students? What are the educational priorities of teachers, administrators, and parents?

## English as a Second Language

As defined by Alatis (1976), *English as a second language* (ESL) is "the field of teaching English to speakers of other languages" (p. 5). The role of ESL in today's elementary and secondary schools has expanded in recent years and is an increasingly varied one. English as a second language is an integral component of bilingual education programs, and where these are not feasible, it provides an essential adjunct to instruction in regular classrooms.

The primary focus of ESL instruction is concentrated in three major areas (TESOL, 1976):

- *Culture*: Integrating students' cultural experiences and background into meaningful language learning
- *Language development*: Teaching structures and vocabulary relevant to students' learning experiences
- *Content area instruction*: Applying techniques from second language learning to subject matter presented in English

Language development in English is a priority in all ESL programs. The extent to which culture and content area instruction are incorporated varies from program to program, by grade level, and with the approach used.

Contemporary approaches to ESL instruction are characterized by diversity and include more than a dozen different methods and approaches emphasizing the development of communicative and/or academic language skills. A survey of ESL teachers by Chamot & Stewner-Manzanares (1985) indicated that most were eclectic, using elements from different approaches found to be effective in meeting student needs. These authors point out that if regular classroom teachers are to complement the efforts of ESL teachers, they should realize the following:

- The transition of limited-English-proficient students into the regular instructional program is facilitated when the two are interrelated.
- Incorporating ESL throughout the total curriculum is more effective than simply treating it as a separate class.
- Providing support in the home language can enhance the effectiveness of ESL programs.
- Limited-English-proficient students benefit from interaction with fluent speakers of English in bilingual and regular classrooms.

Table 4–2 presents a summary of the different types of instructional programs for limited-English-proficient students that were available in U.S. schools in the mid-1980s. These include both bilingual education programs and those classified

**Table 4–2**   Distribution of Instructional Services for Limited-English-Proficient Students

| Type of Service | % of Schools Offering Service | % of LEP Students Receiving Service* |
|---|---|---|
| Primary language of instruction is native language; students also taught native language arts | 3 | 7 |
| Both native language & English used for instruction | 11 | 26 |
| Both native language & English initially used for instruction, but use of native language gradually decreased as use of English increased | 29 | 40 |
| All instruction in English supplemented by "special" instruction in English | 51 | 25 |
| All instruction in English with no "special" supplemental instruction in English | 6 | 1 |

*Column figures do not add to 100 because of rounding.

**Source:** Based on data from Development Associates, Inc., and Research Triangle Institute, 1984, LEP Students: Characteristics and School Services, Washington, DC: U.S. Department of Education. Cited in Hakuta and Gould (1987).

as English as a second language. In the largest proportion of schools (51%), all instruction is in English, but some supplemental instruction in English is provided for language-minority students. Clearly, this represents only a modest accommodation to the special needs of language-minority students. On the other hand, about 66% of students with limited English proficiency are attending schools that provide instruction both in the native language and in English, although in many of these schools use of the native language is phased out as students' proficiency in English increases. These data seem to suggest that at least some schools with a high proportion of limited-English-proficient students are undertaking concerted efforts to respond to their special needs.

## Foreign Language Education

To those involved in teaching languages, it seems almost paradoxical that the United States is so rich in terms of ethnic language resources and yet "notoriously deficient in foreign language skills" among the population as a whole (Simon, 1983, p. 10). Consider the following facts:

- Less than 1% of the 11 million students in U.S. colleges are learning the languages spoken by three quarters of the world's population (Simon cited in Lurie, 1982).
- There are fewer students of Russian in the United States than there are teachers of English in the Soviet Union. Estimates are that almost 10 million students in the USSR are learning English, whereas only about 28,000 students in the United States study Russian (Lurie, 1982).
- In 1980, 85% of all high school students did not participate in foreign language classes (Simon, 1983).
- Until recently, the United States was the only nation in the world where students could graduate from college without having one year of a foreign language preceding or as part of a university program (Lurie, 1982).

In recent years, the extremely small number of Americans who are fluent in foreign languages and the potential negative consequences of this deficit have become increasingly obvious (Lambert, 1985). Foreign policy, diplomacy, and international trade are among the areas in which foreign language skills often are necessary for effective job performance. At the state level, legislators are beginning to respond to concerns that the nation's commercial and strategic position in a highly competitive global community is being undermined by lack of second-language skills (Rohter, 1987). Since the late 1970s, for example, at least 30 states have imposed or restored language requirements in high school, as have major colleges and state university systems. In addition to political and economic considerations, study of a foreign language has been shown to enhance skills and attitudes related to English vocabulary, reading and communication skills, self-concept, cultural enrichment, and creativity (American Council on the Teaching of Foreign Languages, 1984).

Foreign languages can be taught at the elementary and secondary levels. Most programs for high school students provide formal language instruction. An alternative approach effective in developing the foreign language skills of children whose primary language is English is school-based *immersion education*. This approach was originally developed in Canada in the 1960s in response to efforts by English-speaking parents in Quebec to enhance their children's success in learning French. Immersion programs are based on the premise "that people learn a second (or third) language in the same way as they learn their first; that is, in contexts where they are exposed to it in its natural form and where they are socially motivated to communicate" (Lambert, 1984, p. 11). The major goals of immersion education are to promote (a) understanding and appreciation of another language and culture, (b) general academic achievement, and (c) normal language development in the first language and ability to function in the second (Genesee, 1984). Now widespread throughout Canada, immersion language programs also are available in a number of school districts across the United States. Such programs are offered in both large and small communities including Alpine, UT; Baton Rouge, LA; Cincinnati, OH; Holliston, MA; Milwaukee, WI; Montgomery County, MD; Rochester NY; Culver City, Davis, and San Diego, CA; Tulsa OK; and Washington, DC (Campbell, 1984).

In immersion programs, the foreign language serves a dual role as a subject and a medium of instruction. Children are literally "immersed" in the new language for all or part of the school day. Teachers interact with students only in the foreign language, presenting the same content pupils would be expected to learn in the regular classroom curriculum. Classes typically are composed of non-native speakers of the foreign language who all begin the process of language acquisition on an equal basis. Although the foreign language skills pupils develop in immersion programs do not fully match those of native speakers, they tend to be significantly better than the skills acquired in traditional foreign language programs. In addition, immersion education seems to promote cross-cultural understanding without any apparent negative effects on the English language development, content achievement, cultural appreciation, and self-identity of students.

The distinction between immersion programs and the submersion approach described earlier in this chapter is an important one. Immersion programs are additive enrichment programs for English speakers. They are designed for students who already have English language skills and wish to acquire proficiency in another language as well. Ideally, all students in the classroom have comparable skills in the foreign language, and instruction is geared to their level of proficiency. In contrast, the submersion approach involves assignment of language-minority students to classrooms in which teachers' instruction in English is geared to the language skills of native speakers. With this approach, language-minority students receive no instruction in their native language, and many lose proficiency in their first language in the process of developing proficiency in English. Thus, the submersion approach often discourages rather than promotes bilingualism; its practical effect is to substitute one language (English) for another (students' native language) (Hernández-Chavez, 1981).

# Second-Language Acquisition

Classroom instruction is predicated upon knowledge and beliefs about what students must learn, what they can do, and what methods will work best for individual learners. When communication is limited by language differences, teachers may find their task more challenging than usual. By becoming familiar with theoretical concepts and research findings related to second-language acquisition, regular classroom teachers can better understand the abilities and needs of language-minority students.

## Social vs. Academic Language Skills

Cummins (1981) proposes that an important distinction exists between language skills used for communicative and academic functions. Language skills in the social arena (i.e., *basic interpersonal communicative skills*), he suggests, are characterized by interpersonal interaction. Meaning is negotiated between participants and conveyed through language with a relatively high reliance on context. Interpretation is embedded in the situation itself, often amply supported by cues that are situational and nonverbal. Children in the process of learning language associated with classroom routines, for example, can follow the actions of other children and interpret teacher gestures and facial expressions. Imagine all the contextual cues present when a teacher asks children to line up for lunch or recess!

Cummins also identifies a second level of language skills, a cognitive and academic dimension (i.e., *cognitive-academic language proficiency*). In this realm, language, particularly in written form, is primary; little information, if any, can be gleaned from other sources. Reading selections from an anthology or science text demands language skills significantly different from those used in interpersonal communication. Meaning is inherent almost exclusively in the written text itself, and the task of deriving meaning from this source is cognitively demanding. Thus, limitations in language skills are far more likely to inhibit students' performance of academic tasks than their functioning in social situations in which meaning is negotiated, supported contextually, and generally less intellectually demanding.

The distinction between social and academic language skills is an important one for teachers to remember. It helps to explain why students who can function well in a second language in social situations may continue to experience difficulties with academic tasks. In essence, the acquisition of social-communicative language skills is no guarantee that students have developed comparable command of academic-cognitive language. Failure to recognize this distinction has often resulted in misconceptions regarding the "skills" of language-minority students. It has also

Literacy skills are an integral part of cognitive and academic language proficiency.

contributed to assumptions that learners have cognitive deficits rather than limited language skills. Based on examination of 400 referral forms and psychologists' assessments on language-minority students, Cummins (1981) found that such misconceptions were prevalent. Many of those assessing language-minority students concluded that because they "are fluent in English, their poor academic performance and/or test scores cannot be attributed to lack of proficiency in English. Therefore, these students must either have deficient cognitive abilities or be poorly motivated ('lazy')" (Cummins, 1981, p. 6).

How long, then, does it take for language-minority students to develop language skills in English? Although there is no way to predict the length of time an individual will need to acquire proficiency in English, accumulating evidence indicates that, for most students, it may be considerably longer than teachers would expect. Cummins (1981) reports that immigrant students arriving in Canada after age six require approximately 2 years to develop certain aspects of age-appropriate English communicative skills and 5 to 7 years to develop age-appropriate academic skills in English. In other words, the expectation that language-minority students will be completely proficient in English in a matter of months or even a year or two would seem to be totally unrealistic for the vast majority of such students.

## Relationship Between First- and Second-Language Proficiency

In recent years, research has indicated that proficiency in one's first language provides the basis for language acquisition in a second (Cummins, 1981). At an intuitive level, it seems obvious that a high level of competence in the home language would provide a strong foundation for development of a second language. After all, continued development of the first language enhances acquisition of the second by further expanding the cognitive and linguistic resources available to the individual. Command of verb tenses in one language, for example, facilitates their development in the second.

The experiences of language-minority students who have succeeded in the educational system indicate that individuals who are highly proficient in two languages enjoy definite academic, cognitive, and linguistic advantages over those proficient in only one. When the second language represents an addition to the first and both are fully developed, the cognitive effects are positive (Cummins, 1981). This process is one of enrichment. Conversely, second-language acquisition is much less successful when development of the first language is curtailed. In other words, when learning a second language contributes to loss of proficiency in the first, the end result often is low levels of development in both languages (Cummins, 1981). Many now believe that language-minority students will experience negative cognitive effects unless they attain a certain level of bilingualism.

Cardenas' (1986) personal observations illustrate the connection between proficiency in a first and second language:

> It is interesting to note that, almost without exception, those of us who learned the English language grew up in homes with a strong language capability. Although this

capability was usually in a language other than English, the level of language ability within our families was high during our developmental years. This is as true for language-minority persons of my generation who grew up to become legislators, mayors, educators, and successful business people as it is today for the Korean or Vietnamese children who are graduating as valedictorians. The common denominator invariably is extensive competence in the use of some language. (p. 360)

For bilingual teachers, the positive connection between first- and second-language proficiency provides critical support for use of the home language for classroom instruction, not only to facilitate acquisition of academic content but also to enhance language development. For regular classroom teachers, this connection suggests accepting and even promoting development of the first language at school, whenever possible, and in the home. This is justified not only because fluency in the home language aids second-language development, but also because it contributes to self-esteem and cultural identity.

These conclusions may conflict with the beliefs and experiences of some teachers. Popular myths about language have held that the home language should not be maintained if English is to be learned quickly and well; that individuals have a "limited" capacity for language, and thus the first language must make way for the second. Believing this, many teachers have discouraged use of ethnic languages in the classroom, on school grounds, and even at home. Students have been reprimanded for using their first language to interact with others. Although the situation in each school, home, and community is different, mounting evidence indicates that teachers are best advised to adopt a position supportive of continued development in the first language. The role of the first language is especially critical in supporting cognitive and linguistic development during the period in which English language skills are not yet sufficient to do so.

## Effect of Learner Characteristics

Second-language acquisition is a complex cognitive and social process, which involves far more than mere exposure to a different language or the imitation of new sounds, forms, and structures. Those who are learning a second language must "figure out how the sound system of the new language is organized, how units of meaning are organized into words, by what principles these words are put together to form sentences, how these sentences can be used appropriately in given settings, and in what ways meanings can be conveyed in the new language and culture" (Fillmore, cited in Lindfors, 1987, p. 446).

Language-minority students vary considerably in the rate at which they acquire English and the level of proficiency they attain. Although some children are able to learn English in about 2 years, the majority seem to require 4 or 5 years of exposure. A significant proportion require as many as 6 or 7 years, *whether they are in bilingual programs or all-English classes* (Fillmore & Valadez, 1986).

To the task of learning a second language, each student brings a unique combination of cognitive and social abilities (Fillmore, cited in Lindfors, 1987). On the cognitive side, the student must figure out the structure of the new language and determine how meaning is communicated. Aptitude is involved. How well does the individual remember language? How easily is it produced? To what extent is the individual flexible in thinking of alternative ways of saying things? How sensitive to the context and patterns of language? How well does the individual guess at the meaning of what is communicated?

On the social side, the student must also develop strategies for communicating and interacting with speakers of the new language. Personality factors are involved. How outgoing is the language learner? To what extent does the individual seek contact with others? How talkative? Is there a preference for verbal and interactive activities or independent, nonverbal tasks? Thus, both cognitive and social abilities are applied to observing and producing language.

There is no single dimension that teachers can use to predict whether a particular individual will be a good language learner. The extent to which any single characteristic contributes to the development of skills in a given language depends, at least in part, on the situation in which the language is learned. For example,

Cognitive, aptitudinal, and social abilities are applied to observing and producing language.

language acquisition is influenced by the interaction of learner characteristics with instructional and social factors (Fillmore & Valadez, 1986). Sociability and peer orientation are most useful when language-minority students are able to interact with English-speaking children sharing a mutual interest. However, in settings in which there are many language learners and the teacher is the primary source of input in the new language, students who are less sociable and more adult-oriented seem to have a definite advantage.

Learner attitudes toward the first as well as the new language and culture also influence language acquisition. For language-minority students, acquisition of native-like proficiency in a second language depends at least in part upon attitudinal factors related to group identification and perceptions of group status in society. Second-language learning is part of an acculturation process. In this process, individuals differ in the degree to which they identify with and adopt the language and behaviors representative of another language group (Schumann, cited in Ramirez, 1985). In the United States, the more willing individuals are to identify with speakers of English and the more favorable the perceptions of a group's status within American society, the greater the likelihood learners will acquire native-like proficiency in English. The more negative the attitudes toward a language, its speakers, and its culture, the less likely an individual is to be motivated to acquire native-like proficiency (Ramirez, 1985).

## Effect of Classroom Characteristics

The most favorable conditions for language-minority students to learn English occur in a classroom that is linguistically balanced (Fillmore & Valadez, 1986). This is true because the quantity and quality of language that learners are exposed to provide  input for language learning. Students who are trying to learn English as a second language tend to do least well when they are few in number or when they outnumber their English-speaking classmates. Their achievement also is affected when speakers from any one language group predominate (Fillmore & Valadez, 1986). A balanced number of English learners and native English-speaking classmates can best provide the language exposure and interaction needed for second-language acquisition to occur.

Because classroom interactions are an important source of language input for those learning English as a second language, language-minority students must be motivated to take full advantage of the opportunities available in the instructional environment. Interactions must serve not only the purposes of communication and instruction but also of language learning (Fillmore & Valadez, 1986). To ensure that this happens, teachers need to provide structured and informal peer interaction. The following guidelines encourage high levels of peer interaction in ESL classes (Enright & Gomez, 1985) and can be incorporated in regular classrooms as well.

ENCOURAGING PEER INTERACTIONS IN CLASSROOMS

*Planning*

- Consistently include peer interaction in activities.
- Use organized and free-choice peer groupings.

*Room Arrangement*

- Arrange the classroom environment to facilitate various forms of interaction (e.g., areas for listening, meeting, socializing, working).

*Organization*

- Organize large- and small-group activities to promote peer interaction.
- Provide clear instructions describing how students are to interact.
- Use space effectively in organizing activities.

*Atmosphere*

- Create an atmosphere in which students feel they are admirable and valued members of the classroom community.
- Include all students in activities.
- Draw attention to contributions in ways that are culturally appropriate.
- Talk with each student individually.

*Consistency*

- Create opportunities for peer interaction consistently and continually.

*Talk*

- Incorporate verbal and nonverbal dimensions in classroom activities.
- Incorporate language development as a crucial component of the classroom agenda.

## Strategies That Promote Bilingualism in the Classroom*

The development of English language skills by limited-English-proficient students in the regular classroom can be enhanced if teachers pay attention to their own

*Adapted from Barker and Morrisroe (1983), Cantoni-Harvey (1987), Chan (n.d.), Fillmore, cited in Lindfors (1987), Krashen (1981), Saville-Troike (1976), Terrell (1981), and Thonis (1982).

language usage, the classroom environment, and how they correct errors and provide contextual support to help convey meaning. Especially in the elementary grades, many of these same concepts also are beneficial for language development by native English-speaking students.

Teachers should try to speak to limited-English-proficient students in meaningful and comprehensible language. Although students do not have to understand each and every word spoken by their teachers, they should be able to capture the essence of what is said. Ideally, the language used for instruction should be familiar yet challenging to students.

Modifications in speech and vocabulary can be used to make the language of instruction more easily understood. Speaking naturally, perhaps a little more slowly than usual, and keeping the choice of words and sentence structure as simple as possible can help. Teachers should focus special attention on terminology that is specialized. Key terms and concepts should be defined in language that is familiar. Whenever possible, illustrations and concrete objects can be used to help students visualize the meaning of words. Strategies that draw attention to the appearance of words and help students make associations also facilitate recall. One trick some teachers use is to turn the sound track down on films and filmstrips and do the narrations themselves in language that is simpler and more easily understood.

Making mistakes is a normal part of the language-acquisition process. Teachers, therefore, initially should focus on the content of student contributions rather than on their form (e.g., grammar, structure, pronunciation). When corrections are necessary, they should be made covertly (e.g., by repeating or rephrasing what students say), rather than by directly drawing attention to the error.

To the extent possible, instruction should be accompanied by contextual support that provides additional clues to convey meaning. In seminars, teachers can actually see the difference context makes with a very simple demonstration. Suppose that a pencil is described twice in a language other than English. The first time no clues are provided while the pencil is described in terms of color, features, and functions. The second time around, the verbal description is accompanied by display of a pencil and demonstration of its uses. This simple exercise quickly demonstrates to teachers the difference that context makes in understanding what is communicated in a language they do not know. In the classroom, contextual support can be provided through use of gestures, facial expressions, pantomime, and paralinguistic clues. Visuals (e.g., charts, graphs, symbols and diagrams), demonstrations, and concrete objects used as manipulatives also are helpful.

Language-minority students often go through a silent period before they start speaking in English because development of listening comprehension skills normally precedes oral production. Hence, teachers should not be surprised if some students, particularly younger children, go through a silent period as they begin language learning. This period may last from several hours to several months. Teachers should also look for opportunities to provide students with ways to respond with one- or two-word answers or short phrases when they are first beginning to speak English.

To promote language instruction in specific content areas and to facilitate understanding of subject matter, teachers are encouraged to try the following techniques:*

- Preview topics and specialized vocabulary before presenting new material.
- Use introductory activities to pre-teach vocabulary and check for understanding.
- Use structured organizers, outlines, summaries, and charts at more advanced levels of instruction.
- Provide oral recordings of teacher presentations and reading materials.
- Provide directions on the use and interpretation of charts, tables, maps, etc.
- As appropriate, plan some tasks that are less "dependent" on literacy skills (e.g., listening to tapes, interviews, viewing films).

Heath (1986) draws two particularly significant conclusions based on studies of cultural differences in language and their impact on educational outcomes. First, academic success may depend less on children's knowledge of a specific language than on how they use the language they do know. Second, by providing a wide variety of activities for using both oral and written language, schools can promote children's academic and vocational success regardless of their first-language background.

One way teachers can facilitate expanded language use is by incorporating a wide range of language forms in classroom lessons, especially at the elementary level. Although the possible range of language forms available to speakers of any language is large, each cultural group seems to have certain forms that recur in set patterns. Furthermore, although there is considerable continuity between home and school settings across cultural groups, there are also areas in which they have been found to differ. To deal with this diversity, teachers must be aware of how students demonstrate the academic, cognitive, and linguistic proficiency required in school by use of specific forms of language. Then, especially at the elementary level, teachers need to provide students with various ways to acquire and demonstrate proficiency, such as the following (Heath, 1986):

- Naming items; asking for names. *Examples*: "What's this?"; "Who's that?"
- Explaining the meanings of words, pictures, combinations of events, and children's own behaviors (explanations should include what it means, what will happen, how it is to be interpreted). *Examples*: Asking the meaning of passages; inferring what an author means from a written text.
- Providing summaries of known material orally and in writing. *Example*: Test questions that depend upon recounting a reading passage.
- Retelling or performing. *Examples*: Show-and-tell; creative writing.
- Explaining the sequence of steps to be taken to accomplish a current task or future goal. *Examples*: An essay outline; a plan for a group project.

- Providing fictional accounts of animate beings or creatures. *Examples*: Basal texts; literary texts.

It is imperative for students from all sociocultural and class backgrounds to have repeated, reinforced access to multiple uses of language that match those in the school. According to Heath (1986), children's access to these forms of language and the extent to which it involves written texts determines, to a considerable degree, success in school and beyond. Heath suggests that teachers provide opportunities for students to practice and use a variety of language forms in all subject areas and at all levels. Teachers may even incorporate forms of language from the home in the classroom. Use of the "talk story" with Hawaiian children, for example, is just one example of how this approach can enhance achievement in reading. In addition, teachers can try to expand the types of language uses employed in the classroom to incorporate those needed for effective participation beyond the school.

## Did You Know That. . .?

There are approximately 5000 living languages in the world (Ramirez, 1985). Worldwide, it is estimated that bilinguals outnumber monolinguals. It is also believed that more people speak English as a second or foreign language than as a first language.

According to the most recent census, 15% of the total U.S. population has a non-English-speaking background. The minority-language population is over 3 million in California, New York, and Texas; in Illinois, Florida, New Jersey, Pennsylvania, and Massachusetts, it surpasses 1 million (Waggoner, 1984b).

Between 50 and 75% of all limited-English-proficient students in U.S. schools speak Spanish. Large numbers of language-minority students also speak Asian and American-Indian languages, French, German, and Italian (Waggoner, 1984b; Rotberg, 1982).

In the nineteenth century, an estimated 1 million students participated in public school bilingual programs; thousands more enrolled in similar programs in private schools (Zirkel, cited in Baca & Cervantes, 1984).

Projections indicate that in the year 2000, there will be 39.5 million people in the United States whose language background is not English; 3.4 million of these will be between the ages of 5 and 14. Almost half will be found in three states: California, New York, and Texas (Ramirez, 1985).

## Summary

Language diversity has long been an important aspect of cultural diversity in the United States. Students who have limited English proficiency—whose first language is not English—have come both from immigrant and nonimmigrant homes. The number of students in this category and the variety of languages represented are significant, especially in states like California, New York, Texas, New Mexico, Arizona, and Hawaii.

Historically, misconceptions have influenced how people respond to issues associated with the education of language-minority students. These affect perceptions about student experiences and academic performance as well as the use of languages other than English for instruction. In the past, although bilingual programs were instituted in some areas, the dominant approach to the education of language-minority students was submersion, i.e., placement in classes for native English speakers. This did not provide an optimal learning environment for many students despite myths to the contrary.

Recent decades have brought federal and state involvement in educational policy regarding language-minority students. Legislation and court decisions requiring intervention on their behalf now compel school districts to provide equal educational opportunity for students unable to benefit fully from instruction in English.

Bilingual education, English as a second language, and foreign language education are all concerned with the development of bilingualism. In the United States, bilingual education and English as a second language focus primarily on the linguistic and academic development of language-minority students. In bilingual education, two languages and cultures are integrated in an instructional program. English as a second language, in its many variations, provides a bridge to English for language-minority students at all levels. Foreign language skills can be acquired by children whose primary language is English through various foreign language programs.

Teachers working with limited-English-proficient students should be aware of the distinction between communicative and academic language skills, the relationship between first- and second-language development, and the many learner and classroom factors that influence second-language acquisition. Current strategies for teaching limited-English-proficient students emphasize techniques, the language of instruction, contextual support, peer interaction, and ways of using language.

## References

Alatis, J. E. (1976). The compatibility of TESOL and bilingual education. In J. E. Alatis & K. Twaddell (Eds.), *English as a second language in bilingual education* (pp. 5–14). Washington, DC: Teachers of English to Speakers of Other Languages.

American Council on the Teaching of Foreign Languages. (1984). *Second languages and the basics*. Hastings-on-Hudson, NY: Author.

Baca, L. M., & Cervantes, H. T. (1984). *The bilingual special education interface*. St. Louis: Times Mirror/Mosby.

Barker, D., & Morrisroe, S. (1983). Helping content area teachers deal with LEP students in their classes. *Secondary Interest Section Newsletter, 6*(1), 1.

*Basic principles for the education of language-minority students.* (1982). Sacramento: California State Department of Education.

The 1984 Bilingual Education Act. (1985). Rosslyn, VA: National Clearinghouse for Bilingual Education.

Campbell, R. N. (1984). The immersion education approach to foreign language teaching. *Studies in immersion education* (pp. 114–143). Sacramento: State Department of Education.

Cantoni-Harvey, G. (1987). *Content-area language instruction.* Reading, MA: Addison-Wesley.

Cardenas, J. A. (1986). The role of native-language instruction in bilingual education. *Phi Delta Kappan, 67*(5), 359–363.

Chamot, A. U., & Stewner-Manzanares, G. (1985). *A synthesis of current literature on English as a second language: Issues for educational policy.* Rosslyn, VA: InterAmerica Research Associates.

Chan, J. M. T. (n.d.) *Ways to help LEP students survive in the content area classroom.* Long Beach: California State University. Unpublished summary.

Cummins, J. (1981). The role of primary language development in promoting educational success for language minority students. *Schooling and language minority students: A theoretical framework* (pp. 51–79). Sacramento: Evaluation, Dissemination and Assessment Center, California State University—Los Angeles.

Dolson, D. P. (1985). Bilingualism and scholastic performance: The literature revisited. *NABE Journal, X*(1), 1–35.

Enright, D. S., & Gomez, B. (1984). Pro-act: Six strategies for organizing peer interaction in elementary classrooms. *NABE Journal, IX*(3), 5–24.

Fillmore L. W., & Valadez, C. (1986). Teaching bilingual learners. In M. C. Wittrock (Ed.), *Handbook of research on teaching* (3rd ed., pp. 648–685). New York: Macmillan.

Genesee, F. (1984). Historical and theoretical foundations of immersion education. In California State Department of Education, *Studies on immersion education* (pp. 32–57). Sacramento: Author.

Hakuta, K., & Gould, L. J. (1987) Synthesis of research on bilingual education. *Educational Leadership*, Vol. 44, No. 6, 38–45.

Heath, S. B. (1986). Sociocultural contexts of language development. *Beyond language: Social and cultural factors in schooling language minority students* (pp. 143–186). Los Angeles: Evaluation, Dissemination and Assessment Center, California State University—Los Angeles.

Hernandez, H. (1982). Parallels in the history of American bilingual education. *Chabot College Journal, 4*(2), 33–39.

Hernández-Chavez, E. (1981). The inadequacy of English immersion education as an educational approach for language minority students in the United States. *Studies in immersion education* (pp. 144–183). Sacramento: State Department of Education.

Herrick, M. (1971). *The Chicago schools.* Beverly Hills, CA: Sage Publications.

Kloss, H. (1977). *The American bilingual tradition.* Rowley, MA: Newbury House.

Krashen, S. D. (1981). Bilingual education and second language education theory. *Schooling and language minority students: A theoretical framework* (pp. 51–79). Sacramento: Evaluation, Dissemination and Assessment Center, California State University—Los Angeles.

Lambert, R. D. (1985). Foreign language instruction: A national agenda. *Foreign Language Annals, 18*(5), 379–383.

Lambert, W. E. (1984). An overview of issues in immersion education. *Studies on immersion education* (pp. 8–30). Sacramento: California State Department of Education.

Lindfors, J. W. (1987). *Children's language and learning* (2nd ed.). Englewood Cliffs, NJ: Prentice-Hall.

Lurie, J. (1982). AMERICA. . . .Globally blind, deaf and dumb. *Foreign Language Annals, 15*(6), 413–420.

McConnell, B. B. (1982). In grandpa's day. *NABE News, V*(5), 10.

Ochoa, A. M. (n.d.). *Overview of federal regulations impacting national origin minority.* Unpublished workshop presentation.

Ogbu, J. U., & Matute-Bianchi, M. E. (1986). Understanding sociocultural factors: Knowledge, identity, and school adjustment. *Beyond language: Social and cultural factors in schooling language minority students* (pp. 73–142). Los Angeles: Evaluation, Dissemination and Assessment Center, California State University—Los Angeles.

Olson, Lynn. (1984, November 21). Bilingual students are underserved, E.D. report says. *Education Week, IV*(12), 1, 11.

Ramirez, A. G. (1985). *Bilingualism through schooling: Cross-cultural education for minority and majority students.* Albany: State University of New York Press.

Rohter, L. (1987, January 19). Parlez-vous Deutsch, señor? *San Francisco Chronicle,* p.16.

Rotberg, I. C. (1982). Some legal and research considerations in establishing federal policy in bilingual education. *Harvard Educational Review, 52*(2), 149–168.

Saville-Troike, M. (1978). *A guide to culture in the classroom.* Rosslyn, VA: National Clearinghouse for Bilingual Education.

*School Report: Chicago, 1900.* (1900). Chicago: H. Anderson, Printers. pp. 235–241.

Schreiner, T. (1987, December 18). Hispanic students: Educator sees 5 types. *San Francisco Chronicle.*

Secada, W. G. (1987). This is 1987, not 1980: A comment on a comment. *Review of Educational Research, 57*(3), 377–384.

Simon, P. (1983). Is America tongue-tied? *Academe,* (March–April), pp. 9–12.

Terrell, T. D. (1981). The natural approach to bilingual education. *Schooling and language minority students: A theoretical framework* (pp. 117–146). Los Angeles: Evaluation, Dissemination and Assessment Center, California State University—Los Angeles.

TESOL (Teachers of English to Speakers of Other Languages). (1976). *Position paper on the role of English as a second language in bilingual education.* Washington, DC: Author.

Thonis, E. (1982). *No-cost strategies for LEP students.* Presentation for Marysville (CA) Unified School District. Unpublished summary.

Tiedt, P. L., & Tiedt, I. M. (1986). *Multicultural teaching* (2nd ed.). Boston: Allyn and Bacon.

Troen, S. K. (1975). *The public and the schools: Shaping the St. Louis school system, 1838–1925.* Columbus, MO: University of Missouri Press.

Trueba, H. (1981). Bilingual education: An ethnographic perspective. *California Journal of Teacher Education, VIII*(3), 15–41.

Tyack, D. B. (1974). *The one best system.* Cambridge, MA: Harvard University Press.

U.S. Commission on Civil Rights. (1975). *A better chance to learn: Bilingual-bicultural education.* Clearinghouse Publication 51. Washington, DC: U.S. Government Printing Office.

Waggoner, D. (1984a). The need for bilingual education: Estimates from the 1980 Census. *NABE Journal, VIII*(2), 1–34.

Waggoner, D. (1984b). Minority language populations from the 1980 Census. *National Clearinghouse for Bilingual Education, VII*(5), 2, 6–7.

Willig, A. C. (1987). Examining bilingual education research through meta-analysis and narrative review: A response to Baker. *Review of Educational Research, 57*(3), 363–376.

Yang, M. (1987). A very scary experience. Unpublished manuscript.

Zeydel, F. H. (1961). The teaching of German in the United States from colonial times to the present. In *reports of surveys and studies in the teaching of modern foreign languages*. New York: Modern Language Association of America.

# 5

# Special/Gifted Education: Multicultural Connections

*The success of education depends on adapting teaching to individual differences among learners.*

Corno and Snow (1986, p. 605)

✳ On a daily basis, teachers in regular classrooms are challenged to provide an educational environment and experience that meets the individual needs of students from diverse cultural, social, and linguistic backgrounds, including handicapped students and those with learning problems; students achieving at levels not commensurate with their abilities; and students gifted with unique talents and capabilities. This central challenge to the educational enterprise has been recognized for many centuries and in diverse cultures:

> "The success of education depends on adapting teaching to individual differences among learners." This thought, and the admonition to teachers it carries, can be found expressed in some detail in the fourth century B.C. Chinese treatise by Yue-zheng entitled *Xue Ji*, in the ancient Hebrew Haggadah of Passover, and in the *De Institutione Oratoria* of Quintilian in first century Rome. (Corno & Snow, 1986, p. 605)

The discussion in this chapter focuses on students with exceptional abilities and special needs. The intent is to identify aspects of special and gifted education that relate to multicultural education and to examine ways in which teachers can maximize the performance of these and other learners in the regular classroom. As Amos and Landers (1984) suggest, a "marriage" between special and multicultural education would provide teachers with knowledge, skills, and attitudes to increase educational opportunities for *all* learners. "Such a marriage should also enhance the efforts to serve more learners with differences in the mainstreams of our educational system" (p. 146). Likewise, a union of gifted and multicultural education can contribute insights to the teaching of unusually creative and gifted learners.

After completing this chapter, you will be able to

1. Identify major issues facing special and gifted education in general and their implications for culturally diverse student populations in particular.
2. Recognize the influence of federal legislation and legal decisions on the education of the handicapped.
3. Define the major categories of special education students and the areas encompassed within gifted and talented education.
4. Develop practical classroom strategies for dealing with a diversity of student needs.
5. Examine effective instructional practices based upon use of learning styles and learning strategies.

## Special Education

Within the school-age population, rough estimates indicate that almost 11% of all students—nearly 5 million of the approximately 45 million elementary and secondary students enrolled in the 1980s—are in need of some special education services (Gage & Berliner, 1988). These include children and youth with a wide variety of handicaps that require adaptations in their educational programs. Learning disabled, speech impaired, and mentally retarded youngsters account for about 86% of all the school-age handicapped; emotionally disturbed children account for 8%; the remainder have hearing, visual, orthopedic, or other health impairments or are multihandicapped (Gage & Berliner, 1988).

Within the student population that requires special education, many children were still underserved by existing programs in the mid-1980s. In fact, those receiving services probably represented less than half of all handicapped children in the United States (Baca & Cervantes, 1984). Those least likely to receive appropriate services were children 3 to 5 years of age; secondary students and individuals between the ages of 18 and 22; emotionally disturbed, migrant, and foster children; military dependents; and incarcerated youth (Cardenas & First, 1985). Clearly, not all of those in need of services were receiving them, a situation that was still true in the late 1980s.

It is important for teachers to remember that the vast majority of students in special education programs have disabilities that "do not necessarily reflect

An estimated 11% of school-age children are in need of some special education services.

diminished intellectual capacity" (Wang, Reynolds, & Walberg, 1986, p. 30). For example, in the state of New York, about three quarters of the 286,000 students in special education are identified as learning disabled or as having a speech, visual, or orthopedic impairment; these handicaps are not necessarily associated with limitations in the abilities of students to perform academically (Wang et al., 1986). The fact that these students must be identified in order to provide the assistance and resources they need should not—in and of itself—adversely affect teacher and peer perceptions and expectations regarding their mental abilities.

Another general point about students in special education programs is that boys significantly outnumber girls among those classified as mildly handicapped learners. Phipps (1982) reports that about 85% of the students in public school programs for the learning disabled, educable mentally retarded, and behavior disordered are boys. In a study of gender differences in referrals for one California school district, Phipps found that teachers' perceptions of boys' conduct and behavior was a significant factor in their identification for placement in special education. Numerically, boys outnumber girls in programs for the educable mentally retarded by a ratio of 1.2 to 1; in learning disabled programs by 3 or 4 to 1 and even higher (MacMillan, Keogh, & Jones, 1986). To some extent, the decision to refer a student for special education appears to be an index of teacher

tolerance, and a tacit admission that the student is not likely to benefit instructionally in a particular classroom setting (Shinn, Tindal, & Spira, 1987).

## Legislative and Legal Perspectives

As the result of legislation enacted on behalf of the handicapped since the 1960s, the federal government has assumed an increasingly prominent role in special education. Indeed, more has been done to promote the educational rights of the handicapped in recent years than in the entire previous history of the nation (Baca & Cervantes, 1984). During this period, legislation has been marked by an affirmation of handicapped students' educational rights; the convergence of directives for handicapped and limited-English-proficient students; and provisions for non-discriminatory assessment, parental involvement, and expanded instructional services (Fradd & Vega, 1987; Baca & Cervantes, 1984).

From a teacher's perspective, the Education for All Handicapped Students Act of 1975 (PL 94-142) is of particular importance. This landmark law addresses issues of significance to handicapped students in general and to culturally and linguistically different populations in particular. Among the most important provisions of PL 94-142 are those establishing the following (MacMillan et al., 1986):

- *The right to due process*—Provides procedural safeguards in classification and placement; guarantees parental access to school records; and assures parental rights to an impartial hearing on placement and an opportunity for independent evaluation of their child.

- *Protection against discriminatory testing during assessment*—Prohibits use of a single psychometric instrument as the sole criterion for placement and requires administration of tests in a child's native language.

- *Placement in the least restrictive educational setting*—Requires that handicapped students be educated in environments resembling, to the greatest extent possible, the regular classroom.

- *Individualized education programs*—Requires a written description of educational programs for individual learners specifying objectives, services, program schedule, and evaluation criteria.

In essence, PL 94-142 addresses basic rights and equal protection issues with respect to the evaluation, identification, and placement of handicapped children; its intent is to "provide benchmark requirements for the development of assessment criteria that, if properly implemented, will be racially and culturally non-discriminating" (Mercer & Lewis, 1978, p. 3). Under this law, assessment should serve to identify handicapped students and to guide instructional planning based upon established educational needs (Cummins, 1984; Mercer & Lewis, 1978). Safeguards are provided to ensure nondiscriminatory testing and materials, evaluation, and placement practices.

Progress in the nation's response to the special educational needs of the handicapped has been promoted not only by legislation but also by litigation. MacMillan et al. (1986) suggest that the educational system has been dramatically affected by court decisions in two types of cases: Several well-known cases have established the legal right to a free and public education for severely handicapped children (*Pennsylvania Association for Retarded Children (P.A.R.C.) v. the Commonwealth of Pennsylvania*, 1972); others have addressed issues related to the assessment, classification, and placement of low-achieving minority children (*Diana v. State Board of Education*, 1970; *Larry P. v. Wilson Riles*, 1972; and *People in Action on Special Education v. Hannon*, 1980). The thrust of these and other court decisions have considerably influenced educational policy and legislation at the state and federal levels. Based on various court decisions, the following legal findings and standards have been established:

- Assessment of intellectual capabilities using measures in English is inappropriate for limited-English-proficient students.
- Identification of children as mildly retarded requires consideration of factors such as adaptive behavior, sociocultural group, and motivational system in addition to performance on measures of intelligence.
- The degree to which minority-group students have been overrepresented in special education classes for the educable mentally retarded is sufficient to constitute bias. Causes of overrepresentation have included (a) failure to take linguistic and cultural differences into account; (b) failure to appropriately identify and determine the eligibility of handicapped students and to provide proper procedures and special services; and (c) excessive reliance on IQ test results as criteria for placement of culturally and linguistically different children.
- Factors such as item bias on measures of IQ and discriminatory instruments alone do not suffice to account for misplacements and disproportionate representation of minority-group students in special education classes.*

These legislative and judicial actions have provided the impetus for examining the merits of and the basis for educational services provided to special needs students (Wang, Rubenstein, & Reynolds, 1985). This examination has prompted a call for the reform of compensatory and special education services in regular classrooms. Concerns relate to issues such as the fit between assessment practices and instructional treatment; the role of special education in dealing with problems within the regular classroom setting; and compliance with legal mandates.

## The Mildly Handicapped: Educationally Retarded and Learning Disabled

Less than 20% of the children in special education are identified on the basis of objective, medically defined criteria—that is, "rigorous physical or physiological measures" (Wang et al., 1986, p. 27). Classifications such as *educable mentally retarded* and *learning disabled* are to a large extent socially determined. Among recipients of special education services, about 19% are classified as educable mentally retarded and 36% are classified as learning disabled (MacMillan et al., 1986). Thus, the majority of learners in special education are classified by largely subjective criteria, which to some extent may be associated with socioeconomic variables.

---

*Adapted from J. L. Manni, D. W. Winikur, and M. R. Keller, 1984, *Intelligence, Mental Retardation, and the Culturally Different Child*. Courtesy of Charles C. Thomas, Publisher, Springfield, IL.

As Gelb and Mizokawa (1986) note, "Social context. . .is at least as important as the inner qualities of individuals in creating mild 'handicaps' " (p. 552). It is these learners—the "mildly handicapped"—that teachers are most likely to encounter through mainstreaming in regular classrooms. For many of these children, the regular classroom represents the least restrictive educational environment mandated by PL 94-142.

**Educable Mentally Retarded**    As defined by the U.S. government, *mentally retarded* refers to individuals "having significant sub-average general intellectual functioning existing concurrently with deficits in adaptive behavior and manifested during the developmental period" (cited in Baca & Cervantes, 1984, p. 43). Teachers must recognize that to a large extent, mental retardation is a "social status" defined primarily on the basis of two characteristics: social incompetence and cognitive impairment (Manni et al., 1984).

The mildly retarded are those at the lower end of the normal distribution: They are *"normal* in the sense that differences between them and higher-IQ children are differences of *degree,* not *kind"* (MacMillan et al., 1986, p. 687). Learners characterized as severely retarded have intellectual limitations directly attributable to chromosomal anomalies or brain damage (MacMillan et al., 1986). The social incompetence and cognitive impairment of such individuals are evident at home, in the school, and within the community. Overall, however, they represent a relatively small proportion of children and youth in special education.

That the proportion of culturally different students classified as educable mentally retarded on the basis of IQ tests is higher than their representation in the general population has been recognized for some time. Dunn (cited in Baca & Cervantes, 1984) concluded that in the 1960s, about 60–80% of the pupils in classrooms for the "retarded" were from "low-status" backgrounds. These pupils included a disproportionately high number of Afro-Americans, American Indians, Mexican-Americans, and Puerto Ricans; children from broken homes; and youngsters from nonstandard-English-speaking and non-middle-class environments. This same pattern was still prevalent in the early 1980s, according to Ysseldyke, Algozzine, and Richey (cited in Amos & Landers, 1984): "The number of minority and low socioeconomic children thought to evidence academic difficulties and behavior problems was at least twice as high as the number of high-socioeconomic status children and girls; estimates for boys were medial" (p. 145).

This nationwide pattern, however, sometimes is not observed within specific populations. Among some minority groups with a home language other than English, for example, children who are fluent in English may be overreferred to special education programs, whereas those with limited English proficiency (for whom assessment is more problematic) may be underreferred (Ochoa, Pacheco, & Omark, 1983).

In general, there appears to be agreement that although the disproportionately high numbers of minority and limited-English-proficient children classified as educable mentally retarded have been reduced to some extent in recent years, problems persist (Baca & Cervantes, 1984; MacMillan et al., 1986).

**Learning Disabled**    Individuals classified as learning disabled generally are characterized by one or more of the following: "notions of brain damage, hyperactivity, mild forms of retardation, social-emotional adjustment, language difficulties, subtle forms of deafness, perceptual problems, motor clumsiness, and above all, reading disorders" (Farnham-Diggory, cited in Cummins, 1984, p. 82). Estimates of the incidence of learning disabilities among the general population range from 2 to 20%; government estimates place the incidence as high as 26% (Cummins, 1984; MacMillan et al., 1986).

Learning disabled students usually are identified on the basis of (a) a discrepancy between what appears to be their potential and their actual classroom performance or (b) a dysfunction related to the learning process that is not attributable to environmental, cultural, economic, and other conditions (MacIntyre, Keeton, & Agard, cited in Cummins, 1984). In general, the academic problems of the learning disabled primarily involve language and literacy, and most of these students are placed in regular classes.

Students identified as learning disabled account for the largest proportion of Whites placed in special education, nearly 40%; about 26% of Blacks in special education classes are considered learning disabled (Collins & Camblin, 1983). The largely subjective criteria used to classify students as learning disabled have resulted in overidentification in general and variability in identification among different populations. Thus, it is difficult to determine whether minority children as a group are overidentified as learning disabled. Some researchers have reported that they have not been (MacMillan et al., 1986), whereas others cite evidence that some groups (e.g., Hispanics) have been overrepresented (Ortiz & Yates, cited in Cummins, 1984).

At present, students who are learning disabled cannot be consistently differentiated from those who are not (Cummins, 1984; Gelb & Mizokawa, 1986). Some question the multifold increase in the numbers of learning disabled students and hypothesize that this labeling may be an inappropriate response to academic underachievement resulting from instructional inadequacies (Gage & Berliner, 1988). Others question the purposes and needs served by identifying certain students as learning disabled while not identifying others who are "very much their twins" (Ysseldyke et al., cited in Sleeter, 1986).

## Classroom Learning Environment

Because most learning disabled students are mainstreamed in regular classrooms, the learning environment provided by teachers is crucial to their academic achievement. Despite the difficulties in formally identifying learning disabled and other mildly handicapped students, regular classroom teachers should be prepared to recognize and address the special needs of these students. To achieve this objective, Gage and Berliner (1988) recommend careful examination of student behaviors and the instructional context in which they occur.

Specifically, Gage and Berliner (1988) suggest that teachers begin by observing and describing student behaviors in different contexts. After examining the child's behavior and comparing it with that of other children, teachers need to determine whether it falls within the range of typical behavior for the age group. If the child appears to have a learning disability or behavior problem that may require treatment, a decision is made regarding consultation and referral. If a student is eventually classified as learning disabled and treatment is indicated, then an individualized learning plan is developed and implemented.

Teachers also should assess the effectiveness of their own instructional methods and explore alternative instructional strategies before looking for ways "to explain children's academic difficulties in terms of cognitive processing deficits" (Cummins, 1984, p. 5). Pedagogy is increasingly regarded as the key element in promoting academic achievement for students in special education. Appropriate pedagogical approaches, used effectively, can help students assume greater control over their

Pedagogy is increasingly regarded as the key element in promoting academic achievement for students in special education.

own learning and develop what Cummins refers to as a sense of efficacy (i.e., a belief in their own ability to succeed) as learners. Inappropriate or ineffective instructional strategies may unintentionally undermine academic achievement.

If all students are to achieve academically and develop a sense of efficacy, teachers must provide facilitative teaching and learning environments; they must also believe that they can teach all students within that environment. Creating this "ideal" classroom, Cummins argues, requires a realignment of instructional strategies based on the principles of language and knowledge acquisition. Ideally, the classroom environment should empower students, promote academic achievement, and heighten teachers' own sense of effectiveness in promoting the learning of all students. From Cummins' perspective, the promise inherent in emphasizing instructional factors is the belief that these elements, at least in principle, are more easily changed than presumed cognitive deficits in the child.

What would this classroom environment look like? In the context of bilingual special education, an instructional model emphasizing language, literacy, and cognition would have the following characteristics as described by Cummins (1984):

- Substantive and meaningful teacher-student interaction in both oral and written forms
- Promotion of peer interaction through cooperative learning
- Emphasis upon meaningful language use rather than correctness of form
- Incorporation of language development as an integral part of all content areas
- Increased emphasis on development of higher level cognitive skills
- Use of approaches that promote intrinsic rather than extrinsic motivation

## Gifted Education

Gifted and talented students are set apart from others by unique abilities, talents, interests, and psychological maturity; tremendous versatility and complexity; and a special sensitivity to the school environment (Correll, 1978). Under the law, giftedness is defined in terms of capability for high levels of performance in intellectual ability, academic aptitude, creative and productive thinking, leadership, and unusual talent in the visual and performing arts (Cheney & Beebe, 1986); some definitions also have included psychomotor and kinesthetic abilities.

Students who are gifted and talented require specific programs and services to fully develop their abilities. Presently, there are at least 30 distinct program alternatives for teaching gifted and talented students. These include, but are not limited to, Saturday and summer programs, special classes and schools, acceleration, ability grouping, enrichment, resource teachers, televised instruction, tutoring, self-directed and independent study, community-based programs, counseling, mentoring, and parent programs (Getzels & Dillon, cited in Torrance, 1986).

### Identification and Distribution of Gifted Students

As strange as it may seem, gifted children are frequently not recognized in schools. In one study at the junior high school level, more than half of the gifted students identified by researchers were not nominated by teachers (Pegnato & Birch, 1959). To assist teachers in identifying gifted and talented students, Gage and Berliner (1988) recommend that they look for the following attributes and behaviors:

- Demonstrations of talent through creative efforts or performance
- Extensive knowledge and curiosity in diverse areas of interest
- The capacity to focus on problems or activities for prolonged periods of time
- The ability to relate problems to their solutions and to produce ideas that are original and inventive
- The ability to think independently and in abstract terms

Giftedness is manifest in many forms including intellectual ability, academic aptitude, creative and productive thinking, leadership, and the visual and performing arts.

- Command of a large vocabulary and accelerated learning of basic skills and reading

Not only are many individual gifted students overlooked, but certain groups of students have traditionally remained unrecognized and underrepresented in gifted programs. Among these are underachieving, low-socioeconomic, and minority students; creative and/or divergent thinkers whose abilities are not effectively assessed through existing procedures; and learning disabled and handicapped students (Richert, 1985). Despite efforts to establish a rationale and appropriate approaches for identifying and educating creative and gifted learners from diverse populations, current educational responses have been described as ambivalent (Torrance, 1986). In general, state and local authorities have been reluctant to broaden the criteria for identifying gifted and talented students in ways that would assure inclusion of greater numbers of gifted students from these underrepresented populations (Torrance, 1986). Today, the IQ test remains the single most important measure used to identify students for gifted programs; some argue that, even as the end of the twentieth century approaches, educators still rely on "a 1900's definition of intelligence and an IQ test largely unchanged since 1930" (Hatch & Gardner, 1986, p. 147; Sternberg, 1986).

That the participation of minority students in gifted programs is disproportionately small in relation to their numbers in the student population as a whole has been well established (Mercer, 1976). In the mid-1980s, enrollments in gifted programs nationally suggested that groups such as Afro-Americans, Hispanics, and Native Americans were underrepresented by 30–70% (Richert, 1985). The results of one study in New Jersey, for example, indicated that social conditions related to racial and ethnic group and socioeconomic status tended to circumscribe access of minority and low-socioeconomic students to gifted/talented programs (McKenzie, 1986). In another study, Evans de Bernard (1985) found that only one Hispanic child was placed in a gifted class over an 8-year period in a New York City school district in which Hispanic students constitute a large segment of the student population.

## Theory vs. Practice in Gifted Education

As Torrance (cited in Masten, 1985) points out, "There is a great deal of [unrecognized] giftedness among the culturally different and the waste or underuse of these resources is tragic" (p. 83). The tragedy affects not only individuals, whose unusual talents and abilities are not nurtured to fruition, but also society, which is deprived of the fullest possible range of creative, innovative thinking. An important first step in correcting this situation is to compare what is known about identifying and teaching creative and gifted learners with what is typically done in U.S. schools.

Treffinger and Renzulli (1986) made just such a comparison between educational research and theory and common educational practice. Their analysis reveals the following, rather startling, discrepancies:

| *We know that...* | *We continue to...* |
|---|---|
| 1. Ability cannot be represented by a single score or a single measure. | Use scores as the primary basis for determining access to special programs. |
| 2. Many human talents are independent. | Consider giftedness primarily in academic terms. |
| 3. Aptitudes and talents are dynamic potentials, which can be developed in appropriate settings. | Think of giftedness as a fixed and permanent endowment, which individuals either have or do not have. |
| 4. Most students benefit from instruction involving thinking processes at different levels. | View "thinking skills" as the exclusive purview of a select group of students. |
| 5. Broadening the definition of giftedness would promote the identification and development of many more students with special talents and abilities. | Limit special instruction and services to a select few labeled as gifted based on quite restrictive, culturally biased criteria. |

## Learning Styles

The previous discussion has focused on two populations of students—the handicapped and the gifted. These students can be fruitfully viewed as part of the spectrum of the diversity that characterizes multicultural education. This diversity is manifested not only in the cultural, social, and linguistic backgrounds that students bring to the classroom but also in generalized patterns of response to the instructional environment; these patterns have been termed *learning styles*.

Teachers, for example, have long observed that all learners do not respond in exactly the same way to instruction, and some have posited the existence of culturally related variability in learning styles. Laosa (1977) states that "different cultural groups exhibit nonsuperficial differences in such educationally important variables as the manner of approaching and coping with cognitive and perceptual tasks and with interpersonal, motivational, and other learning situations" (p. 26). Recognizing the existence of individual and group variations is one thing; translating what is known about the relationship and interaction between culture, learning, and personality dynamics into educational practice is something else. Given the complexity of this translation process, it is not surprising that few "learning strategies have been associated validly with ethnic group membership" (Laosa, 1977, p. 27).

Learning styles reflect and are one manifestation of individuals' personality. Thus, they are influenced and determined by many of the same elements associated with personality development. According to the model of Garza and Lipton (1982), personality development in a multicultural society involves the interaction of social, ecological, cultural, personal, and behavioral elements, as illustrated in Figure 5–1.

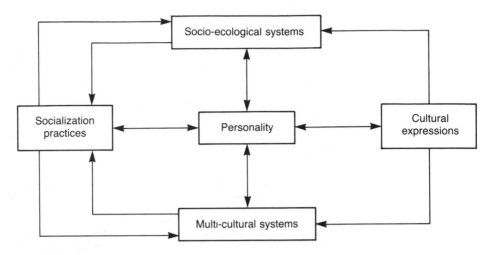

**Figure 5–1**   Interactional model of personality development.

Source: R. T. Garza and J. P. Lipton, "Theoretical Perspectives on Chicano Personality Development," 1982, *Hispanic Journal of Behavioral Sciences, 4*(4), 407–432. Reprinted by permission.

This model relates (a) "personality," which includes affective and cognitive factors, perceptions, aptitudes, and abilities; (b) multicultural systems that bring to bear cultural, social, and environmental influences; and (c) observable behaviors represented through cultural expressions. By focusing on the individual, this model allows for variability within groups: "Even identical cultural, socialization, and situational factors may lead to different personality configurations" (Garza & Lipton, 1982, p. 427). From a teacher's perspective, this model is useful because it emphasizes the interrelationship of elements central to any discussion of personality and learning styles. It also demonstrates that the personality of each learner is a unique expression of the influence and interaction of various elements.

According to Cornett (1983), learning styles are consistent patterns of behavior defined in terms of cognitive, affective, and physiological dimensions. To a certain extent, they are stable indicators of how individuals process information and respond to affective, sensory, and environmental dimensions of the instructional process. Just as cognitive styles encompass consistent patterned responses to the total environment, learning styles represent the characteristic way individuals respond to the instructional environment (Collier & Hoover, 1987).

A useful framework for looking at learning styles is in terms of their cognitive, affective, and physiological dimensions. The *cognitive* dimension refers to how individuals decode, encode, process, store, and retrieve information. The *affective* dimension involves emotional and personality characteristics related to motivation, attention, locus of control, interests, willingness to take risks, persistence, responsibility, and sociability. The *physiological* dimension encompasses sensory perceptions (e.g., visual, auditory, kinesthetic) and environmental characteristics (e.g., noise level, light, temperature, room arrangement) (Cornett, 1983).

## Cognitive and Affective Dimensions

**Effects of Culture**    The relationship between culture and learning styles—although not fully understood—is an important one: "Culture shapes the way we think (cognition), the way we interact (behavior), and the way we transmit knowledge to the next generation (education)" (Collier & Hoover, 1987, p. 7). Cultural and cognitive development are closely intertwined. Social and environmental factors, as well as socialization practices, influence cognitive and affective preferences. These, in turn, are manifested in incentives and motivation, interpersonal relationships, and patterns of intellectual abilities (Ramirez & Castaneda, 1974). For example, *field sensitivity* and *field independence* are two constructs used to describe certain combinations of cognitive and affective behaviors and preferences. By and large, field-sensitive individuals prefer a more global, holistic, and relational approach, whereas field-independent individuals display a more analytic, verbal, and sequential style (Hatch, 1983).

The extent to which members of different cultures and subcultures display certain cognitive and affective tendencies (e.g., to be field sensitive or field independent) has been the subject of debate among educators for many years. Teachers must remember, however, that "it is risky to generalize from *group* findings to *individuals*" (Laosa, 1977, p. 28). Moreover, although some studies have revealed differences in cognitive and affective behaviors or patterns among groups, they have also established that significant differences exist *within* groups as well. For example, differences in maternal teaching behaviors, in both qualitative and quantitative terms, have been found to be much greater within ethnic groups than between ethnic groups (Laosa, 1977).

**Assessment of Learning-Style Preferences**    Cornett (1983) observes that one's teaching style is influenced to some extent by one's learning style. Under most circumstances, the manner in which individuals teach is dictated by the way in which they learn; even the levels and subjects taught can reflect individuals' preferences. For example, field-sensitive individuals tend to gravitate toward elementary teaching; those who are field independent seem to be more attracted to mathematics and science at the secondary level.

Because of the influence that teachers' personal learning style has on their teaching style, it is important that they recognize their own learning-style preferences. This will help them understand how their "natural" teaching style may inadvertently conflict with or be unresponsive to the learning styles of some of their students. Table 5–1 presents an inventory for use by teachers to assess their own learning style.

Obviously, in order for teachers to select and use teaching strategies appropriate to the learning styles of their students, they must be able to recognize and describe those learning styles. Table 5–2 presents an inventory for assessing learning-style preferences of students; definitions of the dimensions in this inventory are given in Table 5–3. Although this inventory was developed by Collier and Hoover (1987) especially for use with minority handicapped students, it is generally applicable to all students.

**Table 5-1**   Informal Learning-Style Inventory

*Directions:*   For the sections dealing with cognitive and affective styles, put an X on the dotted line at the point where you think you fall with regard to each polar concept expressed by each pair of words. For the section dealing with physical aspects of learning style, check your preferences and describe the environment in which you learn best. After completing the inventory, draw a line connecting the X's. This, along with your preferences, will give you a rough profile of your learning and teaching style.

**Cognitive Style** (concerned with processing, encoding, storage, and retrieval of information)

| | |
|---|---|
| sequential | random |
| serial | simultaneous |
| focusing | scanning |
| separating | integrating |
| parts | whole |
| discriminate | generalize |
| abstract | concrete |
| compartmentalization | differentiation |
| narrow categories | broad categories |
| analyze by describing | draw relationships based on functioning and themes |
| reflective | impulsive |
| deductive | inductive |
| convergent | divergent |
| analytic | global |
| splitter | lumper |
| logical | metaphoric |
| words | images |
| time-oriented | nontemporal |
| digital | spatial |
| details and facts | generalizations |
| careful | quick |
| literal | figurative |
| outline | summarize |
| surface approach | deep approach |
| memorize | associate/understand |
| verbal communication | nonverbal communication |
| implications | analogies |

**Affective Style** (concerned with attention, motivation, and personality)

| | |
|---|---|
| objective | subjective |
| practical | theoretical |
| reality | fantasy |
| subject-oriented | people-oriented |
| realistic | imaginative |
| intellectual | creative |
| close-minded | open-minded |
| conformist | individualist |
| concentration | distraction |
| reserved | outgoing |

**Table 5-1**  *continued*

thinker............................intuiter
rigid.............................flexible
Groucho humor                                    Harpo humor
(puns, satire).............................(slapstick)
competitive.............................cooperative
structured.............................unstructured
intrinsically                                    extrinsically
motivated.............................motivated
persistent.............................gives up easily
cautious.............................risk-taking
intolerant of                                    tolerant of
ambiguity.............................ambiguity
internal locus of                                external locus of
control.............................control
leader.............................follower
pessimistic.............................optimistic
future-oriented.............................present-oriented
does not like
pressures.............................likes pressure
likes working alone.............................likes working in a
group

**Physical Style** (concerned with perceptual modes, energy level, time preferences, and environment)

| RECEIVING INFORMATION | | EXPRESSING YOURSELF | |
|---|---|---|---|
| visual (reading/viewing) | _____ | visual (writing/drawing) | _____ |
| auditory (listening) | _____ | oral (speaking) | _____ |
| kinesthetic (feeling/doing) | _____ | kinesthetic (art, demonstrating, showing) | _____ |

Describe the environment in which you learn best (lighting, furniture, room arrangement, noise level, time of day, etc.).

*Interpretation*

Cognitive profile

| To the left: | More left-brain oriented |
|---|---|
| To the right: | More right-brain oriented |
| Neither/mix: | Balance of right and left |

Affective profile

| To the left: | More systematic, structured, organized |
|---|---|
| To the right: | More flexible, group-oriented, creative |
| Neither/mix: | Balance of right and left |

**Source:** C. E. Cornett, *What You Should Know About Teaching and Learning Styles.* Copyright © 1983 by Phi Delta Kappa Educational Foundation. Reprinted by permission.

**Table 5-2**  Inventory for Identifying Student Learning-Style Preferences

*Directions:*  Place an X on each line nearest the description that is characteristic of the student's learning preferences. See Table 5-3 for definitions of terms.

### Field

| FIELD INDEPENDENCE | FIELD SENSITIVITY |
|---|---|
| Analytical | Global |
| Separating | Integrating |
| Parts | Whole |
| Discriminate | Generalize |

### Tolerance

| HIGH TOLERANCE | LOW TOLERANCE |
|---|---|
| Fantasy | Reality |
| Imaginative | Realistic |
| Individualist | Conformist |
| Flexible | Rigid |

### Tempo

| REFLECTIVENESS | IMPULSIVENESS |
|---|---|
| Careful | Quick |
| Sequential | Random |
| Serial | Simultaneous |
| Reflective | Impulsive |

### Categorization

| BROAD CATEGORIZER | NARROW CATEGORIZER |
|---|---|
| Inclusive | Exclusive |
| Lumper | Splitter |
| Generalizations | Details |
| Summarize | Outline |

### Persistence

| HIGH PERSISTENCE | LOW PERSISTENCE |
|---|---|
| Focusing | Scanning |
| Persistent | Gives up easily |
| Concentration | Distraction |
| Structured | Unstructured |

### Anxiety

| HIGH ANXIETY | LOW ANXIETY |
|---|---|
| Cautious | Risk-taking |
| Dislikes pressure | Likes pressure |
| Negative stress response | Positive stress response |
| Finds challenge difficult | Finds challenge motivating |

### Locus of Control

| INTERNAL LOCUS | EXTERNAL LOCUS |
|---|---|
| Attributes success to own efforts | Attributes success to luck or ease of task |
| Attributes failure to own lack of effort | Attributes failure to fate, others, difficulty |
| Blames self for circumstances | Blames others for circumstances |
| Accepts personal responsibility for circumstances | Accepts that circumstances may be due to others |

**Source:**  C. Collier and J. J. Hoover, *Cognitive Learning Strategies for Minority Handicapped Students.* Copyright © 1987 by Hamilton Publications. Adapted by permission.

**Table 5–3**   Definition of Terms Related to Learning Styles

| Term | General Tendency |
|---|---|
| Field independence | See everything as elements making up a whole; emphasize the parts and not the whole. |
| Field sensitivity | See the whole; difficulty separating the whole from its parts. |
| High tolerance | Accept experiences that vary markedly from the ordinary or even from reality or the truth. |
| Low tolerance | Show a preference for conventional ideas and reality. |
| Reflectiveness | Take more time and generate more effort to provide appropriate responses. |
| Impulsiveness | Give first answer that comes to mind even if frequently wrong or inappropriate. |
| Broad categorizer | Include many items in a category and lessen the risk of leaving something out. |
| Narrow categorizer | Exclude doubtful items and lessen the probability of including something that doesn't belong. |
| High persistence | Work until the task has been completed; seek any necessary help. |
| Low persistence | Short attention; inability to work on a task for any length of time. |
| High anxiety | Perform less well when challenged by a difficult task. |
| Low anxiety | Perform better when challenged by a difficult task. |
| Internal locus of control | Think of oneself as responsible for own behavior. |
| External locus of control | See circumstances as beyond one's own control; luck or others are seen as responsible for one's behavior. |

**Source:** C. Collier and J. J. Hoover, *Cognitive Learning Strategies for Minority Handicapped Students.* Copyright © 1987 by Hamilton Publications. Adapted by permission.

**Accommodating Instruction to Diverse Learning Styles**   Students are likely to learn best in instructional environments that are consistent with their learning-style preferences. For this reason, teachers faced with culturally diverse classes and students who differ in their learning preferences must be able to draw upon a variety of teaching strategies appropriate to various learning styles. The following guidelines can help teachers create a classroom environment that is sensitive to many different learning styles (Cornett, 1983):

- Use all types of questions to promote different levels of thinking.
- Provide students with a structured overview of material to be learned using advance organizers (see Chapter 7).
- Establish a routine in which students expect to learn at least one new thing every day and are asked to share what they have learned.

- Explain the purpose for listening, viewing, and reading activities.
- Use brainstorming, pretests, word associations, fantasy journeys, etc., as warm-up activities.
- Incorporate intermittent practice (e.g., rehearsal strategies) to promote recall and skills development.
- Provide opportunities for students to process and retrieve information using multisensory means (e.g., give written and oral directions).
- Bring closure to lessons using different review and reflection techniques such as summarizing, creative writing, reciting, opinion surveys, and drama.

## Physiological Dimension

**Sensory Perception**   The visual, auditory, and kinesthetic senses are the perceptual channels or modalities through which individuals receive, process, and retain information. Research in this area indicates the following (Barbe, 1980; Barbe & Milone, 1981):

- All children have *modality strengths* (single, dual, or mixed); that is, one or another modality is most efficient in receiving and processing information.
- Children at the same grade level (boys and girls; bilinguals and monolinguals) have similar modality strengths.
- Modality strengths change over time. At the primary level, children rely on the auditory modality more than the visual or kinesthetic. By the time pupils reach the upper elementary grades, the visual modality becomes dominant.
- With age, modalities become integrated. Although children rely predominately on a single modality, older learners are able to utilize all three effectively; nonetheless, most individuals continue to exhibit differential modality strengths as adults.
- Student and teacher modality strengths appear to interact.
- Individuals teach in accordance with their personal modality strengths and are most effective teaching in that mode.

By the early 1980s, researchers encouraged teachers to assess students' modality strengths and to develop greater awareness of their own (Barbe & Milone, 1981). Although the relationship between modality strength and achievement is unclear, efforts to determine which materials and approaches are most effective with students displaying certain modality strengths have continued (Carbo, 1987a,b) and remain controversial (Stahl, 1988).

**Environmental Characteristics**   The Learning Styles Inventory developed by Dunn, Dunn, and Price (1975, 1978, 1979, 1981, 1984, 1985) draws attention to a number of environmental, emotional, sociological, physical, and psychological elements

All learners have modality strengths, that is, tendencies to rely on one perceptual channel more than the others.

that can influence the instructional process. Although the environmental characteristics included in this inventory are frequently overlooked, such elements as sound, light, design, and temperature can effect students' performance in the classroom.

## Learning Styles and Educational Outcomes

A diagrammatic illustration of the elements that affect learning style, as visualized by Dunn (1984), is presented in Figure 5–2. Given the seemingly large number

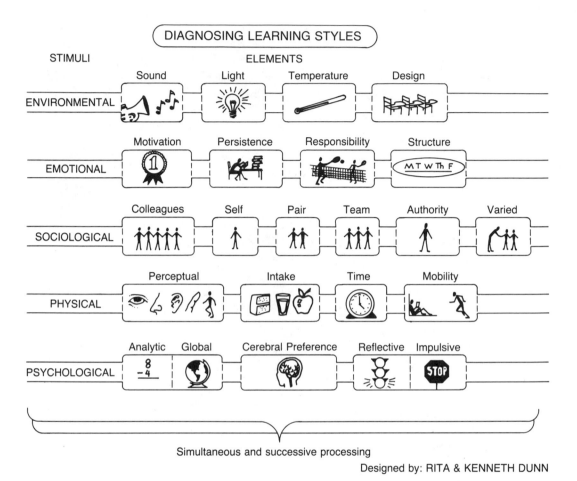

**Figure 5-2** Component elements characterizing learning-style preferences.

**Source:** R. Dunn, "Learning Styles: State of the Science," 1984, *Theory Into Practice, XXIII*(1), 10–19. Published by The Ohio State University, College of Education. Reprinted by permission.

of possible elements to be considered, it is fortunate that the number of elements to which individuals react strongly appears to be relatively small, ranging from 6 to 14 per person (Dunn, 1984). According to Dunn, when strong learning-style preferences are accommodated, academic achievement, attitudes, and behavior will be enhanced.

Teachers should keep several caveats in mind when considering various models proposed to explain and describe learning styles and the relationship of learning styles to academic performance. The first is the danger that constructs may be oversimplified when applied to certain groups (e.g., minority students; males and females) and used to stereotype or label rather than to identify individual behaviors that are educationally relevant. The second involves limitations in the constructs themselves, some of which involve assumptions regarding the importance and universality of culturally relative values. For example, although independence is highly valued by many persons in American society, for others values such as cooperation, mutuality, and respect may take precedence (Hunt, 1981). Such cultural values may well influence students' learning styles and educators' evaluations of them.

Finally, although learning styles may influence academic behavior and performance, overemphasizing individual preferences is not advisable. First, many of the interactions between learner factors and instructional process are not captured by the concept of learning style. Hence, no single, dominant learner dimension should dictate a specific mode of instruction. Second, most teachers intuitively employ multiple teaching approaches, and students demonstrate flexibility and adaptability in dealing with these different modes of instruction (Good & Stipek, cited in Doyle & Rutherford, 1984).

## Learning Strategies

Teachers empower students by helping them become more effective learners; teaching students how to use and apply learning strategies can be an important part of this process. The rationale for looking at what students do while learning is simple: "Good teaching includes teaching students how to learn, how to remember, how to think, and how to motivate themselves" (Weinstein & Mayer, 1986, p. 315). Learning strategies have been defined by Weinstein and Mayer (1986) as behaviors and thinking skills utilized during the learning process to influence how information is processed. These involve affective and motivational states as well as the way learners select, acquire, organize, and integrate new information. According to the cognitive model of learning, the learner is viewed as an active participant in the teaching-learning process, one whose use of mental structures and processes in dealing with information plays a critical role. Hence, what students learn depends jointly upon the efficacy and interaction of both teaching and learning strategies.

The learning strategies children use influence how they approach academic learning, as well as general and interpersonal problem-solving situations (Meyers & Lytle, 1986). Moreover, knowledge of these strategies can be developed and taught. In the long run, heightened recognition that learners' knowledge of their own cognitive processes is an important part of the learning process may lead to improved instruction.

### Types and Developmental Progression

Eight major categories of learning strategies have been identified: basic and complex rehearsal strategies; basic and complex elaboration strategies; basic and com-

What students learn is dependent upon the efficacy and interaction of both teaching and learning strategies.

plex organizational strategies; comprehension monitoring strategies; and affective and motivational strategies (Weinstein & Mayer, 1986). Descriptions and examples of these learning strategies are presented in Table 5–4.

Research reveals that there is a developmental progression associated with many of these strategies (Weinstein & Mayer, 1986). Use of rehearsal strategies, for example, generally is acquired and refined as learners progress through the primary and intermediate grades. Other strategies emerge later, as learners grow older. Researchers hypothesize that various learning strategies can be described and taught to students at appropriate levels of maturity. Indeed, students explicitly taught to use various strategies effectively tend to outperform those in control groups. For example, Weinstein and Mayer (1986) report that reading performance can be significantly improved by teaching students comprehension monitoring. Comparisons of good and poor readers reveal that those with poor comprehension skills do not naturally use the active learning strategies required to monitor understanding.

**Table 5-4** Learning Strategies

| Category | Example | School Task |
|---|---|---|
| Basic Rehearsal Strategies | Repeating names of items in ordered list | Remembering order of planets from sun; order in which characters are introduced in a play |
| Complex Rehearsal Strategies | Copying, underlining, or shadowing material | Underlining main events in a story; copying portions of a lesson on causes of a war or revolution |
| Basic Elaboration Strategies | Forming a mental image or sentence relating items in each pair from a list of paired associated words | Forming a phrase or sentence relating the name of a state and its major agricultural product; forming a mental image of a scene described in a poem |
| Complex Elaboration Strategies | Paraphrasing, summarizing, or describing how new information relates to existing knowledge | Creating an analogy between the operation of a post office and a computer; relating the information presented about the structure of complex molecules to that of simple molecules |
| Basic Organizational Strategies | Grouping or ordering of items to be learned from a list or a section of prose | Organizing foreign vocabulary words into the categories for parts of speech; creating a chronological listing of events leading up to the Declaration of Independence |
| Complex Organizational Strategies | Outlining a passage or creating a hierarchy | Outlining assigned chapters in a textbook; creating a diagram to show the relationship among the stress forces in a structural design |
| Comprehension Monitoring Strategies | Checking for comprehension failures | Using self-questioning to check understanding of material presented in class; using textbook questions at beginning of section to guide reading behavior |
| Affective and Motivational Strategies | Being alert and relaxed to help overcome test anxiety | Reducing external distractions by studying in a quiet place; using thought stopping to prevent thoughts of doing poorly from directing attention away from a test and toward fears of failure |

**Source:** Adapted from C. F. Weinstein and R. F. Mayer, "The Teaching of Learning Strategies. In *Handbook of Research on Teaching*, (3rd ed.). Copyright © 1986 by Macmillan. Used by permission.

## Classroom Applications

The implications of work on learning strategies are relevant for teachers at all levels. Efforts to implement these learning strategies should extend from elementary through university levels and across content areas. These strategies can benefit students of diverse abilities and talents, and they have been incorporated into programs for gifted and talented learners (Torrance, 1986) and into special education programs (Collier & Hoover, 1987).

One example of the use of learning strategies at the elementary level is Reading Recovery, an early intervention program. Based upon a model developed for use with culturally diverse populations in New Zealand, this program provides short-term, intensive, individualized instruction for first-grade pupils identified at risk of failing (Boehnlein, 1987). Students are given 30 to 40 hours of specific instruction about learning strategies characteristic of good readers, that is, techniques for deriving meaning from structure, self-correcting nonsensical errors, self-monitoring through visual and auditory cues, using book language, and developing memory for text. Rather than asking children to sound out words or giving them the word, teachers ask questions like the following (Boehnlein, 1987):

- Does it make sense? (for visual and meaning cues)
- Does that look right? (for visual cues)
- What would you expect to see or hear? (for letter or sound cues)
- Can we say it that way? (for structure or grammar cues)

Thus far, research findings on the effectiveness of the Reading Recovery program appear to be positive. Estimates are that after this intervention, 90% of the students involved in the program—those originally in the lowest 20% of their class on the basis of test scores—equal and even surpass the class average in reading (Boehnlein, 1987).

At the secondary level, learning strategies typical of good students have been incorporated into programs such as Learning to Learn (Heiman, 1985). Good students typically generate questions on new material, discuss content, formulate hypotheses, and check for understanding. They also identify specific instructional goals, develop informal ways to assess their progress, and divide complex content principles, ideas, and tasks into smaller, more manageable units. In Learning to Learn, these behaviors provide the basis for training junior and senior high school students in a broad range of content areas (e.g., chemistry, social studies).

One specialized use of learning strategies is in teaching minority handicapped students. For minority handicapped students, the purpose of strategy instruction is "to increase student control over and use of strategies which increase the capacity for learning" (Collier & Hoover, 1987, pp. 24–25). The following six strategies have been identified as especially effective with this student population (Collier & Hoover, 1987):

- *Active Processing:* Scanning, summarizing, generating questions, clarifying, predicting, and elaborating upon information to be acquired.
- *Analogy:* Recall of familiar patterns similar to new ones; identification of analogous elements between concepts, materials, or experiences.
- *Coping:* Problem-solving by confronting the problem, planning a strategy, seeking assistance, implementing the solution, developing alternatives, and achieving a solution.
- *Evaluation:* Task analysis, strategy identification and implementation, feedback, elaboration, and generalization to other tasks.
- *Organization:* Concept development involving data awareness, grouping, labeling, examining groups, and self-testing.
- *Rehearsal:* Recall of ideas, reading passages, and related elements; use of self-questioning, visualizing, and summarizing.

## Did You Know That. . .?

With the advent of a widespread acceptance of the use of mental tests, the number of immigrant aliens deported for feeble-mindedness increased about 350% in 1913 and 570% in 1914 (Goddard, cited in Cummins, 1984).

According to a 1981 government report, 8.6% of the student population nationwide were receiving special education services; 36% of these students were identified as learning disabled. According to estimates published in 1985, 10.4% of the student population received special education services; 34% of these students were considered learning disabled (Mick, 1985).

Of the approximately 5 million limited-English-proficient students in the United States, an estimated 600,000 are handicapped (Baca & Cervantes, 1984). In the 1980s, Hispanic students tend to be enrolled at significantly higher rates in programs for the learning disabled than in programs for the educable mentally retarded. Of the estimated 10.7% of Hispanic students receiving special education services, 44% were classified as learning disabled (Mick, 1985).

Federal statistics indicate that White students accounted for 75% of the nation's total student enrollment and represented 71% of the population in special education programs in the early 1980s. Blacks accounted for 16% of the total school population and 21% of enrollment in special education classes. Nearly half (46%) of the Black students in special education were classified as mentally retarded, whereas only 22% of the White students were so classified (Collins & Camblin, 1983).

Figures from a government study in the mid-1970s indicated that 13% of all 17-year-olds were functionally illiterate (Levin, 1987).

Famous people with learning disabilities include Thomas Edison, Albert Einstein, Nelson Rockefeller, Hans Christian Anderson, Leonardo da Vinci, Bruce Jenner, Cher, Tom Cruise, and Henry Winkler (Roth & Souza, 1987). On the basis of various existing definitions, over 80% of normal students could be identified as learning disabled (Ysseldyke, cited in Wang et al., 1986).

## Summary

Special, gifted, and multicultural education are related in that all are concerned with maximizing the potential of individual learners with a broad array of talents, aptitudes, and backgrounds. Recognition of this diversity underscores the need for an educational system geared toward "average students" to adequately serve *all* students. Today, many—perhaps most—regular classroom teachers must deal with a student population that is culturally diverse and includes minimally handicapped and gifted students.

The student population served by special education programs is itself widely diverse. It includes students who are learning disabled, mentally retarded, and emotionally disturbed, and those with visual, hearing, speech, and physical impairments. Some populations (e.g., preschoolers, adolescents, and migrant children) generally are underserved by special education programs, whereas others (e.g., ethnic minorities) are overrepresented in these programs. Federal legislation and court decisions have significantly influenced special education policy, particularly as regards due process, protection from discriminatory assessment procedures, regular classroom placements (to the extent possible), and individualized learning programs.

Teachers need to recognize that the majority of children and youth in special education programs do not have disabilities that imply diminished cognitive abilities. Two major categories of mildly handicapped learners are educable mentally retarded and learning disabled. To a degree, both are subjective and socially-determined classifications in which socioeconomic variables are at least as important as individual characteristics. In working with disabled learners, teachers must consider specific behaviors, their prevalence within the age group, and the instructional context in which they occur. They are also advised to focus closely on pedagogy as the key to enhancing the academic achievement of these students.

Students in gifted education also bring unique abilities, talents, and needs to the classroom. As a group, gifted learners are frequently unrecognized, especially among minority populations. Actual educational practice in providing for the gifted and talented appears to be several years behind current research and thinking in the field.

Understanding how to meet the needs of students experiencing learning difficulties or demonstrating behavioral problems requires insight about the relationship between the child's individual abilities, the broader sociocultural context, and the learning environment provided in the classroom. Given the legal mandate that educational services be provided as much as possible in regular classrooms, teachers need to create facilitative teaching and learning environments in which all students can achieve academically to their fullest potential.

Knowledge of learning styles can help teachers in designing classroom environments and instructional strategies that are compatible with individual patterns of behavior along cognitive, affective, and physiological dimensions. Teachers can also use learning strategies to "empower" students, that is, to help them develop effective learning skills so that they can become successful learners.

## References

Amos, O. E., & Landers, M. F. (1984). Special education and multicultural education: A compatible marriage. *Theory Into Practice, XXIII*(2), 144–150.

Baca, L. M., & Cervantes, H. T. (1984). *The bilingual special education interface*. St. Louis: Times Mirror/Mosby.

Barbe, W. B. (1980). The best kept secret in education today: Modality-based instruction. *Aids to Bilingual Communication Report, 1*(1), 1, 5–7.

Barbe, W. B., & Milone, (1981). What we know about modality strengths. *Educational Leadership, 38*(5), 378–380.

Boehnlein, M. (1987). Reading intervention for high-risk first-graders. *Educational Leadership, 44*(6), 32–37.

Carbo, M. (1987a). Reading styles research: "What works" isn't always phonics. *Phi Delta Kappan, 68*(6), 431–435.

Carbo, M. (1987b). Deprogramming reading failure: Giving unequal learners an unequal chance. *Phi Delta Kappan, 69*(3), 197–202.

Cardenas, J. A., & First, J. McC. (1985). Children at risk. *Educational Leadership, 43*(1), 5–8.

Cheney, M., & Beebe, R. J. (1986). Gifted education: Continuing controversies. *ERS Spectrum, 4*(3), 12–17.

Collier, C., & Hoover, J. J. (1987). *Cognitive learning strategies for minority handicapped students*. Lindale, TX: Hamilton Publications.

Collins, R., & Camblin, L. D., Jr. (1983). The politics and science of learning disability classification: Implications for Black children. *Contemporary Education, 54*(2), 113–118.

Cornett, C. E. (1983). *What you should know about teaching and learning styles*. Bloomington, IN: Phi Delta Kappa Educational Foundation.

Corno, L., & Snow, R. E. (1986). Adapting teaching to individual differences among learners. In M. C. Wittrock (Ed.), *Handbook of research on teaching*. (3rd ed., pp. 605–629). New York: Macmillan.

Correll, M. (1978). *Teaching the gifted and talented*. Bloomington, IN: Phi Delta Kappa Educational Foundation.

Cummins, J. (1984). *Bilingualism and special education: Issues in assessment and pedagogy*. San Diego, CA: College Hill Press.

Doyle, W., & Rutherford, B. (1984). Classroom research on matching learning and teaching styles. *Theory Into Practice, XXIII*(1), 20–25.

Dunn, R. (1984). Learning styles: State of the science. *Theory Into Practice, XXIII*(1), 10–19.

Dunn, R., Dunn, K., & Price, G. (1975, 1978, 1979, 1981, 1984, 1985). *Learning styles inventory*. Lawrence, KA: Price Systems.

Evans de Bernard, A. (1985). Why Jose can't get in the gifted class: The bilingual child and standardized reading tests. *Roeper Review, VIII*(2), 80–85.

Fradd, S. H., & Vega, J. E. (1987). Legal considerations. In S. H. Fradd & W. J. Tikunoff. *Bilingual education and bilingual special education* (pp. 45–74). Boston: College Hill Press and Little, Brown.

Gage, N. L., & Berliner, D. (1988). *Educational psychology.* (4th ed.). Boston: Houghton Mifflin.

Garza, R. T., & Lipton, J. P. (1982). Theoretical perspectives on Chicano personality development. *Hispanic Journal of Behavioral Sciences, 4*(4), 407–432.

Gelb, S. A., & Mizokawa, D. T. (1986). Special education and social structure: The commonality of "exceptionality." *American Educational Research Journal, 23*(4), 543–557.

Hatch, E. M. (1983). *Psycholinguistics.* Rowley, MA: Newbury House.

Hatch, T. C., & Gardner, H. (1986). From testing intelligence to assessing competencies: A pluralistic view of intellect. *Roeper Review, VIII*(3), 147–150.

Heiman, M. (1985). Learning to learn. *Educational Leadership, 43*(1), 20–24.

Hunt, D. E. (1981). Learning style and the interdependence of practice and theory. *Phi Delta Kappan, 62*(7), 647.

Laosa, L. M. (1977). Multicultural education—How psychology can contribute. *Journal of Teacher Education, XXVIII*(3), 26–30.

Levin, H. M. (1987). Accelerated schools for disadvantaged students. *Educational Leadership, 44*(6), 19–21.

MacMillan, D. L., Keogh, B. K., & Jones, R. L. (1986). Special education research on mildly handicapped learners. In M. C. Wittrock (Ed.), *Handbook of research on teaching* (3rd ed., pp. 686–724). New York: Macmillan.

Manni, J. L., Winikur, D. W., & Keller, M. R. (1984). *Intelligence, mental retardation and the culturally different child.* Springfield, IL: Charles C. Thomas.

Masten, W. G. (1985). Identification of gifted minority students: Past research, future directions. *Roeper Review, VIII*(2), 83–85.

McKenzie, J. A. (1986). The influence of identification practices, race and SES on the identification of gifted students. *Gifted Child Quarterly, 30*(2), 93–95.

Mercer, J. R. (1976, May). *Identifying the gifted Chicano child.* Paper presented at the First Symposium on Chicano Psychology, University of California, Irvine.

Mercer, J. R., & Lewis, J. F. (1978). Nondiscriminatory, multidimensional assessment for educational placement and planning. *UCLA Educator, 20*(2).

Meyers, J., & Lytle, S. (1986). Assessment of the learning process. *Exceptional Children, 53*(2), 138–144.

Mick, L. B. (1985). Assessment procedures as related to enrollment patterns of Hispanic students in special education. *Educational Research Quarterly, 9*(2), 27–35.

Ochoa, A. M., Pacheco, R., & Omark, D. R. (1983). Addressing the learning disability needs of limited-English-proficient students: Beyond language and race issues. *Learning Disability Quarterly, 6*(4), 416–423.

Pegnato, C. W., & Birch, J. W. (1959). Locating gifted children in junior high schools: A comparison of methods. *Exceptional Children, 25*(7), 300–304.

Phipps, P. M. (1982). The LD learner is often a boy—Why? *Academic Therapy, 17*(4), 425–430.

Ramirez, M., & Castaneda, A. (1974). *Cultural democracy, bicognitive development and education*. New York: Academic Press.

Richert, E. S. (1985). Identification of gifted students: An update. *Roeper Review, VIII*(2), 68–72.

Roth, S., & Souza, P. (1987). *In a different way*. Chico, CA: Chico Unified School District.

Shinn, M. R., Tindal, G. A., & Spira, D. A. (1987). Special education referrals as an index of teacher tolerance: Are teachers imperfect tests? *Exceptional Children, 54*(1), 32–40.

Sleeter, C. E. (1986). Learning disabilities: The social construction of a special education category. *Exceptional Children, 53*(1), 46–54.

Stahl, S. A. (1988). Is there evidence to support matching reading styles and initial reading methods? *Phi Delta Kappan, 70*(4), 317–322.

Sternberg, R. J. (1986). Identifying the gifted through IQ: Why a little bit of knowledge is a dangerous thing. *Roeper Review, VIII*(3), 143–147.

Torrance, E. P. (1986). Teaching creative and gifted learners. In M. C. Wittrock (Ed.), *Handbook of research on teaching* (3rd ed., pp. 630–647). New York: Macmillan.

Treffinger, D. J., & Renzulli, J. S. (1986). Giftedness as potential for creative productivity: Transcending IQ scores. *Roeper Review, VIII*(3), 151–154.

Wang, M. C., Reynolds, M. C., & Walberg, H. J. (1986). Rethinking special education. *Educational Leadership, 44*(1), 26–31.

Wang, M. C., Rubenstein, J. L., & Reynolds, M. C. (1985). Clearing the road to success for students with special needs. *Educational Leadership, 43*(1), 62–67.

Weinstein, C. F., & Mayer, R. F. (1986). The teaching of learning strategies. In M. C. Wittrock (Ed.), *Handbook of research on teaching* (3rd ed., pp. 315–327). New York: Macmillan.

# 6

# Instructional Materials in Multicultural Education

*Curriculum materials profoundly affect learners and their learning—in the way they view themselves and their social groups;. . .in the way they are motivated to work and play and learn and live.\**
*Rosenberg (p. 44)*

Implementation of a multicultural curriculum requires instructional materials that reflect the diverse character of American society. The "density of diversity"—to borrow from Cortes (1981)—is a reality in the 1990s, one that cannot be ignored. At the national level, the U.S. population is becoming increasingly diverse along many dimensions, including ethnicity. On a global scale, interdependence is a major characteristic of relationships among nations and peoples of the world. Students' knowledge of and attitudes toward people in other parts of the world have more implications than ever. Moreover, as students from all ethnic groups find themselves in classrooms with students whose backgrounds are considerably different from their own, "global understanding and related intercultural sensitivity attain a growing significance here at home, as well as in our relations with the rest of the world" (Cortes & Fleming, 1986a, p. 384).

---

\*From M. Rosenberg, "Evaluate Your Textbooks for Racism, Sexism." In M. Dunfee (Ed.), *Eliminating Ethnic Bias.* Reprinted with permission of the Association for Supervision and Curriculum Development. Copyright © 1974 by the Association for Supervision and Curriculum Development.

Although teachers cannot control what students know and learn about diversity, they will have to deal with it. It's inescapable. The purpose of this chapter is to assist teachers in looking at curriculum materials with an eye to dealing with diversity. Because of the centrality of textbooks and other materials in the teaching of content, teachers must be aware of the inherent attitudes, values, and perspectives these materials convey to students. Skills are needed to examine and analyze materials for manifestations of bias—overt and covert—towards various ethnic, gender, class, age, religious, and other groups. Teachers should attempt to provide students with accurate, fair, and objective representations of diverse groups in content, illustrations, and language. They also should help students develop the skills needed to be critical users of instructional materials.

After completing this chapter, you will be able to

1. Recognize ways in which textbooks affect students.
2. Identify different forms of bias in textbooks and other instructional materials.
3. Recognize specific elements that characterize less than adequate and appropriate portrayals of minorities, women, and other groups.
4. Analyze and evaluate the treatment of diverse groups in textbooks and other instructional materials.
5. Implement strategies for helping students develop critical reading skills.
6. Use literacy tests to explore knowledge of ethnic groups and women's history.

## Textbooks: Diversity and Controversy

Instructional materials in general and textbooks in particular are central to the educational process. In the nineteenth century, reliance upon textbooks set U.S. schools apart from the educational establishment in other countries. Today, an estimated 80–90% of the school curriculum is based upon textbooks (Honig, 1985). Textbook-oriented activities account for about 75% of all classwork and 90% of all homework. By the time students complete high school, they will have read about 32,000 textbook pages (Black, cited in U.S. Commission on Civil Rights, 1980).

### Public Concern Over Textbook Content

Historically, textbooks have been a focal point of public attention. This is understandable when one considers the political, social, cultural, and economic content, values, and beliefs that textbooks convey. Following World War I, for example, the mayor of Chicago and the Hearst newspapers led a major public protest over charges of pro-British bias in history texts. To please critics, one author is said to have offered to change part of his account of the battle of Bunker Hill, transforming "Three times the British returned courageously to the attack" into

It is estimated that 80–90% of the school curriculum is based upon textbooks.

"Three times the cowardly British returned to the attack" (FitzGerald, 1979, p. 35). According to FitzGerald, over the years the range of issues exciting public interest has varied from emphasizing military history and temperance to promoting the interests of utilities, advertising, and industry; in science, protests over evolutionary theory—past and present—have been well publicized and documented.

How different groups are portrayed in textbooks has also been a concern for many years. In 1939, the National Association for the Advancement of Colored People (NAACP) issued a statement highly critical of the treatment of Blacks in textbooks. A decade later the American Council on Education undertook the first major study of how minorities were being portrayed. Depictions were found to be "distressingly inadequate, inappropriate, and even damaging to intergroup relations" (cited in Kane, 1970, p. 1). In the same period, an examination of reading textbooks indicated that females were also underrepresented and stereotyped (Child, Potter, & Levine, cited in U.S. Commission on Civil Rights, 1980).

With the civil rights and women's movements of the 1960s, awareness turned to action. This period was marked by the first successful, large-scale protests by minority groups. In 1962, the Detroit Board of Education withdrew a textbook because it was racially biased against Blacks; a short time later, the Newark Textbook Council took a similar action. Native Americans, Mexican-Americans, Puerto Ricans, Asian-Americans, Armenian-Americans, and others soon protested biased textbook portrayals in school districts across the nation (FitzGerald, 1979; U.S. Commission on Civil Rights, 1980). In the ensuing years, individuals, groups, and organizations undertook literally hundreds of studies analyzing textbooks. Attention also focused on how textbooks portrayed older persons, religious minorities, and the handicapped.

Today, the proposition that the United States is a multicultural, multilingual, and multiracial society and should be represented as such in textbooks has gained acceptance. State laws to ensure fair textbooks, although not always enforced, have been enacted. A multitude of guidelines have been drafted and implemented by those selecting, evaluating, and developing textbooks and other instructional materials. Although recent studies show that textbooks published in the 1980s are more accurate, fair, and objective than those from earlier decades, they also reveal areas in which bias persists. Hence, it is imperative that teachers regard instructional materials from a multicultural perspective, with a critical eye to the multiple messages they convey.

## Effect of Textbooks on Student Attitudes and Achievement

How minorities, women, and members of other groups are treated in textbooks is of considerable importance to teachers. If textbooks taught only "factual information," their impact on students' attitudes and beliefs would be limited, their content less controversial. In reality, however, textbooks also influence ideas and transmit "officially-sanctioned" cultural values. "The words and pictures children see in school influence the development of the attitudes they carry into adult life. These words and pictures not only express ideas—they are part of the educational experience which shapes ideas" (Association of American Publishers, 1984, n.p.).

The United States Commission on Civil Rights (1980) examined the treatment of minorities, women, religious groups, and the elderly in textbooks. In its review of research on the effects of textbooks, the Commission found studies indicating that textbooks affect student attitudes; personality development and behavior; academic achievement; and career aspirations and attainment.

The influence of textbooks on student attitudes is significant. It appears, not surprisingly, that children's attitudes are affected by what they read. Perceptions of specific minorities are influenced by whether the treatment in reading material is positive or negative. Favorable stories engender more positive attitudes, unfavorable stories more negative perceptions. This also applies to attitudes toward cultural pluralism in general. In one study, for example, the attitudes of 6- and 7-year-old children exposed to different types of reading material were compared. Materials emphasizing cultural pluralism promoted acceptance of diversity as normal. Those reflecting what was described as a "culturally parochial" viewpoint reinforced existing prejudicial attitudes (Trager & Yarrow, cited in Saunders, 1982). It appears that children recognize a story for what it is but absorb without question "the values and attitudes of the author" (Klein, 1985, p. 14).

How children react to characterizations in textbooks is influenced by a number of factors, according to studies cited in U.S. Commission on Civil Rights (1980). First, the extent to which attitudes and stereotypes are internalized and retained seems to be determined, at least in part, by the amount of time spent interacting with materials. As one would suspect, the longer the contact, the greater the effect. Second, children vary in their emotional involvement and identification with individuals and situations portrayed. In reading, mathematics, and social studies, for example, student performance is enhanced when content is perceived to be relevant and interesting. On the positive side, culturally relevant materials can facilitate the process of learning to read, making it both easier and faster. On the negative side, the absence of characters and situations with which children are able to identify may contribute to and reinforce feelings of insecurity, inferiority, or superiority depending upon an individual's group identity. These nonacademic aspects of textbook content affect variables associated with academic achievement (e.g., motivation, retention, and skills development).

Finally, the career aspirations and attainment of students are sensitive to representations in textbooks ranging from messages about occupational interests (especially for girls, minorities, and children from low-income backgrounds) to perceptions related to future employment and expectations for success. What students see and don't see in teaching materials affects the way in which they define the possibilities and opportunities available to them. Rosenberg (1974) summed up these effects on students as follows:

> [Instructional] materials are relevant to the students' life experiences, or they are not. These materials give the students the clear feeling that this education is intended for them, or it is not. These materials make the students aware that they are part of the mainstream of American education and American life, or that they are not. (p. 44)

## Bias in Instructional Materials

In that textbooks and other instructional materials inevitably reflect a point of view—a particular perspective that determines what is to be included and how material is to be presented to a specific student population—all are biased. The bias may be positive or negative, intentional or unintentional, subtle or pronounced. Such bias often reflects particular social and cultural values and beliefs associated with ethnicity, gender, religion, class, age, region, and exceptionality.

In recent decades, many forms of bias in educational materials have been reduced significantly. A teacher need only compare contemporary textbooks with

Textbooks can influence student attitudes; personality development and behavior; academic achievement; and career aspirations and attainment.

those of a generation ago to see that important changes have taken place. As noted already, however, even though current texts are generally more accurate and representative of cultural diversity, problems remain: Some groups continue to be underrepresented; imbalances, omissions, and problems with perspective still exist. As a result, ongoing evaluation of educational materials is as relevant and necessary today as in the past. Teachers using newer textbooks and other materials need to be aware of the persistence of more subtle forms of bias; those using older instructional materials must also be sensitive to the presence of more overt forms of bias.

Under ideal circumstances, replacement cycles would provide current textbooks in every classroom. Unfortunately, timely replacements are not a reality in all schools; outdated and obsolete texts often remain in use years beyond "retirement" age (Luty, 1982). Thus, teachers are likely to encounter examples of social and cultural bias that have disappeared from more contemporary texts. In addition, teachers using classical works of children's and adolescent literature or original

Textbooks and literary works inevitably reflect the attitudes and values of the period in which they were written.

historical documents need to consider how these and similar materials reflect the attitudes and values of the period in which they were written.

## Types of Bias

Bias in textbooks and other instructional materials is conveyed in several different ways. The intent of this section is to help teachers recognize three of the most common forms of bias: stereotyping, omissions and distortions, and biased language usage.

**Stereotyping**    Stereotyping occurs when all individuals in a particular group are depicted as having the same attributes; the result is that diversity *within* groups is obscured, whereas differences *between* them are exaggerated (Klein, 1985). In textbooks, stereotyping has been common in the portrayal of ethnic minorities, women, elderly persons, and members of other groups. For example, Native Americans have been stereotyped as warlike; Puerto Ricans, as violent and poor. Stereotyping by role has been particularly widespread in reading materials (e.g., Blacks depicted only in service work, sports, and entertainment). Depictions provide for limited development of characters, and a narrow range of activities, occupations, and experiences (U.S. Commission on Civil Rights, 1980).

The presence of stereotyping in textbooks has been well documented. Although there is less stereotyping now than in the past, it has not yet disappeared. Consider, for example, the nature of portrayals for different groups. If children were asked to complete the following sentences with information gleaned only from their textbooks, which, if any, specific attributes and characteristics do you think would prevail?

Girls are _____ .

Boys are _____ .

Older persons are _____ .

Members of group X are _____ .

**Omissions and Distortions**   In this context, *omission* refers to information left out of an account presented in a textbook. *Distortions* often result from the lack of balance occasioned by systematic omissions. Because of omission, members of certain groups have remained virtually "invisible" in textbooks. Even today, efforts at inclusion and integration have been more balanced and thorough for some groups than others. Hispanic-Americans, Asian-Americans, Native Americans, and women continue to be among those commonly underrepresented in educational materials.

When the impression conveyed through the omission of information is inaccurate or unbalanced, distortions occur. For example, history and reading materials that ignore the presence and realities of certain groups in contemporary society, confine treatment to negative experiences, or provide only a single point of view on events and issues may be technically correct but nevertheless misleading. What is left unsaid can be as important as the information actually presented. For example, the use of general referents (e.g., Native American, Hispanic-American, Asian-American) when the specific names of ethnic groups (e.g., Navajo, Hopi, Mexican-American, Cuban-American, Puerto Rican, Japanese-American, Chinese-American) are called for gives a false impression of uniformity in heritage, culture, values, and beliefs.

**Biased Language Usage**   Specific aspects of language usage can convey bias in subtle, often unintended ways. Of particular importance in relation to textbook bias are the nuances of meaning associated with particular words, selection of proper nouns to refer to groups, and the gender attitudes reflected in language.

Words or phrases with the same denotative meaning often convey quite different connotations reflecting positive or negative evaluations or an implicit viewpoint. For example, the impression created about a particular group differs substantially depending on whether members are referred to as "terrorists" or "freedom fighters." In many situations, several different words or phrases can be used to identify or denote the same referent, and the writer's specific choice of words carries meaning above and beyond simple identification.

Descriptions of conflicts are particularly sensitive to word choice: the "Yom Kippur War" and the "Ramadan War" refer to the same conflict; and religious differences dictate whether Richard the Lionhearted battled in a "Christian Crusade" or Saladin in an "Islamic Holy War" (Griswold, 1986). In terms of U.S. history, consider the different perspectives embodied in the terms "Civil War" and "War Between the States." What about Bull Run and Manassas (First and Second)? Antietam and Sharpsburg? How many students realize that the same battles were given different names by the armies involved—one side using adjacent towns, the other the streams that marked the landscape?

Other good examples of the influence of word choice can be found in accounts of the outcomes of struggles for basic rights and independence. The difference between women being "given" the right to vote as opposed to their "winning" it is perhaps subtle, but definitely significant (Gollnick, Sadker, & Sadker, 1982). Such differences in connotation also occur in descriptions of national independence movements, in which colonial powers "give" or "grant" independence as opposed to people having struggled to achieve or regain their freedom (Crofts, 1986).

In some instances, proper names have not been used appropriately in identifying certain peoples. In essence, the name people use to refer to themselves is replaced by one ascribed to them by others. With respect to groups of people in Africa, for example, the San have often been referred to as Bushmen. The latter term, however, comes from the Afrikaans "boesman," and is a name Europeans gave to the people they encountered in the bush (Klein, 1985). Similarly, the Mbuti and Khoi peoples have often been referred to as Pygmies and Hottentots (Bennett, 1986).

Language has been described as a "social mirror" (Chaika, 1982). It is not the cause of societal attitudes but rather a reflection of the prevailing and changing attitudes and realities of society. Teachers can demonstrate one effect of linguistic bias relating to gender by asking students to draw an "early caveman" (Gollnick et al., 1982). The completed drawings are then examined to see whether males or females are portrayed and the types of activities represented. The results of such an exercise generally suggest that terms traditionally considered generic are apparently less all-encompassing than once assumed, at least in the minds of children. For example, especially at the elementary school level, children given this task draw only pictures of cave-*men*. In contrast, when instructed to draw "cave people," the children generate drawings of men, women, and children. In classrooms, teachers can point out to students words that appear to exclude women as full participants in society or to limit their occupational options. This includes sensitivity to occupational terms (e.g., mail carrier and police officer as alternatives to mailman and policeman) and use of the generic *he* pronoun (Gollnick et al., 1982).

## Portrayal of Various Groups

In addition to the forms of bias just described, teachers also need to be cognizant of group-specific concerns regarding treatment in textbooks and other instructional materials. As members of multiple groups defined according to ethnicity, gender, class, and other dimensions, students may be sensitive about how the groups to which they belong are depicted in history, literature, and other areas of the curriculum. Teachers, however, need a broader awareness, one that provides the basis for incorporating content reflecting this diversity.

In 1980, the U.S. Commission of Civil Rights reviewed hundreds of studies on the treatment of minorities, religious groups, older persons, and females in textbooks. The findings of the Commission are summarized in Table 6–1.

**History Textbooks**  Studies of textbooks in the 1980s suggest both change and persistence in some of the patterns outlined in Table 6–1. A study of U.S. history textbooks by Davis, Ponder, Burlbaw, Garza-Lubeck, & Moss (1986) rated most 1986 texts as very good and some as excellent. These researchers found that although the United States was consistently presented in a positive light, the country's history was described in human terms with credibility and generally without obscuring the blemishes. On the other hand, the treatment of minorities (specifically, Hispanics, Asians, and Native Americans) and women continued to perpetuate "their invisible roles in building this nation" (Davis et al., p. 51). These research-

**Table 6–1**  Portrayal of Groups in U.S. Textbooks Before 1980

*Blacks*
- Persistence of stereotypes in occupational roles, primarily in service work, sports, and entertainment
- .Continued tendency to present romanticized versions of Black life
- Avoidance or denial of the actual conditions in which many Blacks have lived
- "Token" representation

*Native Americans*
- Inclusion limited primarily to historical contexts
- Rarely depicted in contemporary settings
- Failure to present the rich intragroup diversity of cultures and traditions
- Failure to include the group's own perspective of its history and cultures in accounts of events and experiences

*Hispanics (Puerto Ricans and Mexican-Americans)*
- Generally depicted as living in poverty in segregated neighborhoods
- Frequent associations of both groups with violence

*Asian and Pacific Island Americans*
- Depictions in reading and social studies textbooks often stereotypic and limited
- Representations of contemporary Asian-Americans promoting the image of a "model minority"

ers call for greater recognition of women in history textbooks and more emphasis on the roles of ordinary women in America's development:

> Textbooks must portray how women have engaged in the roles they have, how they have influenced and participated in the great sweep of historical events, and how they have felt and feel about their lives. The ever-changing roles that average as well as exceptional women have played in our society are no less important to our nation's development than those of ordinary as well as exceptional men. (Davis et al., 1986, p. 52)

Others also are challenging traditional historical perspectives and conceptualizations. In an analysis of high school history textbooks, Tetreault (1984, 1986) found that women were indeed incorporated in the textbooks examined. However, these accounts inevitably emphasized contributions, movements, and events limited to the public arena. What is needed, Tetreault argues, is an approach that would integrate the experiences of men and women into a more holistic view of the human experience. Knowledge of events in the public sphere would be balanced with greater knowledge of the private sphere. Such an approach would avoid the impression that the relationship of men and women throughout American history has been an adversarial one.

With respect to religious groups, studies representing both liberal and conservative views have agreed that textbooks "largely ignore the importance of religion and religious freedom in U.S. history and life" (American School Board

**Table 6-1**  *continued*

---

- Occupational roles most commonly portrayed as service work (e.g., laundry, culinary skills) and railroads

*Religious Groups*
- Rarely depicted

*Older Persons*
- Portrayed in children's literature mostly by images of individuals described as little, old, and poor; individuals neither as healthy nor as self-reliant as younger adults
- Failure to feature a full range of behaviors and roles; employment limited to a number of occupations, mostly service-related
- Impression that old age is not an enjoyable time of life

*Females*
- Central characters in stories with themes of dependency and domesticity; portrayed in a limited range of occupational roles
- Some stereotyping in mathematics texts (particularly in word problems and illustrations) but less than in past
- In science, indications of stereotyping in types of activities and occupations (e.g., girls cast more often in the role of observers rather than scientists, as recipients rather than initiators of actions)

---

**Source:** U.S. Commission on Civil Rights, 1980.

Journal, 1987, p. 46). Overall, references to contemporary religious events, church-state issues, and the concept of religious liberty (except during the colonial period) are rare or nonexistent. One study characterized the general treatment of religion in history textbooks as brief and simplistic at best, exclusionary at worst: "Honest treatment of religion in American history seems to be equated with advocacy of particular religious ideas and practices" (Davis et al., 1986, p. 50).

**Reading Materials** Some researchers have focused upon the treatment of minority groups and women in reading materials. Garcia and Florez-Tighe (1986) analyzed the portrayal of three minority groups—Blacks, Hispanics and Native Americans—in basal readers. They concluded that the percentage levels of minority content were acceptable but that the portrayals were less than fully accurate and balanced. There seemed to be a tendency, for example, to overrepresent members of minority groups in certain contexts (e.g., Hispanics in rural settings; Native Americans as a pre-Columbian phenomenon).

A review by Bordelon (1985) of studies on sexism in reading materials suggests that basal material in the 1970s and 1980s reflected more equal male-female representation than in the past but no substantial changes in the nature of female activities. Independence, initiative, strength, and ambition remained exclusively male traits. Others also have found changes in the numbers of minorities and females depicted as major characters but not in the types of choices presented as career role models (Britton & Lumpkin, 1984). Although the proportion of female to male central characters in basal readers has more than doubled since the 1960s, the current ratio still is not representative of the population as a whole.

It should be noted that teachers must also take cultural considerations into account in dealing with some of the values and attitudes inherent in the changes reflected in today's instructional materials. For some students, for example, the nonsexist orientation emphasized in current children's literature may reflect a set of values incompatible with those in their traditional home community (Cantoni-Harvey, 1987). In such communities, Cantoni-Harvey observes, boys may be reticent to participate in activities involving cooking and dishwashing, and girls may find it difficult to identify with female characters aspiring to nontraditional roles. She suggests that teachers faced with such situations may want to explain that although equality of the sexes is valued in American society, family members can establish and enact the roles they feel are most appropriate for themselves from the many options available.

## Ethnocentric Perspectives: Effects and Limitations

As discussed in Chapter 2, ethnocentrism is the belief that one's culture is superior to the cultures of others and that the perspective it provides is the optimal platform from which to view and evaluate other people. Because members of *all* groups tend to perceive their own culture as primary and superior, ethnocentrism is not unique to any particular cultural group. The essence of an ethnocentric's attitude is captured in the following description: "The ethnocentric says: our religion is

✳ the only true one, our language is more refined, our material objects are more sophisticated, our artifacts are more beautiful, we have better clothes, food, literature and theatre" (Preiswerk, cited in Klein, 1985, p. 59).

Educators face a troublesome paradox in dealing with ethnocentrism in the classroom. At one end of the spectrum, as Garcia (1984) notes, ethnocentrism can reflect a "mild ethnic pride," which may be "benevolent" and a positive, cohesive societal force. However, taken to extremes, ethnocentrism has negative social implications, which often are manifested as stereotyping, bias, and discrimination. In response to this paradox, Garcia (1984) suggests that teachers "learn to understand the many forms of ethnocentrism; through understanding perhaps we can better control ethnocentrism among ourselves and our students" (pp. 105–106).

Ethnocentrism can be perpetuated in textbooks and other instructional materials in ways that may be difficult for teachers to recognize. After all, a perspective consonant with one's own attitudes and values is likely to be accepted at face value and not be questioned. It may not even occur to teachers that another perspective even exists. Geography provides some interesting examples. The common terminology used to refer to regions of the world still reflects Eurocentric views: "When the British Empire stood at the heart of matters geographical, the Holy Land was 'Near,' the Persians were 'Middle,' and India and China were 'Far' east of the Greenwich Meridian" (Griswold, 1986, p. 357). To this day, these regions are referred to as the Near East, the Middle East, and the Far East. That New Zealand is "down under" is a matter of perspective, ours not theirs. Americans and Europeans are accustomed to maps of the world that split "Asia in half in order to put Europe and the Americas front and center" (Levstik, 1985, p. 42). In fact, different map projections of the world (Figure 6–1) may seem strange and unsettling to some.

The powerful impact of such ethnocentric perceptions can be demonstrated to students through an exercise described by Mukhopadhyay (1985). When asked to draw maps of the world from memory, most students depict the United States as considerably larger than it should be in relation to the rest of the world, and they ignore or recall inaccurately areas of the world with which they are less familiar. Students need to recognize how the common perceptions of American society can influence their conceptions of the relative importance of different countries and their notions of what is near and far, familiar and strange (Levstik, 1985). The 7-year-old Korean child's drawing of the world shown in Figure 6–2 dramatically illustrates how ethnocentric societal perceptions can influence views of the world.

That ethnocentrism affects how students perceive other nations has been documented in several countries. In the 1960s, an international study reported on the nationality preferences of U.S. children (Lambert & Klineberg, cited in Cortes & Fleming, 1986b). Children in elementary grades responded that if they were not Americans, they would most prefer to be British, Canadian, or Italian; they would least like to be Chinese, Russian, German, Indian, or Japanese. Older students (age 14) indicated that they would least like to be Russian or African. In a more recent British study, children age 9 to 10, were asked to think about countries they would like to visit; Europe, America and the "White" Commonwealth were by far the most popular choices. Given an opportunity to write about a place in which

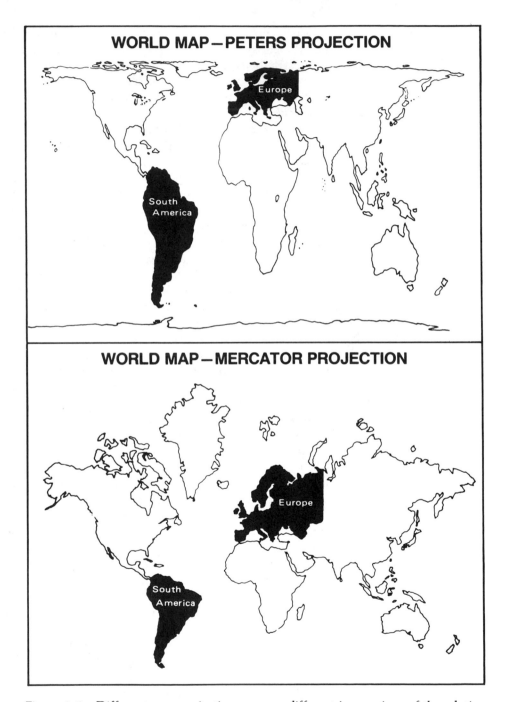

**Figure 6–1** Different map projections convey different impressions of the relative size, shape, and importance of various regions.

**Source:** From A. Peters, *The New Cartography*. Copyright © 1983 by Friendship Press. Reprinted by permission.

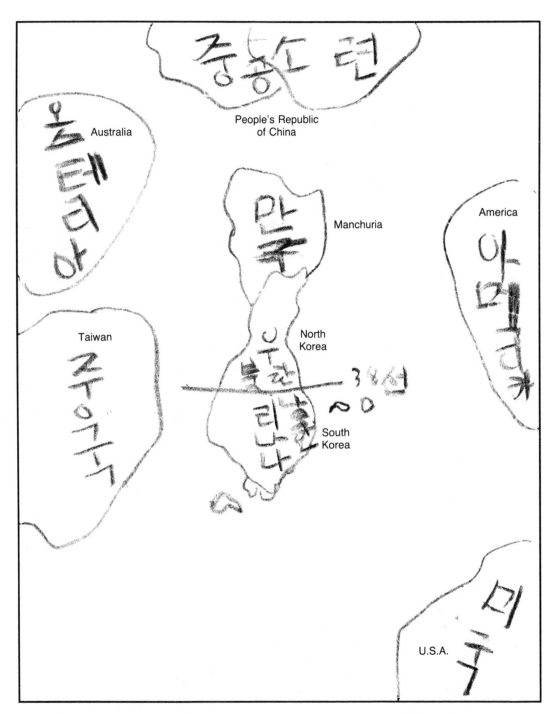

**Figure 6–2**  Map of the world as drawn by a 7-year-old Korean child.
**Source:** T. W. Johnson, personal collection. Reprinted by permission.

they did not want to land by mistake, "they produced a narrow range of stereotype descriptions of jungles, 'primitive' natives brandishing spears and dirty thin people" (Worral, cited in Klein, 1985, p. 8).

## Geocultural and Global Perspectives

Perspective is a critical element in how content is treated in any subject area. Dealing with cultural diversity sometimes requires that teachers use a frame of reference different from the one traditionally used. Ideally, the way teachers organize concepts should facilitate incorporation of the myriad cultural experiences that make up the history and heritage of the United States. Ethnocentric perspectives, like blinders, can limit rather than expand this vision. The geocultural and global perspectives described in this section are educationally and conceptually valid alternatives to ethnocentric points of view, which distort views of American society and the rest of the world. Both are appropriate for elementary and secondary levels and useful in subject areas such as history, literature, economics, music, and art.

The history and heritage of the United States have traditionally been characterized as largely the product of a movement of people and European culture from east to west—the Atlantic coast westward to the Pacific coast and beyond (Cortes, 1976, 1981). For years, this unidirectional approach has permeated the curriculum in U.S. schools. This approach, by limiting discussion of historical developments primarily to those falling within existing national political boundaries, has imposed constraints on thinking and teaching.

Describing this common conceptual framework as a "straightjacket," Cortes contends that its effect has been twofold. First, some aspects of the history and heritage of the United States have been largely ignored in the curriculum. For example, the treatment of Native American, African, Asian, Hawaiian, Hispanic, and Mexican cultures and civilizations prior to their incorporation into the fabric of the nation has generally been limited and without depth. In a review of history texts, FitzGerald (1979) found that the real distortion was less in what textbooks said than in what they did not say. For example, students reading a typical history textbook would have no way of knowing that while English settlers struggled to survive on Roanoke Island, 300 poets were in competition for a prize in Mexico City, or that when Jefferson was President, Mexico City was regarded by a leading European scientist as having "the most solid scientific institutions" of any city in the Western Hemisphere (FitzGerald, 1979, p. 96).

Second, inherent in the theme of an advancing frontier is the tendency to describe established territorial groups (e.g., Native Americans and Mexicans) first as obstacles to westward progress and later as problems in society. From this perspective, resistance to encroachment and territorial conflicts cast those obstructing the westward advance in a negative light.

There is an alternative to this European-oriented, westward-bound perspective—one based upon a multidirectional frame of reference. As defined by Cortes, this *geocultural perspective* encompasses the entire area now part of the United States, subsuming all of the cultures and experiences therein. Such an approach traces "the northwesterly flow of civilization from Africa to America, the northerly flow of Hispanic and Mexican civilization into what is today the U.S. Southwest, and the easterly flow of civilization and cultures from Asia" (Cortes, 1981, p. 15). The geocultural approach also allows for greater continuity in dealing with multiple group perspectives (e.g., racial, ethnic, cultural, gender, age, religious) as an integral part of the nation's development, not merely as addendums.

Working from a geocultural perspective, Cortes (1981) suggests, teachers can deal effectively with the following topics, which often are overlooked or treated in a culturally biased way:

(1) the varieties of Native American civilizations in what was to become the United States;

(2) the northward movement of men and women to explore and establish communities in northern New Spain and Mexico (later the U.S. Southwest), westward movement of English, French, and Dutch, in parallel with the other European and African peoples onto the Atlantic coast;

(3) the relations of Native American civilizations with expanding U.S. society from the east and Mexican society from the south;

(4) the westward expansion of the United States, including the relations of Anglo-Americans and Mexicans as the United States took over half of northern Mexico by conquest and annexation;

(5) the continuous immigration of peoples from Asia, Africa, Latin America, Europe, and Australia, including the adaptations and perspectives of immigrant women and men of diverse national, religious, and linguistic heritages;

(6) the response to immigration and to increasing ethnic diversity by U.S. institutions and people (including former immigrants and their descendants)

Just as a geocultural perspective can enhance teaching of the American experience, so too a *multiple-faceted global perspective* can facilitate students' understanding of the world's many complexities. Unfortunately, ethnocentrism continues to pervade the treatment of other peoples and nations, particularly those involving the Third World, in U.S. curricula. When textbooks overemphasize modernization in their treatment of other nations, for example, students learn to define cultures solely or primarily in terms of technological and material achievements and to devalue other important aspects of culture, such as the positive aspects of tradition (Cortes & Fleming, 1986a; Crofts, 1986). Societies that are highly technical and productive are assumed, from this perspective, to be "superior" and "better"; those that are "less advanced" technologically are also considered to be "less civilized."

Often more subtle than in the past, ethnocentrism remains a powerful influence on how areas outside the United States are presented in instructional materials. Partly as the result of such curricula, "many students come to view the world with knowledge drawn almost entirely from Western and middle-class perspectives. But the majority of Earth's people are not white; although they may be influenced by the West, their cultures are neither Western nor dominated by a middle class" (National Council for the Social Studies, cited in Cortes & Fleming, 1986b, p. 340).

Some of the specific effects and limitations of ethnocentric textbooks and curricula were described in the previous section. One antidote to such ethnocentrism is the inclusion of a better balance between the outsider perspective of Americans towards other countries and the insider perspectives of the inhabitants of those countries. Although the use of one's own cultural frame of reference to present realities, events, and experiences of other cultural groups and nations appears "logical" and "normal," it is not always conducive to understanding what is observed (Cortes & Fleming, 1986a). Customs, attitudes, and actions that from the vantage points of American society may seem shortsighted, senseless, or simply exotic may appear perfectly rational and appropriate when viewed from within another society. Inclusion of such insider perspectives offers American students an opportunity to understand how people in other countries see themselves; how groups within other countries see each other; and how they see the outside world, including their neighbors and the United States (Cortes & Fleming, 1987).

All societies hold somewhat inaccurate views of people living far away: "Accounts report that some early Japanese authors described Americans as people who 'had bushy tails somewhere hidden in [their] garments' " (Bullard, 1986, p. 367). If this outsider view seems preposterous to us as Americans, consider our outsider view of the Middle East. What physical resource do you believe is most important to inhabitants of the region? Did you say "oil"? Griswold (1986) points out that the resources that appear most important to the West (e.g., oil, minerals, agricultural products) are not necessarily the most valued by inhabitants of other regions. In many countries of the Middle East, "water exceeds oil in importance because its scarcity limits the growth of. . .economies, both agricultural and industrial" (Griswold, 1986, p. 358). Obviously, the misrepresentations that may result from an outsider's view can extend to all aspects of another country's culture and society. The growing recognition of the importance of insider views to a true understanding of other countries has led to guidelines for curricular reform that stress teaching about cultural and national groups from within their own perspective.

Both geocultural and global perspectives provide numerous and different interpretations of reality. The dilemma that faces teachers is perhaps best expressed in the words of Ortega y Gasset: "The sole false perspective is that which claims to be the only one there is" (cited in Smith & Otero, 1982, p. 10).

## Guidelines for Bias-Free Instructional Materials

Implementation of a multicultural program requires instructional materials that provide for fair treatment of all people. As the previous discussion in this chapter indicates, many of today's textbooks are strong in a number of areas but uneven in others. General guidelines can help teachers to evaluate and select textbooks that are relatively free from bias and to develop their own materials. The following guidelines, adapted from the Association of American Publishers (1984), address the content, illustrations, and language of instructional materials:

*Content*

- Represent diverse groups of people in a variety of activities, occupations, and careers, including positions of leadership.

- Represent fairly and accurately the historic and contemporary achievements of people in society within a wide range of areas.

- Integrate materials by and about minorities, women, and members of other cultural groups that provide a range of perspectives and reflect intragroup diversity.

- Include materials that honestly convey the positive and negative political, social, and economic realities that have been part of the American experience for members of various cultural groups and segments of society.

- Depict all men and women as displaying a full range of human emotions and behaviors.

- Represent all groups in a variety of settings—urban, suburban, and rural— and socioeconomic levels.

*Illustrations*

- Provide a fair, reasonable, and balanced representation with respect to race, religion, ethnicity, age, socioeconomic level, sex, and national origin.

- Include positive role models for male and female students of different ethnic backgrounds.

- Avoid stereotyping groups and individuals.

- Show men and women from different cultural groups in positions of prominence and leadership.

*Language*

- Encompass members of both sexes by (1) avoiding use of terms that exclude women and (2) designating occupations by work performed.

- Reflect cultural diversity through inclusion of varied ethnic names as well as more common Anglo-Saxon ones.

- Avoid words that are loaded or convey biased connotations and assumptions.*

## Critical Use of Instructional Materials

Because there is no single, universally accepted body of knowledge that all students must learn, textbooks play an important role in defining the ideas, concepts, and

*__Source:__ From Association of American Publishers, *Statement on Bias-Free Materials*. Copyright © 1984 by Association of American Publishers. Used by permission.

skills that constitute a major part of the curriculum. From a teacher's perspective, providing students with all available information in any subject area is neither feasible nor even desirable.

Given the ever-expanding nature of information in today's society, students must learn to use textbooks analytically and to develop skill in evaluating materials for accuracy and perspective (Cortes & Fleming, 1986a; Klein, 1985). In relation to children's literature, history, and other content areas, there is agreement that teaching such critical skills is a most significant component of multicultural education. If such skills are not taught, the product is a generation of "adults who believe everything they read—or read only what they wish to believe" (Klein, 1985, p. 115). If teachers are to instill critical thinking skills in their students, they, too, must deal with instructional materials analytically.

For many teachers, a critical approach is already at the heart of their teaching. FitzGerald (1979) describes a teacher in rural Maine who intentionally uses a "conservative," 10-year-old history text because its viewpoint is diametrically opposed to his own. For some teachers, however, using textbooks critically, as they would other readings, represents a major departure from their usual practices. Based on studies in several areas including social studies, researchers have concluded that textbooks are the dominant instructional tool for most teachers. Moreover, "teachers tend not only to rely on, but to believe in, the textbook as the source of knowledge" (Shaver et al., cited in FitzGerald 1979, p. 19).

## Strategies for Demystifying Print

Teachers have found several strategies effective in the process of "demystifying print" (Klein's term is apropos). One is to help students learn to challenge what they read through guided questioning: Do you believe that is true? Why did the author say that. . .? More probing questions can be used to direct analysis of specific topics in different content areas (Klein, 1985). Another strategy is to make published writing accessible to students, their families, and communities. In many elementary and secondary schools, student efforts are compiled into class and school "publications." Bilingual high school students translate children's stories for use by pupils in elementary schools. In some English schools, parents and community members write and illustrate stories for children which are bound, laminated, and displayed in classrooms and school libraries (Klein, 1986). Such texts, Klein observes can provide a wide range of languages, dialects, orthographies, and viewpoints.

Analyzing, comparing, and contrasting texts and readings is a third strategy teachers can use. This technique requires "the application of critical thinking to the reading process" (Saunders, 1982, p. 114). Through critical reading, students become actively involved with a written text by examining its attitudinal, functional, and evaluative elements. According to Saunders, critical reading encompasses a range of skills from distinguishing between factual information, opinions, and propaganda to analyzing the language used to convey ideas. On occasion,

Demystifying print includes making published writing accessible to students.

for example, accounts in different textbooks, particularly in history, appear to be contradictory. Such discrepancies can be revealed by analyses of different text-books published during the same period, different editions of the same text, and texts selected from different periods. To illustrate this point, consider the follow-ing excerpts about the beginning of the Crusades from two different sources:

TEXT ONE

The first Crusade. . .was the result of an appeal for Western help from the hard-pressed Emperor Alexius of Byzantium. His territories in Asia Minor had been captured by the Moslems in 1071, and the Saljuk's spreading power had put [an end] to the relatively peaceful relations he had enjoyed with the Arab occupiers of Palestine. . .He was attracted by the idea of getting foreigners to recapture his territories for him. (*The Invaders*, cited in Klein, 1985, p. 118)

TEXT TWO

About 900 years ago, the Christian pilgrims met trouble in the Holy Land. They were cruelly treated by the Saracens who had conquered Jerusalem. This made Christian people everywhere very angry. Alexius sent to the Head of the Christian Church, Pope Urban II, for help against the Saracens. (*The Crusades*, cited in Klein, 1985, p. 118)

One variation on this strategy involves its use with textbooks and materials from other countries. In accordance with local guidelines and practices, students could compare accounts of periods, events, and individuals in U.S. textbooks with appropriate materials from other nations. They may be intrigued by the English version of the American Revolution (or was it a rebellion?) or the War of 1812. How are past and present leaders and events portrayed? Students might also find it useful to compare the treatment of countries like Canada, Australia, and New Zealand in foreign and domestic texts. Bilingual students can assist in doing the same with comparable texts in other languages.

Finally, students can analyze how various evaluative terms are used in depictions of different groups in textbooks and readings. In general, approximately 300 common nouns and adjectives are believed to account for about 88% of the evaluative terms (favorable and unfavorable) commonly found in textbooks (Saunders, 1982). One list developed in the early 1970s included brave, civilized, hardworking, intelligent, honorable, proud, honest, bold, clean, noble, and victorious as examples of positive terms; negative terms included hostile, ignorant, primitive, savage, backward, barbarian, blood-thirsty, corrupt, dirty, lazy, warlike, and treacherous. By using scales of such evaluative terms, students can rate how different groups are depicted along various dimensions. As an example, the following scale could be used to assess how the elderly are portrayed (Sorgman & Sorenson, 1984, p. 122):

| | |
|---|---|
| Kind | Mean |
| Healthy | Sick |
| Happy | Sad |
| Quiet | Aggressive |
| Poor | Rich |
| Wise | Senile |

## Cultural "Literacy" Tests

Time for a test! "Literacy" tests are an effective way to draw attention to what students know and do not know about different groups in American society. By addressing those groups whose textbook treatment has traditionally been limited and uneven, such exercises provide opportunities for discussion of common misconceptions about the nation's development as a pluralistic society. Such literacy tests are readily available, applicable in most content areas at the secondary level, and versatile.

The two variations reprinted here will also enable teachers to "test" their own knowledge of history from what is perhaps a different perspective than usual. After completing the exercises, compare your performance on the two tests and, if possible, discuss the results with others. Which test was easier? Why? How well did you know the material? How would you rate your knowledge in these areas?

The Ethnic Literacy Test developed by Banks (1987) assesses knowledge about specific historical events related to ethnic groups in the United States and some aspects of their culture and role in American society. This test is presented in Table 6–2.

"Literacy" tests are an effective technique for drawing attention to what students know and do not know about different groups in American society.

**Table 6–2  Ethnic Literacy Test**

*Directions*: Indicate whether each of the statements is TRUE or FALSE by placing a "T" or "F" in the preceding space.

1. _____ The percentage of Whites in the United States, relative to non-Whites, decreased between 1970 and 1980.

2. _____ The first Chinese immigrants who came to the United States worked on the railroads.

3. _____ In 1980, there were more than 26 million Afro-Americans in the United States.

4. _____ Puerto Ricans on the island of Puerto Rico became U.S. citizens in 1920.

5. _____ Between 1970 and 1979, the Mexican-American population increased by slightly more than 60%.

6. _____ Between 1820 and 1930, 15 million immigrants came to the United States.

7. _____ White Anglo-Saxon Protestants are the most powerful group in the United States.

8. _____ Rosh Hashanah, which in Hebrew means "end of the year," is a Jewish holiday that comes early in the fall.

9. _____ Between 1820 and 1971, Germans were the largest European group immigrating to the United States.

10. _____ The first law to limit immigration to the United States was passed in 1882 to restrict the number of African immigrants.

11. _____ Puerto Ricans in New York City tend to identify strongly with Afro-Americans in that city.

12. _____ Between 1820 and 1971, more individuals from Canada and Newfoundland immigrated to the United States than from Mexico.

13. _____ Most Afro-Americans came from the eastern parts of Africa.

14. _____ The internment of the Japanese-Americans during World War II was opposed by President Franklin D. Roosevelt.

15. _____ In 1980, there were more than 14 million Hispanic-Americans in the United States.

16. _____ More than 270,000 immigrants came to the United States from the Philippines between 1971 and 1980.

17. _____ Congress passed a Removal Act that authorized the removal of American Indians from east to west of the Mississippi in 1830.

18. _____ A Japanese settlement was established in California as early as 1869.

19. _____ The United States acquired a large part of Mexico's territory under the terms of the Treaty of Guadalupe Hidalgo in 1848.

20. _____ Agriculture dominates the economy of the island of Puerto Rico.

21. _____ The first Blacks to arrive in North America came on a Dutch ship that landed at Jamestown, Virginia, in 1619.

22. _____ Ethnic minorities comprised about 17% of the U.S. population in 1980.

**Table 6-2**  *continued*

23. _____  *Paper sons* is a custom that is associated with Chinese-Americans.

24. _____  In 1980, there were about one and one-half million American Indians, Eskimos, and Aleuts in the United States.

25. _____  Some of the bloodiest riots involving Afro-Americans and Whites occurred in the early 1900s.

26. _____  More than 110,000 Vietnamese immigrated to the United States between 1971 and 1980.

27. _____  The United States acquired the island of Puerto Rico from Spain in 1898.

28. _____  There are only 438 Japanese surnames.

29. _____  Chinese immigrants to the United States became distinguished for their outstanding work on truck farms.

30. _____  The only large Puerto Rican community on the U.S. mainland is in New York City.

31. _____  A third-generation Japanese-American is called a *Sansei*.

32. _____  More than 46,000 Iranians immigrated to the United States between 1971 and 1980.

33. _____  More than one half of American Indians lived in central cities in 1980.

34. _____  Most Chinese immigrants to the United States came from western China.

35. _____  Eleven Italian-Americans were lynched in New Orleans in 1892.

36. _____  Nativism directed against southern and eastern European immigrants was intense when the Statue of Liberty was dedicated in 1886.

37. _____  In 1980 there were more than three-quarters of a million Cubans living in the United States.

38. _____  More than 58,000 Haitians immigrated to the United States between 1971 and 1980.

*Answer Key:*

| | | | | | |
|---|---|---|---|---|---|
| 1. T | 8. F | 15. T | 22. T | 29. F | 36. T |
| 2. F | 9. T | 16. T | 23. T | 30. F | 37. T |
| 3. T | 10. F | 17. T | 24. T | 31. T | 38. T |
| 4. F | 11. F | 18. T | 25. T | 32. T | |
| 5. T | 12. T | 19. T | 26. T | 33. T | |
| 6. F | 13. F | 20. F | 27. T | 34. F | |
| 7. T | 14. F | 21. F | 28. F | 35. T | |

**Source:** From J. A. Banks, *Teaching Strategies for Ethnic Studies* (4th ed.). Copyright 1987 by Allyn and Bacon. Reprinted with permission.

**Table 6-3** "Susan B. Who?"

*Directions*: Match each individual with her contributions and achievements by placing the appropriate letter before her name.

| | | |
|---|---|---|
| _____ | 1. Prudence Crandall | a. An organizer of the Underground Railroad during the Civil War |
| _____ | 2. Mary Berry | b. First woman president of a major state university |
| _____ | 3. Sor Juana Inés de la Cruz | c. Nuclear physicist |
| _____ | 4. Patricia Harris | d. Winner of Nobel Prize for Physics in 1963 |
| _____ | 5. Dixie Lee Ray | e. Established a school for Black girls in Connecticut prior to the Civil War |
| _____ | 6. Harriet Tubman | f. Responsible for the creation of several Hispanic women's coalitions |
| _____ | 7. Alice Paul | g. Classic ballet dancer in the 1940s and 1950s |
| _____ | 8. Lupe Anguiano | h. Author of a rationale for educating women in the fifteenth century |
| _____ | 9. Susan B. Anthony | i. Governor of Washington, former head of Atomic Energy Commission |
| _____ | 10. Betty Friedan | j. Anthropologist, psychologist, writer, lecturer, and teacher |
| _____ | 11. Maria Tallchief | k. Leader in the struggle for women's rights during the nineteenth century |
| _____ | 12. Maria Goeppert-Mayer | l. U.S. runner who won three Olympic gold medals in 1960 for field and track |
| _____ | 13. Wilma Rudolph | m. Militant suffragist who organized parades and demonstrations in the nation's capital |
| _____ | 14. Chien-Shiung Wu | n. First Black woman to be appointed an ambassador and later a member of the U.S. Cabinet |
| _____ | 15. Margaret Mead | o. Author of *The Feminine Mystique* and one of the founders of the National Organization for Women |

*Answer Key:*

1. e    4. n    7. m    10. o    13. l

**Table 6-3**  *continued*

| 2. | b | 5. | i | 8. | f | 11. | g | 14. | c |
|---|---|---|---|---|---|---|---|---|---|
| 3. | h | 6. | a | 9. | k | 12. | d | 15. | j |

Source: From D. M. Gollnick, M. P. Sadker, and D. Sadker, "Beyond the Dick and Jane Syndrome: Confronting Sex Bias in Instructional Materials." Cited in M. P. Sadker and D. M. Sadker (1982).

The "Susan B. Who?" test, developed by Gollnick et al. (1982), assesses knowledge about the contributions of specific women to the development of the United States. This test is presented in Table 6-3.

## Did You Know That. . .?

The National Education Association has identified 24 different kinds of instructional materials: textbooks, workbooks, pamphlets, anthologies, encyclopedias, tests, supplementary texts, paperbacks, programmed instructional systems, dictionaries, reference books, classroom periodicals, newspapers, films, records and cassettes, transparencies, realia, games, filmstrips, audio- and videotapes, slides, globes, manipulatives, and graphics (e.g., maps, photographs, posters). It is estimated that there are over one half million different instructional materials available (Gollnick et al., 1982).

In a Roper poll of students 8 to 17 years of age, 40% indicated that better textbooks were one important way to improve the quality of education. This figure is higher than those who cited the need for better teachers (cited in Sewall, 1988).

Following a review of textbook presentations of wars in 1889, the International Peace Conference recommended that for the sake of global understanding, "textbooks be purged of false ideas about nations and causes of wars" (UNESCO, cited in Reynolds & Reynolds, 1974).

Today, the older population—65 years and above—represents approximately 12% of the population of the United States. The life expectancy of a child born in 1984 is about 74.7 years—27 years more than it was for children born in 1900 (American Association of Retired Persons, 1985). Descriptions of older people in textbooks focus primarily on the age factor: 75% of descriptive terms applied to the elderly are variations of "old" (Sorgman & Sorenson, 1984).

## Summary

Appropriate curricular materials are central to the process of multicultural education. Historically, textbooks have occupied a major role in classrooms across the United States. Student involvement with textbooks accounts for major portions of students' time in class and almost all of the time engaged in homework. The fact that textbooks and other instructional materials overtly and covertly convey political, social, and cultural values and beliefs generates considerable debate from a wide range of groups.

Within multicultural education, particular interest has been directed at how different cultural groups are portrayed in textbooks. The civil rights movement brought attention to bear on the treatment of ethnic groups, especially Afro-Americans, Hispanics, Native Americans, and Asian-Americans. The women's movement emphasized bias in the depiction of females. Consideration of social content now covers a broad range of categories, including age, handicap, religion, socioeconomic level, etc. Concern over the effects of how issues and groups are depicted goes beyond mere academic debate. The implications are serious because student attitudes, personality development and behavior, academic achievement, and career aspirations are affected by the instructional materials they use.

Bias in textbooks has traditionally taken a variety of different forms. From a teacher's perspective, perhaps the most important practices that contribute to bias are stereotyping, omissions and distortions, and biased language usage. Although bias in textbooks, especially in its most blatant forms, has been considerably reduced in recent years, some remains. Its manifestations are often subtle and differ to some extent depending on the group involved. Perspective is also an integral element in the evaluation of instructional materials. The effects and limitations of ethnocentrism can be mitigated to a degree by adopting geocultural and global perspectives, which recognize the existence of diverse viewpoints.

As teachers use textbooks and other instructional materials they need to examine and use them critically and analytically. This requires evaluation of content, illustrations, and language. It also means teaching students to be critical users of texts and reading materials, learners willing to challenge what they read by questioning, contrasting, comparing, and evaluating information from different sources.

## References

American Association of Retired Persons. (1985). *A profile of older Americans: 1985.* Brochure available from AARP, 1909 K Street, NW, Washington, DC, 20049.

American School Board Journal. (1987). Textbooks ignore religion in American history. *Education Digest, LII*(7), 46–47.

Association of American Publishers. (1984). *Statement on bias-free materials* (rev. ed.). Brochure available from School Division, AAP, 220 E. 23rd St., New York, NY 10010.

Banks, J. A. (1987). *Teaching strategies for ethnic studies* (4th ed.). Boston: Allyn and Bacon.

Bennett, C. I. (1986). *Comprehensive multicultural education.* Boston: Allyn and Bacon.

Bordelon, K. W. (1985). Sexism in reading materials. *The Reading Teacher, 38*(8), 792–797.

Britton, G., & Lumpkin, M. (1984). Females and minorities in basal readers. *Education Digest, L*(2), 48–50.

Bullard, B. M. (1986). Asia. *Social Education, 50*(5), 367–375.

Cantoni-Harvey, G. (1987). *Content-area language instruction.* Reading, MA: Addison-Wesley.

Chaika, E. (1982). *Language: The social mirror.* Rowley, MA: Newbury House.

Cortes, C. E. (1976). Need for a geo-cultural perspective in the bicentennial. *Educational Leadership, 33*(4), 290–292.

Cortes, C. E. (1981). Dealing with the density of diversity: Groupness and individuality in the California history/social science framework. *Social Studies Review, 21*(1), 12–18.

Cortes, C. E., & Fleming, D. B. (1986a). Changing global perspectives in textbooks. *Social Education, 50*(5), 376–384.

Cortes, C. E., & Fleming, D. B. (1986b). Global education and textbooks. *Social Education, 50*(5), 340–344.

Cortes, C. E., & Fleming, D. B. (1987). Social studies texts need a global perspective. *Education Digest, LII*(7), 42–45.

Crofts, M. (1986). Africa. *Social Education, 50*(5), 345–350.

Davis, O.L., Jr., Ponder, G., Burlbaw, L. M., Garza-Lubeck, M., & Moss, A. (1986). A review of U. S. history textbooks. *Education Digest, LII*(3), 50–53.

FitzGerald, F. (1979). *America revisited.* Boston: Atlantic Monthly Press/Little, Brown.

Garcia, R. (1984). Countering classroom discrimination. *Theory Into Practice, XXIII*(2), 104–109.

Garcia, J., & Florez-Tighe, V. (1986). The portrayal of Blacks, Hispanics, and Native Americans in recent basal reading series. *Equity and Excellence, 22*(4–6), 72–76.

Gollnick, D. M., Sadker, M. P., & Sadker, D. (1982). Beyond the Dick and Jane syndrome: Confronting sex bias in instructional materials. In M. P. Sadker & D. M. Sadker, *Sex equity handbook for schools* (pp. 60–95). New York: Longman.

Griswold, W. J. (1986). Middle East. *Social Education, 50*(5), 357–366.

Honig, W. (1985, November 18). "Last chance" to teach culture. Interview. *U.S. News and World Report, 99*(21), 82.

Kane, M. B. (1970). *Minorities in textbooks.* Chicago: Quadrangle Books.

Klein, G. (1985). *Reading into racism.* London: Routledge and Kegan Paul.

Levstik, L. S. (1985). Literary geography and mapping. *Social Education, 49*(1), 38–43.

Luty, C. (1982). Tight budgets keep outdated texts in use past normal "retirement" age. *NEA Today,* December, p. 5.

Mukhopadhyay, C. C. (1985). Teaching cultural awareness through simulations: Bafa Bafa. In H. Hernandez & C. C. Mukhopadhyay, *Integrating multicultural perspectives into teacher education* (pp. 100–104). Chico: California State University—Chico.

Peters, A. (1983). *The new cartography.* New York: Friendship Press.

Reynolds, D. A. T., & Reynolds, N. T. (1974). The roots of prejudice: California Indian history in textbooks. In G. D. Spindler (Ed.), *Education and cultural process* (pp. 506–541). New York: Holt, Rinehart and Winston.

Rosenberg, M. (1974). Evaluate your textbooks for racism, sexism. In M. Dunfee (Ed.), *Eliminating ethnic bias* (pp. 43–47). Washington, DC: Association of Supervision and Curriculum Development.

Saunders, M. (1982). *Multicultural teaching.* London: McGraw-Hill.

Sewall, G. T. (1988). American history textbooks: Where do we go from here? *Phi Delta Kappan, 69*(8), 552–558.

Smith, G. R., & Otero, G. (1982). *Teaching about cultural awareness*. Denver: University of Denver, Center for Teaching International Relations.

Sorgman, M. I., & Sorenson, M. (1984). Ageism. *Theory Into Practice, XXIII*(2), 117–123.

Tetreault, M. K. (1984). Notable American women: The case of United States history textbooks. *Social Education, 48*(7), 546–550.

Tetreault, M. K. (1986). Integrating women's history: The case of United States history high school textbooks. *The History Teacher, 19*(2), 211–262.

U.S. Commission on Civil Rights. (1980). *Characters in textbooks*. Clearinghouse Publication 62. Washington, DC: U.S. Government Printing Office.

# C H A P T E R

# 7

# Development of a Multicultural Curriculum

*No one should make the claim of being educated until he or she has learned to live in harmony with people who are different.*

A. H. Wilson
*(cited in Cole, 1984, p. 151)*

The purpose of this chapter is to facilitate development of an integrated, interdisciplinary multicultural program appropriate to diverse classroom settings in elementary and secondary schools. To accomplish this task, teachers must adopt a sound and systematic approach. As Gay (1977) observes, "It will be virtually impossible for [multicultural] programs to command academic respect if their formulation ignores the acceptable principles of curriculum design" (p.94). Thus, teachers involved in the development of multicultural programs must consider the accepted components of curriculum design: needs assessment; goals and learning outcomes; implementation; teaching strategies; and evaluation (Gay, 1977).

After completing this chapter, you will be able to

1. Assess student and programmatic needs related to multicultural education.
2. Identify major goals and learner outcomes for multicultural education.
3. Draw upon a variety of models and approaches in developing a curriculum that is multicultural.

4. Use different teaching strategies and techniques to attain stated objectives.

5. Evaluate learning outcomes related to multicultural goals and objectives.

## Needs Assessment

Teachers integrating multicultural perspectives into an existing curriculum need to examine various facets of the existing program. This examination usually includes an initial assessment of student knowledge, attitudes, and skills and an evaluation of the curriculum as a whole. To proceed without such assessment can result in programs that are less sensitive than they otherwise could be to variations in student population, school environment, and community setting.

### Assessing Student Attitudes and Perceptions

In general, two key questions underlie the assessment of student knowledge, attitudes, and skills in relation to multicultural education. They can be stated as follows (California State Department of Education, 1979):

- What knowledge, attitudes, and skills do students already demonstrate in areas identified within multicultural education?

- What knowledge, attitudes, and skills do they need to develop?

Although assessment of knowledge and skills is an accepted part of teaching, assessment of attitudes and perceptions is much less common. Many of the goals and objectives in multicultural education involve efforts to examine and even change how students see themselves, how they are viewed by others and, in turn, how they view others. Needs assessment, especially as it relates to student attitudes and perceptions, is a critical, yet often ignored aspect of program development (Kehoe, 1984a).

Information regarding student attitudes about ethnicity, cultural diversity, and self-concept is particularly relevant to curriculum development. Kehoe (1984a) has found that the more negative the attitudes of students are toward a specific minority group, the less receptive they will be to inclusion of that group's history and culture in the curriculum. In one study involving Canadian high school students, for example, student attitudes differed toward the inclusion of history and culture related to Japanese, Chinese, and East Indian immigrant groups in the curriculum. Minority-group students overwhelmingly supported incorporation of ethnic content about all groups; majority-group students were favorably disposed to including content related to the Japanese and Chinese but not to East Indians. In view of these attitudes, Canadian educators designed an elementary curriculum that emphasized cultural differences in the Japanese-Canadian content and cultural similarities in the East Indian-Canadian content (Kehoe, Echols, & Stone, cited in Kehoe, 1984b).

Teachers also need to be sensitive to student self-concept. In some schools, students belonging to identifiable groups—whether defined by ethnicity, ability, class, or other dimensions—may view themselves quite differently. This was the case in a Canadian study of junior high school students (Perry, Clifton, & Hryniuk, cited in Kehoe, 1984a). In this study, British-Canadian students rated themselves very positively, whereas Native Indian students rated themselves less positively on several measures and were rated by others in some relatively negative terms. When educators developing a multicultural program are faced with this type of situation, Kehoe suggests that they include in the program (a) culturally appropriate ways to promote self-esteem among those who rate themselves less positively and (b) strategies to change the attitudes of other students. In such cases, improving the self-evaluations of students whose self-concept is high and who are favorably perceived by others would not appear to be a major priority.

Student attitudes—positive and negative—are likely to influence how specific ethnic material in a multicultural program is received. For this reason, curriculum development must involve not only selection of appropriate content but also identification of student attitudes toward culturally relevant concepts. Formal and informal indicators of prevailing attitudes in the classroom, school, and community are needed in order to select the combination of strategies and materials most likely to be effective. Although there are limitations and problems inherent in the assessment of attitudes, a number of measures can provide teachers with useful information. Among these, Kehoe recommends opinion questionnaires, semantic differentials, social distance scales, and surveys.

In an *opinion questionnaire*, students are asked to indicate the extent to which they agree or disagree (e.g., strongly, moderately, slightly) with a series of 15 to 20 statements. In the context of multicultural education, statements such as the following would be relevant (Kehoe, 1984a, pp. 131–132):

1. Foreign languages often sound pleasing to the ear.
2. I enjoy being around people who are different from me.
3. You can learn a lot from people whose backgrounds are different from yours.
4. People with different backgrounds don't usually have a great deal in common.
5. A country where everyone has the same background is a lot better off than a very mixed one.
6. Because differences among people mainly divide them, people should try to be more alike.

Positive responses to items 1–3 indicate a generally favorable attitude toward cultural diversity; students with this type of attitude are likely to be receptive to program content related to different ethnic and cultural groups. In contrast, positive responses to items 4–6 indicate a negative attitude toward diversity; students with this attitude are likely to be disinterested in, perhaps even hostile toward, minority-oriented content.

A *semantic differential scale* can be used to measure the extent to which students associate certain attributes and qualities with various groups defined by ethnicity, gender, age, and other dimensions. This type of measure consists of a series of paired contrasting adjectives (e.g., friendly and unfriendly, cooperative and uncooperative) that reflect perceptions of and attitudes toward other people. In the context of multicultural education, students might be asked to think of a specific group (e.g., the Canadian people) and then to place an X at the point on the scale between each pair of polar adjectives corresponding to their view of that group. Kehoe (1984a, pp. 133–134) gives the following example:

CANADIAN PEOPLE

| | | |
|---|---|---|
| honest | . . . . . . . . . . . . . . . . . . . . . . . . . . | dishonest |
| friendly | . . . . . . . . . . . . . . . . . . . . . . . . . . | unfriendly |
| pleasant | . . . . . . . . . . . . . . . . . . . . . . . . . . | unpleasant |
| clean | . . . . . . . . . . . . . . . . . . . . . . . . . . | dirty |

By comparing patterns of student responses on a semantic different scale, educators can assess their relative general attitudes toward various groups and also identify any specific negative attributes that students, through ignorance or prejudice, associate with a specific group. Clearly, this type of information could be extremely useful in selecting appropriate content and strategies for multicultural programs in individual communities.

A *social distance scale* is helpful in evaluating how young children feel toward other people and countries. With this technique, a physical object—commonly, a ladder—is used as an indicator rather than a paper-and-pencil scale. In practice, the top of the ladder is used to indicate the most favored choice; the bottom, the least favored. In the context of multi-cultural education, children might be asked to rank specific nations, people from different countries, or children with certain characteristics by going to the rung of the ladder that corresponds to their preference. Kehoe (1984a), for example, asks children to indicate parts of the world in which they would like to live; people they would like to have immigrate to their country; families they would like to have living next door; children they would invite to their birthday party; and children they would select as a close friend. Depending on the items that children are asked to rank, their patterns of social distance rankings, like responses on a semantic differential scale, can be used to assess general attitudes, within a class or school, toward various groups.

An *information survey* can be used to assess student willingness to have the ethnic history and culture of specific groups incorporated into the curriculum. Such surveys can be used to provide information about the extent to which students in a particular school or school district are willing to have the history and culture of a specific group included and the specific topics that students consider most interesting and relevant. The two following questions are examples of the type of questions an information survey contains (Kehoe, 1984a, pp. 141–142):

1. It would be better if the history (or present-day culture) of East Indians in Canada (a) was omitted, (b) was given brief mention, or (c) was given a lot of attention in the curriculum.

2. If East Indian history and culture are included in the curriculum, then the following topics should receive mention:
(a) The performance of East Indian soldiers on the side of Canadians during World War II.
(b) A discussion of the East Indian concept of beauty in men and women.
(c) Possible conflict between East Indians and majority Canadians because of differences in social customs (e.g., East Indians sometimes go to the front of lined-up people).
(d) A discussion of physical attacks against East Indians in Toronto.

As these sample questions indicate, an information survey can be designed to provide specific information relevant to a particular school and community and to students of different age levels.

In addition to formal measures of prevailing attitudes, informal observation, discussion, and interviews can uncover helpful supplementary information. The objective of both formal and informal assessment is to gather information useful in developing programs that are culturally and locally relevant in terms of goals and objectives, content, strategies, and evaluation procedures.

## Assessing Program Needs at the Elementary Level

Evaluation of the strengths and weaknesses of the existing curriculum as it relates to multicultural education can help educators identify the types of changes that are needed. Initially, general questions such as the following can be asked (California State Department of Education, 1979): How is the current program helping students develop knowledge, attitudes, and skills relevant to individual and group differences? How effective is the current program? In what ways is it effective? In what ways is it not effective?

From these general questions, assessment can move to more specific areas of the curriculum. The multicultural needs assessment survey presented in Table 7–1 was designed to identify special program needs. It provides elementary teachers with a practical tool for examining their school's multicultural program and serves as a model for those wishing to develop their own.

## Assessing Program Needs at the Secondary Level

Surveys in the early 1980s found fairly consistent patterns in the nature of multicultural programs in secondary schools (Freedman, 1983). The findings indicate that, although proponents of multicultural and multiethnic education

**Table 7-1** Multicultural Needs Assessment (Elementary)

### Multicultural Instruction

*Content related to human dignity and self-worth:*

1. To what degree do pupils exhibit pride and acceptance of self and abilities?
2. To what degree do pupils recognize the basic similarities among members of the human race and the uniqueness of individuals?
3. To what degree do pupils accept each other on the basis of individual worth regardless of gender, race, religion, or socioeconomic background?
4. To what extent do pupils have opportunities to experience success in learning?

*Content related to ethnic studies:*

1. To what extent do pupils know about their own heritage, history, and contributions to America?
2. To what degree do pupils feel pride in their ethnic heritage?
3. To what degree do pupils recognize and accept the fact that America has been enriched by the contributions of all its ethnic groups?

*Content related to intercultural studies:*

1. To what extent do pupils have knowledge of universal characteristics of cultures?
2. To what extent do pupils have knowledge of the various groups (religious, ethnic, cultural, etc.) in the United States?
3. To what extent do pupils have positive attitudes toward ethnic groups that are not based on stereotypes?
4. To what extent do pupils recognize and know the significance of events, customs, and traditions that are special for different groups?
5. To what degree do pupils accept and appreciate the diversities of the American culture?

*Content related to understanding and acceptance of differences and similarities:*

1. To what extent do pupils participate in activities in which they learn to value both individual and group differences?
2. To what extent do pupils have knowledge of similarities and differences in ways individuals express themselves (e.g., in art, music, literature)?
3. To what degree do pupils recognize and accept differences as positive?

*Content related to human and intergroup relations:*

1. To what extent do pupils engage in positive social interaction among all students of the school?
2. To what extent do pupils have knowledge and understanding of cultural pluralism?
3. To what extent do pupils recognize prejudice as a block to communication and interaction?
4. To what extent do pupils acknowledge that people of different backgrounds have common concerns and can work together to solve common problems?

### Instructional Approaches and Strategies

1. To what extent is multicultural instruction in your classroom cross-disciplinary, drawing from and contributing to other curriculum areas?

**Table 7-1**  *continued*

2.  To what extent is multicultural instruction in your classroom cross-cultural in nature instead of structured around separate ethnic groups?

3.  To what extent does the multicultural instruction in your classroom involve acquisition of knowledge and attitudes?

4.  To what extent is multicultural instruction in your classroom appropriate to the maturity level of the pupils?

### School Climate

1.  To what extent are the multicultural classroom experiences interrelated with school-wide experiences?

2.  To what extent are the approaches and strategies for multicultural classroom instruction evident in the total school multicultural program?

3.  To what extent are self-concept and attitudes toward learning equally positive in all pupils at the school?

4.  To what extent do students of all ethnic groups have the opportunity to be integrated into the social system of the school so that they share comparable status and roles within the school?

5.  To what extent does the physical environment of the school (bulletin boards, displays, etc.) reflect the racial/ethnic composition of the student population?

### Parent/Community Involvement

1.  To what extent have multicultural resources among parents and in community been identified?

2.  To what extent have such resources been utilized at the school?

3.  To what extent do the multicultural objectives of the school reflect the concerns of the parents and community surrounding the school?

**Source:** Adapted from *Multicultural Needs Assessment—Teacher Survey*. Long Beach (CA) Unified School District, Education Department, Special Projects Branch. Used with permission.

emphasize the importance of systematic integration across the disciplines, the majority of programs were confined to one area, namely, social studies (primarily, American history and ethnic studies classes). Only one fourth of the schools responding to surveys indicated that a multicultural approach was included in the area of English literature. As Freedman (1983) puts it, most programs are "serially mono-ethnic": that is, specific groups are treated sequentially and in isolation from one another.

Freedman found, however, that programs differed greatly with respect to the priority given specific educational objectives. Although the highest-ranking general objective was the development of attitudes associated with tolerance and mutual respect, specific objectives varied considerably depending on the composition of the student population. Schools with significant numbers of racial minorities tended to emphasize enhancing the self-esteem of minority-group students; those with large nonminority enrollments gave priority to changing student perceptions and images of minority groups and to understanding the causes of prejudice. In most programs, understanding ethnicity and culture, stereotyping, and intergroup perceptions were the least important objectives.

Freedman (1983) concluded that the primary focus of the programs evaluated was narrowly defined, being directed primarily at racial prejudice and injustice. Consistent with this focus, content emphasis was on minority groups. Unless a specific group was numerically significant within the local community, white ethnic groups were considered only in the treatment of immigration. Issues related to cultural groups along dimensions defined by gender or socioeconomic status, for example, were not usually included.

Given this background, teachers at the secondary level may find the questions in Table 7–2 useful for evaluating existing programs from a multicultural perspective (the applicability of specific items may vary according to subject area).

## Educational Goals and Learning Outcomes

Any instructional program that is multicultural should be consistent with the following general guidelines (Banks, 1981; California State Department of Education, 1977, 1979):

- *Emphasize multiple groups* (e.g., ethnic, religious, regional, socioeconomic, language) rather than treating individual groups separately or in isolation. Such

**Table 7–2** Multicultural Needs Assessment (Secondary)

1. To what extent do multiple cultural perspectives permeate the total school environment?
2. To what extent do school policies and procedures encourage positive interaction between students from different cultural groups?
3. To what extent does the curriculum reflect and accommodate the learning styles of the students?
4. To what extent does the curriculum provide for continued development of student self-esteem and positive self-identity?
5. To what extent does the curriculum help students to develop an understanding of the commonalities and differences in experiences within and across cultural groups?
6. To what extent does the curriculum help students to recognize and understand the conflict in society?
7. To what extent does the curriculum promote values, attitudes, and behaviors that support cultural diversity?
8. To what extent does the curriculum help students to develop decision-making abilities and the necessary skills for participating in society socially, economically, and politically?
9. To what extent does the curriculum help students develop skills for effective interpersonal and intercultural interaction?
10. To what extent is the multicultural curriculum comprehensive in scope and sequence, integrating holistic views of cultural groups across the curriculum?

multiple-group emphasis diminishes the likelihood of stereotyping and facilitates integration of multicultural content into the overall curriculum.

* *Provide an interdisciplinary focus* for the integration of multicultural perspectives, as appropriate, in all content areas. Although most frequently associated with the social sciences, language, literature, art, and music, multicultural perspectives are valid and applicable in areas such as mathematics, science, home economics, and physical education.

* *Use a variety of instructional approaches and materials* appropriate to the maturity level of students. In particular, teaching strategies should aim to accommodate differences in learning styles and to maximize academic achievement.

* *Focus on the development of both cognitive and affective skills.* Learning outcomes should be assessed in terms of knowledge, attitudes, and skills.

* *Emphasize school and area populations,* locally oriented activities, and community resources.

Articulating goals and desired learning outcomes is an essential part of developing instructional programs. Gay (1977) recommends that the curriculum teachers develop include both general goals and specific objectives (as determined by programmatic emphases and the needs of the student population to be served). The statement of goals and objectives in Table 7–3 illustrates the types of learning outcomes frequently specified in multicultural education programs.

**Table 7-2**  *continued*

11. To what extent does the curriculum provide for ongoing study of the culture, experiences, social situation, and conditions of diverse cultural groups?

12. To what extent are interdisciplinary approaches used in developing and implementing the multicultural curriculum?

13. To what extent does the curriculum use comparative approaches in the study of cultural groups?

14. To what extent does the curriculum help students to examine and analyze events, situations, and conflicts from diverse cultural perspectives?

15. To what extent does the curriculum conceptualize and present development of the United States as multidirectional?

16. To what extent does the school provide opportunities for participation in different cultural experiences and activities?

17. To what extent does the school promote a positive attitude toward ethnolinguistic diversity?

18. To what extent does the school utilize home and community resources?

19. To what extent are assessment procedures culturally appropriate for all students?

20. To what extent does the school evaluate goals, methods, and materials used for multicultural education?

**Source:** Adapted from J. A. Banks, C. E. Cortes, G. Gay, R. Garcia, and A. S. Ochoa, *Curriculum Guidelines for Multiethnic Education* (Washington, DC: National Council for the Social Studies, 1976). *Cited in J. A. Banks, Teaching Strategies for Ethnic Studies* (4th ed.). Reprinted with permission.

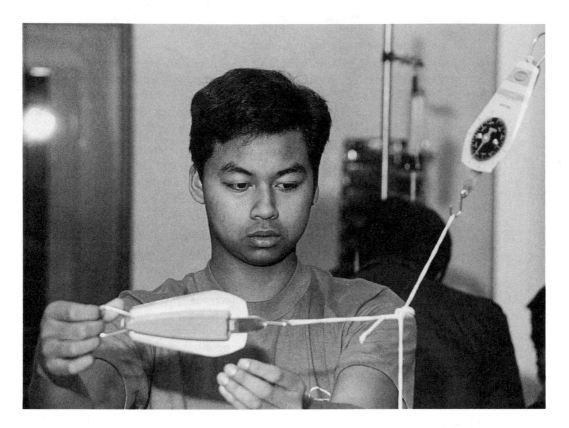

Multicultural perspectives can be integrated across content areas such as mathematics, science, home economics, and physical education, as well as social studies, literature, art, and music.

**Table 7–3** Multicultural Goals and Objectives

### General Goals

*Goal 1.0*  To be aware of ethnic ancestry and cultural heritage in relation to self-definition

*Objectives:*

1.1  To demonstrate appreciation of the characteristics of one's own ethnic, cultural, and linguistic heritage

1.2  To analyze the influence of one's ethnic/cultural heritage and experiences on one's values and lifestyle

1.3  To define personal strengths, capabilities, and limitations (self-esteem)

1.4  To demonstrate the ability to present to others aspects of one's own cultural heritage

*Goal 2.0*  To be aware of the similarities and differences among individuals from diverse ethnic, cultural, linguistic, and religious groups within the community, the United States, and the world

**Table 7-3**  *continued*

*Objectives:*

2.1  To recognize similarities and differences among diverse socioeconomic, ethnic, cultural, linguistic, and religious groups

2.2  To recognize similarities and differences in sex roles within diverse groups in society

2.3  To tolerate alternative beliefs, manners, customs, linguistic traditions, and lifestyles of individuals and groups different from self

2.4  To develop an awareness of and appreciation for cultural diversity in our society and globally

2.5  To understand how people within the United States and from various places in the world differ in their views on issues (e.g., resource use, environmental pollution)

*Goal  3.0*  To be aware of the elements of different cultures

*Objectives:*

3.1  To describe the elements that make up different cultures and recognize those that are common to all humanity

3.2  To compare the elements of diverse cultures

3.3  To recognize that cultures change over time and as the result of contact with other cultural groups

*Goal  4.0*  To demonstrate skills in maintaining positive relationships with other individuals or groups and in responding constructively to conflict in relationships

*Objectives:*

4.1  To develop sensitivity to problems of others through learning and practicing interpersonal skills

4.2  To analyze factors that contribute to conflicts

4.3  To demonstrate the ability to cooperate with others (e.g., males and females; mainstreamed students; members of diverse racial, ethnic, cultural, linguistic, and religious groups) in performing a variety of tasks

*Goal  5.0*  To identify various forms of stereotyping, prejudice, and discrimination

*Objectives:*

5.1  To identify causes and consequences of stereotyping, prejudice, and discrimination

5.2  To confront behavior in self and others that is based on stereotyping, prejudice, and discrimination

5.3  To identify biases in textbooks and other instructional materials and in the media

*Goal  6.0*  To achieve academically in all basic subject areas

**Specific Content-Area Goals**

**Literature and Fine Arts**

*Goal  6.0*  To develop knowledge of and appreciation for the multicultural nature of the literary and fine arts (literature, art, theater, and music) in our society, historically and currently

**Table 7–3** *continued*

---

*Objectives:*

6.1 To develop an awareness of the major movements, traditions, and cultural contexts of various forms of expression, past and present

6.2 To explore how the writer, artist, dramatist, and musician (male and female) have communicated the timelessness and universality of the human condition

6.3 To develop the ability to use awareness of multicultural history and tradition in literary and artistic expression

6.4 To recognize the value and role of the literary and fine arts in the lives of individuals in different cultural groups

**Foreign/Second Language**

*Goal* 7.0 To appreciate the similarities and diversities among languages, cultures, and value systems within the United States and throughout the world

*Objectives:*

7.1 To recognize language patterns that are different from the native language

7.2 To recognize behavioral patterns (attitudes, values, customs, traditions, and taboos) of cultures that are different from the native culture

7.3 To function in the sociocultural contexts in which the language is used

**Mathematics**

*Goal* 8.0 To develop an appreciation for and understanding of the contributions that various cultures have made to mathematical concepts and applications

*Objectives:*

8.1 To relate the contributions of other cultures to the development of the modern Western number system and other areas of mathematics

8.2 To recognize similarities and differences between the counting system used in the United States and systems used in other countries

8.3 To identify variations in computational algorithms as performed in different cultures

8.4 To use computational instruments from other cultures

8.5 To play mathematical games from other cultures

**Science**

*Goal* 9.0 To develop appreciation for and understanding of the contributions that various cultures have made to scientific concepts and applications

*Objectives:*

9.1 To give attention to and value science as an endeavor of human beings from all ethnic and cultural backgrounds

9.2 To demonstrate knowledge of contributions to science and technology made by men and women of various nationalities

**Social Sciences**

*Goal* 10.0 To enable and encourage students to understand and respect individual and cultural differences and similarities

**Table 7-3**  *continued*

*Objectives:*

10.1  To understand and appreciate the United States in particular and the world in general as multicultural phenomena

10.2  To understand and appreciate universal as well as alternative ideas about beauty, ideological beliefs, sex roles, moral standards, and value systems

10.3  To be aware of the wide diversity of occupational choices available and the ways in which individuals make these choices

10.4  To analyze behavior and attitudes for biases against the characteristics of specific groups (e.g., sexual, ethnic, economic)

10.5  To understand different units of human organizations such as world organizations, nation states, ethnic groups, business and labor groups, kin groups, and families

**Source:**  Adapted from J. Browne and J. P. Perez, *Multicultural Education Course of Study for Grades Kindergarten Through Twelve 1979–1981.* Used with permission of the Los Angeles County Superintendent of Schools.

# Implementation

Many options are available to teachers interested in integrating multicultural content into the elementary and secondary curriculum. This section focuses on several principles that are critical to effective integration of multicultural perspectives into the curriculum.

## Balance and Complementarity

Teaching that is multicultural is eclectic by nature. It involves a balanced use of approaches in which the relative strengths of one complements the relative weaknesses of another. According to Nixon (1985), the critical task centers on integration: how to combine and coordinate approaches, faculty, and resources to fashion an effective cross-curricular response. Because multicultural education must be responsive to the uniqueness of each school and each classroom, the development and application of a single, all-encompassing model is precluded. Teachers must use elements of different approaches in tandem to achieve a balance of essential concepts, perspectives, and experiences, which are incomplete when presented in isolation.

For example, teachers can promote more positive attitudes toward cultural diversity by focusing less attention on differences that appear exotic and bizarre (and conducive to stereotyping) and greater attention on similarities among people and cultures in terms of family life and everyday living. It is also advantageous to balance treatment of historical and contemporary hardships and injustices with consideration of positive achievements and developments associated with various groups (Kehoe, 1984b). An effective multicultural curriculum is likely to include the following balanced elements: content about racism awareness *and* cultural diversity; experiential learning *and* the acquisition of facts and skills; contemporary perspectives *and* historical perspectives; and content about local issues *and* global issues (Nixon, 1985).

The planning matrix presented in Table 7–4 can help educators to achieve balance and complementarity in terms of the basic types of learning, specific topics addressed, and subject areas that are incorporated into a multicultural curriculum.

### Structure and Organization

It bears repeating that teachers need to systematically incorporate multicultural content into the curriculum. The question is how this can best be accomplished? Over the years, some of the curricular design approaches used in multicultural education have been criticized because they lead to poorly integrated, narrowly focused programs (Gay, 1977). Among the least acceptable are approaches that include content about specific ethnic groups by use of separate components and those that deal with social, economic, and political realities from a "problems" perspective.

Gay (1975, 1977, 1979) has described several basic organizational strategies appropriate for incorporating multicultural content at the elementary and secondary levels. The curriculum emphasis and basic instructional approach for each of these design strategies are summarized in Table 7–5. Gay regards the thematic and conceptual strategies as most promising. The first provides a framework based on recurrent universal themes; the second, a framework based on concepts drawn from different disciplines. Both have the advantage of allowing for multiple perspectives and comparative, interdisciplinary analyses.

## Teaching Strategies

Given the nature of its curricular goals and objectives and the commitment to meeting the needs of a diverse student population, multicultural education requires a broad repertoire of instructional methods and techniques. Because teaching methods are culturally influenced, certain methods work better with some students than others. Teachers who assume that the same methods work effectively with all students ignore the influence of culture as well as other factors on the instructional process.

To identify methods that work for students in a particular classroom, teachers must use strategies with an analytical eye. Although research may suggest what works, it often does not indicate what works for whom, when, and under what specific conditions. When selecting and applying a particular instructional method, teachers should consider whether it works effectively with all students or only with certain groups of students (as defined by culture, gender, ability, age, learning style, or other relevant dimensions). For example, the inquiry method, though wide-

**Table 7–4** Planning Matrix for Multicultural Curriculum Development

| Kind of learning | TOPIC | Academic activities | | | | | | | | | |
|---|---|---|---|---|---|---|---|---|---|---|---|
| | | Reading | Oral, written language | Mathematics | Social studies | Science | Health | Foreign language | Art, music, drama, dance | Physical education | Practical arts, vocations |
| I. Understand concepts | A. Self<br>B. Lifestyle<br>C. Culture<br>D. Changes in individuals and groups<br>E. Cultural contact as agent in change<br>F. Personal heritage<br>G. Similarities/differences among individuals and groups<br>H. Competence<br>I. Occupational diversity<br>J. Stereotypes/prejudice/discrimination | | | | | | | | | | |
| II. Acquire values | A. Self-esteem<br>B. Appreciation of self and others<br>C. Respect for values/dignity/worth of self and others<br>D. Respect for similarities/differences<br>E. Acceptance of cultural pluralism<br>F. Acceptance of diversity of lifestyles<br>G. Desire to bring about equity/reduce stereotypes<br>H. Positive attitude toward school and life | | | | | | | | | | |
| III. Develop skills | A. Analyzing influence of heritage<br>B. Analyzing similarities/differences<br>C. Distinguishing between myths/stereotypes and facts<br>D. Recognizing prejudiced behavior<br>E. Identifying biases in media<br>F. Interpreting personal heritage<br>G. Clarifying personal values<br>H. Using skills of conflict resolution | | | | | | | | | | |
| IV. Demon-strate behaviors, personal and social | A. Working to reduce inequities<br>B. Confronting prejudiced behavior<br>C. Cooperating with diverse others<br>D. Using community persons as resources<br>E. Using persons in school as resources<br>F. Working to resolve conflicts<br>G. Participating/involving others in life of school<br>H. Using interpersonal skills | | | | | | | | | | |

**Source:** California State Department of Education, 1979, *Planning for Multicultural Education as a Part of School Improvement.* Reprinted by permission.

**Table 7–5**  Strategies for Incorporating Multicultural Content into Curriculum

| Approach | Emphasis | Basic Features |
|---|---|---|
| Integrative Multicultural Basic Skills (elementary) | Social skills<br>Intellectual skills<br>Literacy skills<br>Functional survival skills | Use cultural perspectives content, material, and experiences to teach basic educational skills |
| Modifed Basic Skills | Fundamental skills<br>Social action skills<br>Decision-making skills<br>Ethnic literacy | Use ethnic materials to teach basic skills, enhance student ethnic identity, and expand awareness of multiethnic perspectives; address ethnic/gender stereotypes and racial attitudes |
| Conceptual Approach | Concepts from multiple disciplines (e.g., social sciences such as power, identity, ethnicity, culture, survival, communication, change, racism, socialization, acculturation) | Analyze concepts within an interdisciplinary framework using comparative and multiethnic perspectives |
| Thematic Approach | Themes characterizing the human condition, social realities, and cultural experiences of ethnic groups in the United States (e.g., ethnic identity; the role of ethnic groups in society; struggles against injustice; the quest for freedom) | Focus on themes rather than ethnic groups and treat themes from interdisciplinary perspectives; examine inter- and intragroup diversity |
| Cultural Components | Culture and traditions of ethnic groups including perceptions, behavior and communication patterns, socialization processes, value systems, interpersonal interaction styles | Emphasize identification of cultural features for specific groups; rely on ethnic source materials (e.g., literature, histories, folklore, customs, traditions, religious heritage) |
| Branching Designs | Idea, issue, concept, or problem extended from one discipline to another (e.g., analysis of protest as manifested in civic, literary, and artistic areas) | Organize the curriculum to allow for more integrated, in-depth, and cohesive treatment of content |

**Source:**  G. Gay, "Organizing and Planning Culturally Pluralistic Curriculum," 1975, *Educational Leadership, 33*(3), 176-183; and G. Gay, "On Behalf of Children: A Curriculum Design for Multicultural Education in the Elementary School," 1979, *Journal of Negro Education, XLCIII(3)*, 324-340.

ly used, is based upon assumptions about questioning and problem-solving that are not universally shared (Payne, 1977). Consequently, as presently implemented, the inquiry method may be quite effective in certain cultural contexts but relatively ineffective in others. In general, attainment of instructional objectives depends in large part on the use of teaching strategies that are suitable and effective for a specific purpose, time, and student population. The effective teacher "is the one who can make the right judgment as to what teaching device is the most valuable at any given moment" (Politzer, 1970, pp. 42–43).

Joyce and Weil (1986) observe that "when we teach well, we help students learn well" (p. iii). They suggest that effective teaching strategies (a) help students learn academic skills, ideas, and information; develop values and social skills; and understand themselves and their environment; and (b) provide students with repertoires of powerful tools for acquiring education. Among the wide variety of effective teaching strategies used in multicultural education are the four discussed here: concept attainment, advance organizers, simulations, and role playing.

Effective teachers are skilled in choosing instructional strategies that are appropriate for a specific purpose, time, and student.

### Concept Attainment

The teaching strategy known as concept attainment is designed to facilitate the learning of concepts through concept formation and hypothesizing (Joyce & Weil, 1986; Tenenberg, 1978). A teacher using this strategy presents examples, some of which have attributes of a well-defined target concept. Students are asked to compare and contrast the examples, attempting to distinguish those containing essential characteristics of the target concept from those that do not. Through this process students eventually learn the attributes that define the concept. Figure 7–1 presents an illustration of concept attainment in which visual examples are used to convey attributes of the target concept.

In some cases, verbal examples are used. For example, if the concept to be taught is "doublespeak" (i.e., deceptive language that is evasive and euphemistic), the following exemplars and nonexemplars might be used (Lutz, cited in Shearer, 1988):

| EXEMPLARS | NONEXEMPLARS |
|---|---|
| incomplete success | failure |
| safety-related occurrence | accident |
| experienced automobile | used car |
| unauthorized withdrawal | bank robbery |
| downsizing personnel | firing employees |
| ultimate high-intensity warfare | nuclear war |
| advanced downward adjustments | budget cuts |
| digital fever computer | thermometer |
| social-expression products | greeting cards |

In this case, the teacher presents a few examples in random order and encourages students to compare them and begin hypothesizing about which essential attributes differentiate one group from the other. As the activity continues, additional examples are provided and hypotheses tested until the concept is identified. Students then are given a chance to practice and think of examples of their own. In the final phase of the exercise, students can discuss their individual strategies for developing and testing hypotheses. Additional information on concept attainment and related generic teaching strategies is presented by Tenenberg (1978) and Joyce and Weil (1986).

### Advance Organizers

Advance organizers are structured overviews describing the hierarchy of related concepts within a discipline or subject area (Joyce & Weil, 1986). These "intellec-

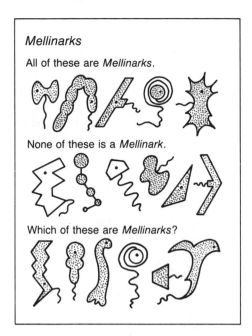

**Mellinarks**

All of these are *Mellinarks*.

None of these is a *Mellinark*.

Which of these are *Mellinarks*?

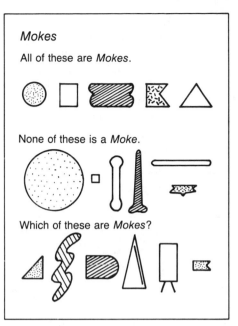

**Mokes**

All of these are *Mokes*.

None of these is a *Moke*.

Which of these are *Mokes*?

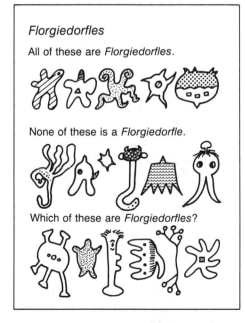

**Florgiedorfles**

All of these are *Florgiedorfles*.

None of these is a *Florgiedorfle*.

Which of these are *Florgiedorfles*?

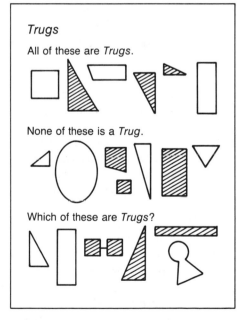

**Trugs**

All of these are *Trugs*.

None of these is a *Trug*.

Which of these are *Trugs*?

**Figure 7-1** Sample visual exemplars and nonexemplars used with concept attainment approach. The criterial attributes of Mellinarks are spots, a black dot, and a tail. Mokes share only one defining attribute—height. All the Florgiedorfles have the same height and number of arms. Trugs may be either shaded triangles or unshaded quadrilaterals.

**Source:** *Teachers Guide for Attribute Games and Problems.* Copyright © 1968 by McGraw-Hill. Used with permission.

tual maps" can facilitate student acquisition and retention of new, abstract information by providing a visual, conceptual framework for learning activities. By enhancing the clarity and organization of knowledge, they enable students to better relate, integrate, and remember new information.

Earle and Barron (cited in Smith & Kepner, 1981) have outlined a procedure for developing structured overviews. The first four steps focus on the preparation of instruction; the last two promote active student involvement in the lessons presented.

### DEVELOPING AND USING AN ADVANCE ORGANIZER

1. Analyze the learning task and required vocabulary. List key words representing the major concepts to be learned.

2. Arrange the key words in a diagram that displays the relationship among concepts.

3. Add familiar vocabulary concepts to illustrate the relationship between what students know and what they are to learn.

4. Examine the advance organizer. Are major relationships depicted clearly and concisely? Does it focus only on the most essential relationships between concepts?

5. In introducing the content, display the diagram and briefly explain the arrangement of the key words. Ask students to contribute as much information as they can.

6. During the presentation and related activities, make the connection between new information and the structured overview.

Advance organizers have been used in a variety of subject areas. They are also effective in adapting instruction at more advanced levels to meet the needs of limited-English-proficient learners (Cantoni-Harvey, 1987). Figure 7–2 is an example of an advance organizer dealing with mathematical concepts.

## Role Playing

Role playing is an experiential learning activity in which students act out behavior in real-life situations. In theory, "dramatizing" problems enables students to scrutinize feelings, attitudes, and values; develop problem-solving strategies; and experience greater empathy toward others (Joyce & Weil, 1986). Classroom re-creations elicit responses that can be directed purposefully in subsequent group discussions of human relations and intercultural communication. Role playing provides a way of integrating social and personal as well as emotional and intellectual elements. In fact, students appear to experience greater changes in attitude when they voluntarily assume roles opposed to their own beliefs (Kehoe, 1984a).

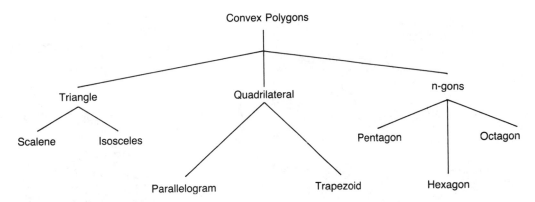

**Figure 7-2**   Advance organizers for presentation on convex polygons.
**Source:** C. F. Smith, Jr., and H. S. Kepner, Jr., *Reading in the Mathematics Classroom*. Copyright © 1981 by National Education Association. Reprinted by permission.

Role plays are appropriate for presenting a number of topics at both elementary and secondary levels. For example, Hoopes and Pusch (1979) use role play to demonstrate that social status is culturally based and manifested in behavior on a daily basis. To make their point, they suggest that teachers themselves role-play the following encounters (Hoopes & Pusch, 1979, pp. 148-149):

- Going before a judge in traffic court for running a red light.
- Requesting an extension on a term paper from a professor.
- Ordering a sandwich at a small restaurant.
- Ordering dinner with wine at an elegant restaurant.
- Scheduling an appointment with a busy doctor, dentist, or lawyer.
- Meeting the Governor at an official occasion.
- Discussing a disciplinary problem in your classroom with the principal.

## Simulations

Simulations are a second type of experiential learning activity widely used in multicultural education, most often in the social sciences. These activities are designed to be used as a basis for viewing human behavior and examining situations in the real world. Psychologically, effective simulations provide sensory learning, insight about the consequences on one's behavior, and an opportunity for self-correction (Joyce & Weil, 1986). They range from short, simple exercises to complex activities requiring extended periods of time and can be applied to diverse areas such as competition and cooperation, critical thinking and decision making, and development of concepts and skills.

Good teaching helps students develop repertoires of powerful strategies for acquiring an education.

Among the simulations most frequently associated with multicultural education are Bafa Bafa, Star Power, Win As Much as You Can, and Albatross. Other commercially prepared and teacher-developed simulation games also are available (for a guide to references on simulation games, see Mukhopadhyay & Cushman, 1985). Descriptions of existing simulation games, instructions for teachers interested in developing their own, and critiques of some of the most widely used models are presented in Batchelder and Warner (1977), Hoopes and Ventura (1979), Mukhopadhyay (1985), Mukhopadhyay and Cushman (1985), Pusch (1979), and Sawyer and Green (1984).

# Evaluation

After a multicultural education program is developed and implemented, its effectiveness can be assessed in several ways. A relatively simple evaluation method is teacher observation of student behaviors. For purposes of informal evaluation, a sampling of students is sufficient. The following examples illustrate how attainment of specific program objectives is indicated by various student behaviors (California State Department of Education, 1979):

| Objective 1: | The student will demonstrate recognition of the dignity and worth of individuals and groups different from himself/herself. |
| Behaviors: | Interacting with students within same group and from different groups. Interacting cooperatively in small groups. Sharing of materials, time and space. |
| Objective 2: | The student will develop feelings of self-worth and self-acceptance. |
| Behaviors: | Requesting assistance when needed. Participating voluntarily in a range of activities. Providing assistance to other students (e.g., tutoring). |
| Objective 3: | The student will desire and be willing to reduce or eliminate inequalities and conflicts caused by stereotyping, prejudice, discrimination, and inequality of opportunity. |
| Behaviors: | Choosing partners freely regardless of their ethnicity, gender, socioeconomic status, etc. Participating in activities across lines defined by socioeconomic level or other factors. Avoiding behaviors demeaning to other students (e.g., jokes, name calling). |

Other recommended measures of program effectiveness include oral and written tests (teacher-made and standardized), sociograms, questionnaires, surveys, student projects, interviews, anecdotal information, and discussion groups. Indicators such as attendance records, class participation, and incidence of disruptive behavior also provide clues about student acceptance of and interest in the program. Many of these procedures are conducive to staff, parent, and student involvement. Whatever combination of evaluation tools is used, the information collected should be well documented, relevant, and useful. The validity of evaluation depends upon the questions asked, behaviors observed, and effort made to sample randomly and apply common standards (California State Department of Education, 1979).

# Did You Know That. . .?

By the late 1970s, over half of the states required development of multiethnic programs and materials in their public schools (American Association of Colleges of Teacher Education, cited in Garcia & Garcia, 1980).

By the mid-1970s, an estimated 600 or more simulation games were available for use with different age levels and in a wide range of subject areas (Heyman, 1975).

In a study in which Canadian students were shown slides of Canada and Thailand, those shown slides emphasizing similarities between the countries evaluated Thailand more favorably than those shown slides highlighting the differences (Salyachivin, cited in Kehoe, 1984a).

Courses of study limited to providing information about other cultures do not appear to significantly affect individuals who have a tendency to be ethnocentric or to engage in stereotyping. Hence, the goal of developing appreciation for cultural diversity cannot be achieved simply by transmitting information because the acquisition of knowledge does not necessarily bring empathy and respect (Kehoe, 1984a,b).

## Summary

Five components are essential in the development of a curriculum that is multicultural: needs assessment; goals and learning outcomes; implementation; teaching strategies; and evaluation. Needs assessment should focus on student knowledge, attitudes, and skills and analysis of the existing curriculum as a whole. Student attitudes and perceptions are especially important because they directly and indirectly influence the teaching of content and skills.

Teachers also need to evaluate how existing programs address different content areas and to what extent this is satisfactory. Common program needs at the secondary level include systematic integration of multicultural content across disciplines, expansion of program objectives, and a focus on cultural groups and issues. Program goals and objectives should incorporate a multiple-group approach in an integrative, interdisciplinary framework emphasizing cognitive and affective skills. Special attention should be given to school populations, locally oriented activities, and community resources. Learner outcomes need to be defined in terms of general as well as discipline-specific goals and objectives.

During implementation of multicultural curriculum, teachers need to consider balance and complementarity, structure and organization. Concepts, themes, and basic skills need to be brought together in a cohesive, well-integrated program of instruction. Effective teaching requires identification of methods that work for a specific student population and use of general instructional strategies such as concept attainment, advance organizers, role playing, and simulations. Finally, information useful for evaluation of program outcomes can be obtained by a combination of indicators that may include observation of student behaviors, interviews, tests, surveys, and discussion groups.

## References

Banks, J. A. (1981). *Multiethnic education*. Boston: Allyn and Bacon.

Banks, J. A. (1987). *Teaching strategies for ethnic studies*. (4th ed.). Boston: Allyn and Bacon.

Batchelder, D., & Warner, E. G. (Eds.). (1977). *Beyond experience*. Brattleboro, VT: The Experiment Press.

California State Department of Education. (1977). *Guide for multicultural education*. Sacramento:

California State Department of Education. (1979). *Planning for multicultural education as a part of school improvement*. Sacramento:

Cantoni-Harvey, G. (1987). *Content-area language instruction*. Reading, MA: Addison-Wesley.

Cole, D. J. (1984). Multicultural education and global education: A possible merger. *Theory Into Practice*, *XXIII*(2), 151–154.

Freedman, P. I. (1983). A national sample of multiethnic/multicultural education in secondary schools. *Contemporary Education, 54*(2), 130–133.

Garcia, J., & Garcia, R. (1980). Selecting ethnic materials for the elementary school. *Social Education, 44*(3), 232–236.

Gay, G. (1975). Organizing and planning culturally pluralistic curriculum. *Educational Leadership, 33*(3), 176–183.

Gay, G. (1977). Curriculum design for multicultural education. In C. Grant (Ed.), *Multicultural education: Commitments, issues and applications* (pp. 94–104). Washington, DC: Association for Supervision and Curriculum Development.

Gay G. (1979). On behalf of children: A curriculum design for multicultural education in the elementary school. *Journal of Negro Education, XLCIII*(3), 324–340.

Heyman, M. (1975). *Simulation games for the classroom.* Bloomington, IN: Phi Delta Kappa Educational Foundation.

Hoopes, D. S., & Pusch, M. D. (1979). Teaching strategies: The methods and techniques of cross-cultural training. In M. D. Pusch (Ed.), *Multicultural education: A cross cultural training approach* (pp. 104–204). LaGrange Park, IL: Intercultural Network.

Hoopes, D. S., & Ventura, P. (Eds.) (1979). *Intercultural sourcebook: Cross-cultural training methodologies.* LaGrange Park, IL: Intercultural Network.

Joyce, B., & Weil, M. (1986). *Models of teaching* (3rd ed.). Englewood Cliffs, NJ: Prentice-Hall.

Kehoe, J. (1984a). *Achieving cultural diversity in Canadian schools.* Cornwall, Ontario: Vesta Publications.

Kehoe, J. (1984b). Achieving the goals of multicultural education in the classroom. In R. J. Samuda, J. W. Berry, & M. Laferriere (Eds.), *Multiculturalism in Canada* (pp. 139–153). Toronto: Allyn and Bacon.

Long Beach Unified School District. (n.d.) *Multicultural needs assessment—teacher survey.* Long Beach, CA: Special Projects Branch, Education Department.

Los Angeles County Superintendent of Schools. (1979). *Multicultural education course of study for grades kindergarten through twelve 1979–1981.* J. Browne and J. B. Perez (developers). Los Angeles: Office of the Los Angeles County Superintendent of Schools, Educational Services Group.

Mukhopadhyay, C. C. (1985). Teaching cultural awareness through simulation: Bafa Bafa. In H. Hernandez & C. C. Mukhopadhyay, *Integrating multicultural perspectives into teacher education: A curriculum resource guide* (pp. 100–104). Chico: California State University—Chico.

Mukhopadhyay, C. C., & Cushman, R. (1985). A guide to references on simulation games. In H. Hernandez & C. C. Mukhopadhyay, *Integrating multicultural perspectives into teacher education: A curriculum resource guide* (pp. 291–293). Chico: California State University—Chico.

Nixon, J. (1985). *A teacher's guide to multicultural education.* Oxford: Basil Blackwell.

Payne, C. (1977). A rationale for including multicultural education and its implementation in the daily lesson plan. *Journal of Research and Development in Education, 11*(1), 33–45.

Politzer, R. L. (1970). Some reflections on "good" and "bad" language teaching behaviors. *Language Learning, XX*(1), 31–43.

Pusch, M. (Ed.). (1979). *Multicultural education: A cross cultural training approach*. LaGrange Park, IL: Intercultural Network.

Sawyer, D., & Green, H. (1984). *The NESA activities for Native and multicultural classrooms*. Vancouver, British Columbia: The Tillacum Library.

Shearer, L. (1988, January 10). Intelligence report. *Parade Magazine*, p.16.

Smith, C. F., Jr., & Kepner, H. S. (1981). *Reading in the mathematics classroom*. Washington, DC: National Education Association.

Tenenberg, M. (1978). *Generic teaching strategies series: Modules and videotapes*. Hayward: California State University, Department of Education.

# 8

# Beyond the Classroom: Home, Neighborhood, and Community

*To teach them all is to know them all.*

*Etlin (1988)*

Teaching is a process of getting to know the students. . .of learning about them and learning from them. That's what most of this chapter is about. What occurs in the classroom clearly is an important part of education, but the curriculum imparted in the schools is only part of the picture. All students experience a very pervasive and influential "education" outside the classroom. The purpose of this chapter is to help teachers learn about the broader, sociocultural context in which their students live and learn outside the classroom. It is also intended to help teachers make connections between the classroom, home, community, and society.

After completing this chapter, you will be able to

1. Pose questions that reveal educationally relevant features of students' cultural background.
2. Use home and neighborhood visits as well as community studies to better understand students and their environment.
3. Recognize the role of parental involvement in promoting school performance.

4. Define the concept of a *societal curriculum*.

5. Use life history projects as a strategy for making the home, neighborhood, and community part of the school experience.

6. Incorporate media analysis as part of a multicultural curriculum.

## Students' Cultural Backgrounds: What Teachers Need to Know

To better understand the lives of their students, teachers need to learn about the history and culture of different groups represented in their classrooms. When confronted with such a task, however, they may find it difficult to decide just how to begin. What areas of culture are important? What kinds of information are most useful? In addition to general information about various cultural groups in the United States, teachers will want to know more about those in their local community. Saville-Troike (1978) has developed a set of questions that can help teachers identify what they need to know (Table 8–1). Applicable to a wide range of groups, the questions focus on sociocultural elements relevant to education—differences related to language, ethnicity, religion, and other cultural characteristics.

Because these questions cover areas central to any discussion of culture in the classroom, they have many possible applications. First, teachers can use the questions to reflect on their own culture. In fact, Saville-Troike suggests that teachers answer some of the questions, based on their own experiences, before trying them out with others. Such introspection might be followed by comparing and contrasting answers with family, friends, and colleagues. In this manner, teachers can become more aware of their own beliefs, behaviors, and values and can see how such concepts as real and ideal culture and implicit and explicit culture apply in their own lives. In the process, the relationship between culture and context will become more clearly defined.

Second, Saville-Troike also recommends use of these questions to guide observations in the classroom, around the school, and in other settings. Informed observation can increase teachers' understanding of classroom events and form the basis for modified teaching strategies that are culturally appropriate and instructionally sound. Some of the questions in Table 8–1 are especially useful as the focal point of observations: What constitutes a positive response by a teacher to a student? What methods do parents use when teaching children at home? What genres of language are most common in the home? One question, for example, addresses the role of language in social control and the significance of using the first as opposed to the second language. A common observation among teachers in bilingual classrooms is that some students respond better when reprimanded in their home language. In this situation, observation can be used to guide language choice in the disciplining of students.

Third, the questions in Table 8–1 can also be used to enhance instruction in a wide range of subjects. Activities incorporating some of the questions can be exciting and rewarding, and the possibilities for student projects are endless. Adding a cultural perspective on foods, for example, can give added depth to a unit on nutrition. At the secondary level, students from cultural groups that traditionally use herbal medicines may enjoy doing research to trace the origin of folk remedies used in the home.

Saville-Troike (1978) offers some guidelines and precautions for use of the questions in Table 8–1. there are no correct or incorrect responses to the questions—only answers that are different. There are no absolutely safe questions about culture. Any question that focuses on culture—even one that appears to be objective and innocuous on the surface—may touch upon areas that individuals (e.g., students, parents, community members) feel are personal, sensitive, or even threatening under certain circumstances. Use of ethnographic techniques such as interviewing, observation, and participation is highly recommended.

**Table 8–1**  Survey of Cultural Group Characteristics

---

**General**

1. What are the major stereotypes that you and others have about each cultural group? To what extent are these accepted by members of the group being typed?
2. To what extent and in what areas has the traditional culture of each minority group changed in contact with the dominant American culture? In what areas has it been maintained?
3. To what extent do individuals possess knowledge of or exhibit characteristics of traditional groups?

**Family**

1. Who is in a "family"? Who among these (or others) live in one house?
2. What is the hierarchy of authority in the family?
3. What are the rights and responsibilities of each family member? Do children have an obligation to work to help the family?
4. What are the functions and obligations of the family in the larger social unit?
5. What is the degree of solidarity or cohesiveness in the family?

**The Life Cycle**

1. What are criteria for the definition of stages, periods, or transitions in life?
2. What are the attitudes, expectations, and behaviors toward individuals at different stages in the life cycle?
3. What behaviors are appropriate or unacceptable for children of various ages? How might these conflict with behaviors taught or encouraged in the school?
4. How is language related to the life cycle?
5. How is the age of children computed? What commemoration is made of the child's birth (if any) and when?

**Roles**

1. What roles within the group are available to whom, and how are they acquired? Is education relevant to this acquisition?
2. What is the knowledge of and perception by the child, the parents, and the community toward these roles, their availability, and possible or appropriate means of access to them?

**Table 8-1** *continued*

3. Is language use important in the definition or social marking of roles?

4. Are there different class differences in the expectations about child role attainment? Are these realistic?

**Interpersonal Relationships**

1. How do people greet each other? What forms of address are used between people in various roles?

2. Do girls work and interact with boys? Is it proper?

3. How is deference shown?

4. How are insults expressed?

5. Who may disagree with whom? Under what circumstances?

**Communication**

1. What languages, and varieties of each language, are used in the community? By whom? When? Where? For what purposes?

2. Which varieties are written? How widespread is knowledge of written forms?

3. What are the characteristics of "speaking well"? How do these relate to age, sex, context, or other social factors? What are the criteria for correctness?

4. What roles, attitudes, or personality traits are associated with particular ways of speaking?

5. What is considered "normal" speech behavior?

6. Is learning language a source of pride? Is developing bilingual competence considered an advantage or a handicap?

7. What is the functionality of the native language in the environment?

8. What gestures or postures have special significance or may be considered objectionable? What meaning is attached to making direct eye contact? To eye avoidance?

9. Who may talk to whom? When? Where? About what?

**Decorum and Discipline**

1. What counts as discipline in terms of the culture and what doesn't?

2. What behaviors are considered socially acceptable for students of different age and sex?

3. Who (or what) is considered responsible if a child misbehaves?

4. Who has authority over whom? To what extent can one person's will be imposed on another? By what means?

5. How is the behavior of children traditionally controlled, to what extent, and in what domains?

6. What is the role of language in social control? What is the significance of using the first versus the second language?

**Religion**

1. What is considered sacred and what secular?

2. What religious roles and authority are recognized in the community? What is the role of children in religious practices?

**Table 8-1**   *continued*

3.   What taboos are there? What should *not* be discussed in school? What questions should *not* be asked? What student behaviors should *not* be required?

**Health and Hygiene**

1.   Who or what is believed to cause illness or death?

2.   Who or what is responsible for curing?

3.   How are specific illnesses treated? To what extent do individuals utilize or accept modern medical practices by doctors and other health professionals?

4.   What beliefs or practices are there with regard to bodily hygiene?

5.   If a student were involved in an accident at school, would any of the common first aid practices be unacceptable?

**Food**

1.   What is eaten? In what order? How often?

2.   What foods are favorites? What taboo? What typical?

3.   What rules are observed during meals regarding age and sex roles within the family, the order of serving, seating, utensils used, and appropriate verbal formulas (e.g., how, and if, one may request, refuse, or thank)?

4.   What social obligations are there with regard to food giving, preparation, reciprocity, and honoring people?

5.   What relation does food have with health? What medicinal uses are made of food, or categories of food?

6.   What are the taboos or prescriptions associated with the handling, offering, or discarding of food?

**Dress and Personal Appearance**

1.   What clothing is typical? What is worn for special occasions? What seasonal differences are considered appropriate?

2.   How does dress differ for age, sex, and social class?

3.   What restrictions are imposed for modesty?

4.   What is the concept of beauty or attractiveness? What characteristics are most valued?

5.   What constitutes a compliment? What form should it take?

6.   Does the color of dress have symbolic significance?

**History and Traditions**

1.   What individuals and events in history are a source of pride for the group?

2.   To what extent is knowledge of the group's history preserved? In what forms and in what ways is it passed on?

3.   Do any ceremonies or festive occasions commemorate historical events?

4.   How and to what extent does the group's knowledge of history coincide with or depart from scientific theories of creation, evolution, and historical development?

5.   To what extent does the group in the United States identify with the history and traditions of their country of origin? What changes have taken place in the country of origin since the group or individuals emigrated?

**Table 8–1** *continued*

6. For what reasons and under what circumstances did the group or individuals come to the United States (or did the United States come to them)?

### Holidays and Celebrations

1. What holidays and celebrations are observed by the group and individuals? What is their purpose (e.g., political, seasonal, religious)?
2. Which are especially important for children and why?
3. What cultural values are they intended to inculcate?
4. Do parents and students of immigrant children know and understand school holidays and behavior appropriate for them (including appropriate nonattendance)?

### Education

1. What is the purpose of education?
2. What methods for teaching and learning are used at home (e.g., modeling and imitation, didactic stories and proverbs, direct verbal instruction)? Do methods vary with the setting or according to what is being taught or learned?
3. What is the role of language in learning and teaching?
4. Is it appropriate for students to ask questions or volunteer information?
5. What constitutes a positive response by a teacher to a student?
6. How many years is it considered normal for children to go to school?
7. Are there different expectations by parents, teachers, and students with respect to different groups? In different subjects? For boys versus girls?

### Work and Play

1. What range of behaviors are considered "work" and what "play"?
2. What kinds of work are prestigious and why? Why is work valued?
3. Are there stereotypes about what a particular group will do?
4. What is the purpose of play?

### Time and Space

1. What beliefs or values are associated with concepts of time? How important is punctuality? How important is speed of performance when taking a test?
2. Is control or prescriptive organization of children's time required (e.g., must homework be done before watching television; is bedtime a scheduled event)?
3. How do individuals organize themselves spatially in groups (e.g., in rows, circles, around tables, on the floor)?
4. What is the spatial organization of the home?
5. What is the knowledge and significance of cardinal directions (North, South, East, West)? At what age are these concepts acquired?
6. What significance is associated with different directions or places (e.g., heaven is up, people are buried facing West)?

**Table 8-1** *continued*

**Natural Phenomena**

1.  What beliefs and practices are associated with the sun, moon, comets, and stars?
2.  Who or what is responsible for rain, lightning, thunder, earthquakes, droughts, floods, and hurricanes?
3.  Are particular behavioral prescriptions or taboos associated with natural phenomena? What sanctions are there against individuals violating restrictions or prescriptions?
4.  How and to what extent does the group's beliefs about natural phenomena coincide with or depart from scientific theories?
5.  To what extent are traditional group beliefs still held by individuals within the community?

**Pets and Other Animals**

1.  Which animals are valued, and for what reasons? Which animals are considered appropriate as pets? Which are inappropriate and why?
2.  Are particular behavioral prescriptions or taboos associated with particular animals?
3.  Are any animals of religious significance? Of historical importance?
4.  What attitudes are held toward individuals or groups holding different beliefs and behaviors with respect to animals?
5.  Which animals may be kept in the classroom? Which may not, and why?

**Art and Music**

1.  What forms of art and music are most highly valued?
2.  What media and instruments are traditionally used?
3.  What forms of art and music are considered appropriate for children to perform or appreciate?
4.  Are there any behavioral prescriptions or taboos related to art and music (e.g., depiction of the human form; desecration of living things)?
5.  How and to what extent may approval or disapproval be expressed?

**Expectations and Aspirations**

1.  How is success defined?
2.  What beliefs are held regarding luck and fate?
3.  What significance does adherence to the traditional culture of the group have for the individual's potential achievement?
4.  What significance does the acquisition of the majority culture and the English language have?
5.  Do parents expect and desire assimilation of children to the dominant culture as a result of education and the acquisition of English?
6.  Are the attitudes of community members and individuals the same as or different from those who speak for the community?

**Source:** M. Saville-Troike, 1978, *A Guide to Culture in the Classroom.* National Clearinghouse for Bilingual Education.

These questions have been widely used by teachers for over a decade. Of course, the relative importance of specific information in any of the 20 areas covered will vary for individuals within and across different groups as well as by subject and grade level. In physical education, for example, the questions listed under Health and Hygiene have been of particular interest. As Swisher and Swisher (1986) argue, however, promoting equity in physical education requires that teachers consider more than motor development; they also need to understand relevant student attitudes, values, and beliefs, which can be revealed by asking additional questions such as the following (Swisher & Swisher, 1986, p. 37):

- Why do some students approach competition differently from other members of their peer group?
- Why do certain students prefer to watch activities before demonstrating that they can do the task?
- How culturally appropriate a mode of interaction is coeducational participation?

In other content areas, teachers can supplement the questions in Table 8–1 with some of their own designed to provide information relevant to instruction in specific areas.

## Home, Neighborhood, and Community: What Teachers Need to Know

Learning about students' homes, neighborhoods, and communities is essential for all teachers. When teachers and students come from different ethnic or socioeconomic levels, such knowledge is "critically" important (Grant, 1981). This section focuses on how teachers can develop a better understanding of the family and community context beyond the school.

### Home Visits

The teacher's task has been described as that of determining for each student what is known, what is possible, and what is important (Wallace, 1981). Home visits are one of the best ways teachers can learn what is familiar and significant to their students. As Wallace points out, "When you know the articles, personal space, names of personalities, family members, smells, and shades of color and light that surround a person, a whole new perspective on that person opens up and you can greatly increase your teaching potential" (p. 92). I still remember many of the home visits I made as a teacher: the people, the sights, the sounds, the smells, and the tastes. Whether to make a "social call" or to report on a student's progress, the home visit can have a positive impact on teaching and enhance rapport with students and parents alike.

For those thinking about making home visits, Grant (1981) offers the following suggestions:

- Determine whether home visits are welcome in your school community.
- Schedule an appointment ahead of time.
- Dress as you would for school.
- Keep the visit short, from 20 to 30 minutes.
- Avoid questions that may be regarded as "prying."
- Say something positive about the student.

For many teachers, scheduling a home visit for each student is an unrealistic goal (e.g., at the secondary level). If this is the case, one or two visits per month to selected students' homes usually is feasible and can provide valuable information. The following account from a Vo-Ag teacher eloquently captures the change in perspective that can result:

> Karl's dad was crippled in a tractor accident, but it never occurred to me that Karl would be living in a trailer on two acres. When he told me he lived in the country and talked about his prize lambs I had pictured a big farm. He dressed the part and obviously was a friend of the other boys whose parents were farmers and ranchers. Now I know that in order to keep those hopes alive, I must build carefully on their (Karl and his dad's) well-tended sheep project crowded carefully onto that small acreage. (cited in Wallace, 1981, p. 92)

## Neighborhood Visits and Community Study

Neighborhood visits enable teachers to become familiar with the neighborhood and community environment experienced by their students (Wallace, 1981). In some cases, much can be learned about an area by walking or driving through it; if students are bused to the school, a bus ride may provide useful information about their neighborhoods. In schools with extended service areas, teachers may choose to focus on a single neighborhood, one they do not know well.

The need for the information such visits provide is becoming increasingly evident. In one study, most teachers surveyed did not know how and where students were spending their time outside school, nor were they aware of available community resources (Grant, 1981). Careful and directed observation and analysis of students' immediate surroundings—the places they spend their time out of school—can have educational payoffs. "Tying into and building onto" what students already know "yields high educational gain and is a way of subtly showing respect for the background and lifestyle of every student" (Wallace, 1981, p. 96).

There are different ways of planning neighborhood walks according to the time available and specific interests. Teachers who are apprehensive about visiting an unfamiliar neighborhood can arrange to be accompanied by someone who is familiar with the area. For example, two teachers who were hesitant about visiting a particular area in a large city arranged to walk through the neighborhood with a doctor whose office was located there. They later reported that their neighborhood walk "gave us a different feeling about the area, a different attitude" (Hays & Hays,

1981, p. 102). Another strategy is to use student "tour guides." For example, one teacher who toured the favorite haunts of junior high students guided by student volunteers observed, "I immensely enjoyed the walks with the kids, they were quite enlightening" (Elner, 1981, p. 108).

In undertaking these visits, teachers will want to identify the physical surroundings familiar to students and consider their possible classroom applications. To facilitate the observation process, Wallace (1981) encourages teachers to note such things as homes, fences, doors, windows, architectural styles, lot sizes, paths, streets, gardens, animals, buildings, stores, industries, junk, water, mail, fire, police, furniture, lighting, religious institutions, music, art, toys, gathering places, landmarks, foods, and cars. The number and age of people visible in the area and their activities also should be noted. For those with an inclination to map the area, color codes can be used to distinguish the location of various types of structures and areas around the school (Anderson, 1979). These features include public community agencies, religious or political organizations, housing, places where children and teenagers play, places where adults gather (e.g., unemployed, senior citizens), major industries and businesses, etc.

Teachers may even find it useful to ask students to map their own neighborhoods. Information gleaned from such an activity can provide valuable insights about areas and structures that are familiar to the students and those that are not. What do children know about their own neighborhoods and the surrounding areas? What appears to be most important and meaningful? From their perspective, what are the "boundaries" of their neighborhood? Finally, if teachers want even more detailed information, questionnaires can be used to assess student and parental attitudes toward the school; the racial and ethnic composition of the community; and community concerns (Anderson, 1979).

## Connections Between School and the World Beyond

The discussion in the first part of this chapter has focused on how teachers can become familiar with the sociocultural context in which their students live—their culture, home, neighborhood, and community. In this section, the emphasis is on making connections between the classroom and that part of students' learning environment that lies beyond.

### Parent Involvement

The very nature of the educational process makes the relationship between home and school an important one. Although opinion surveys indicate that both the public and teachers generally favor increased contact between parents and school (Hoover-Dempsey, Bassler, & Brissie, 1987), actual levels of parent involvement are generally regarded as low. This is true despite the potential benefits of parent involvement on the achievement, behavior, attendance, attitudes, and study habits of students.

In the school setting, parents can provide a role model when they serve as resource persons for classroom activities.

Generally speaking, parent involvement refers to activities by parents, both in the home and school, that are intended to support and promote students' school performance and well-being (Simich-Dudgeon, 1987). Within the school setting, parents typically provide classroom assistance, serve as resource persons, accompany classes on field trips, and participate in parent-teacher organizations, advisory committees, and other decision-making bodies. At home, they provide tutoring and an environment conducive to learning. Overall, teachers at the elementary level try harder and in more diverse ways to encourage parent involvement than do those at the secondary level (Epstein & Becker, cited in Simich-Dudgeon, 1987).

It is believed that the degree to which parents participate in school-based efforts is related to factors such as school socioeconomic status and teachers' belief in their ability to teach effectively and in students' capacity to learn (Hoover-Dempsey et al., 1987). In general, the higher the socioeconomic status and teachers' belief in themselves and their students, the greater the levels of participation. By contrast, these factors do not appear to affect rates of parent involvement at home. For this reason, researchers suggest that efforts to increase and improve home-school linkages—particularly in areas serving predominantly low-income families—should complement school-based activities with "specific, task-related parent-child involvement at home" (Hoover-Dempsey et al., 1987, p. 432).

Recent research supports the importance of home-based parent involvement and school efforts to encourage and enhance parents' efforts. Simich-Dudgeon (1987) mentions the following pertinent findings:

- Parental encouragement, activities, and interest at home, as well as parental participation in schools and classrooms, have a positive influence on achievement, even after accounting for student ability and socioeconomic status.

- Parents involved in academic activities with their children at home gain knowledge that makes them better able to assess the quality of teaching their children receive and to help with academic tasks.

- The results of parent involvement in tutoring limited-English-proficient students are consistent with those for native English-speaking students and their families. To be most effectice as home tutors, all parents—regardless of ethnic language—need school support and direct teacher involvement.

Teachers can encourage parent involvement at home in numerous ways. One approach is the use of materials specifically designed for home use; a good example is *Family Math* by Stenmark, Thompson, and Cossey (1986). This book contains many enjoyable activities that parents and children (K–8) can work on together to develop problem-solving skills and math understanding.

Another useful technique is having children read aloud to their parents. The effectiveness of this practice, long recognized by teachers, was confirmed by a project conducted in England. In this 2-year experiment, children in schools in multiethnic and linguistically diverse areas of London read aloud to their parents on a nightly basis. Their progress was compared with that of children working with a reading specialist and with others receiving no intervention treatment at all. Findings revealed just "how powerful the sharing of literacy experiences can

Parent involvement can have a positive influence on the development of literacy and math skills.

be" (Cummins, 1984, p. 238). First, the researchers found that parental involvement was feasible and practical for virtually all parents, including those who were nonliterate and limited-English proficient. The willingness of parents to participate in home collaboration was not hindered by limitations in their own reading or English language skills, nor did these factors impede children's ability to progress. Second, children who regularly read to their parents outperformed those receiving instruction from a reading specialist and those who did not participate. Teachers observed greater interest in learning and improved behavior among the home readers. Third, parents, for the most part, "expressed great satisfaction" with this type of involvement, and teachers reported that home collaboration was beneficial for pupils regardless of performance level. The practice was considered so worthwhile that after the experiment was over, teachers chose to continue home collaboration and were joined by teachers from the other groups (Cummins, 1984).

## The Societal Curriculum

Education is a lifelong process, a complex combination of formal and informal learning and experiences. That portion of an individual's education acquired outside the classroom is transmitted via the "societal curriculum" (Cortes, 1981, 1986). As described by Cortes, it comprises the massive, informal curriculum of home, community, and society—the sum total of socializing forces that "educate" individuals throughout their lives. For each individual, the societal curriculum embodies the lessons learned from family, peer groups, neighborhood, institutions, organizations, mass media, and personal experiences. Because it involves elements that are of primary importance to individuals, the societal curriculum exerts considerable influence (both positive and negative) on intercultural and interethnic attitudes, values, and beliefs. Its effects are felt before one reaches school age and continue beyond the period of formal education throughout one's entire life.

Because of its pervasiveness and influence, the societal curriculum must be given serious consideration in the design and implementation of multicultural education. Awareness of its existence and content is the first step. To this end, Cortes (1981) suggests that students begin by observing and keeping a record of the number and variety of topics they encounter in the course of daily contact with different sources: family members, friends, community organizations, media, and so forth. From my own experience, teachers have found this activity to be quite revealing. Building on this initial level of awareness, teachers can use strategies such as community study and multicultural analysis of media to integrate elements of the societal curriculum into the school program.

## Community Study Through Life History

A community's most important resource is its people. One way teachers can effectively tap this resource is through oral accounts of individuals' life experiences known as *life history*. In the context of multicultural education, this technique enables students to develop a deeper understanding of culture and community by participating in "the systematic collection of a uniquely personal history—the history of common people" (Mehaffy, 1984, p. 470). Use of life histories helps students to recognize and understand the changes and constants elders have experienced over a lifetime and the ways people cope with problems and conflicts. From a cultural perspective, life histories serve a dual purpose by illustrating both the *commonality* and *diversity* of roles, values, and experiences within groups (Gibson & Arvizu, 1978). Within the family context, they are a record of family heritage and traditions for younger generations, providing "a sense of belonging, of identity,. . .a place in space and time" (Grenier, 1985, p. 6A).

The following guidelines for teachers and students can enhance the effectiveness and educational value of life history projects:*

- *Begin by interviewing someone you know*. Create an atmosphere that is informal and comfortable.

---

*Adapted from Gibson and Arvizu (1978), Mehaffy (1984), and Smith and Otero (1982).

A community's most important resource is its people.

- *Prepare for the interview*. Meet with the person before doing an interview. Explain the purpose of the interview and how the information will be used. Find out about the person's life so that you can guide the interview without being directive.
- *Develop an outline of topics to be covered in the interview*. Common topics include personal items (e.g., place of birth; information regarding parents, schooling, and work); recollections of major historic events that occurred during the person's life (e.g., where were you when. . .); and special qualities, knowledge, or experiences. Topics relevant for family research include the origin of the family surname and its meaning; naming traditions; stories; famous or notorious family members; family recipes; and family members' childhood experiences, religion, politics, schooling, marriage, courtship, etc.
- *Use questions sparingly*. Although useful for providing structure and clarification, questions tend to produce a stilted interview if used in excess. In general, keep questions short, and avoid those that can be answered by a simple "yes" or "no." "Who, what, where, when, and how" questions elicit more elaborate answers and hence, more information.
- *Take notes during the interview*. Check information for accuracy.

- *Limit the length of the interview to no more than 1 hour.* If all areas of interest cannot be covered in one session, schedule a series of interviews. Doing a complete life history requires a considerable amount of time. Students may want to focus upon a particular period in or aspect of an individual's life (e.g., the experiences of international students, immigrants, or longtime residents in the community; the educational experiences and orientations of several generations in the same family).

- *Practice the interviewing technique.* Students can start by interviewing their teacher or each other. Once skills are developed, invite a community elder to the classroom for an interview. Ask students to record information and work together to check its accuracy. Encourage students to interview family members such as grandparents, aunts, and uncles.

Life histories are an effective tool for family and community study. Multiple histories can provide the basis for preparation of a local history, documenting the experiences of a cross-section of the community's population. The technique also serves as a vehicle for integrating multicultural concepts with skills development in history, language arts, and other subject areas. Life history projects also enhance students' self-identity, awareness of their neighborhood and history, and research and writing skills (Mehaffy, 1984). The products of these projects can be shared with other classes, published in school literary publications, incorporated in library collections, displayed in community museums, and used as the basis for other activities.

One of the earliest life history programs instituted in the public schools is the Foxfire project in rural Georgia, which began with a focus on Appalachian traditions; similar projects now number more than 200 nationwide (Mehaffy, 1984). Elementary school students in North Carolina and California have published texts based upon oral history projects, and others have initiated Living History programs. In an old California mining town, a project is underway to preserve the rich cultural heritage of the small community by collecting oral histories from longtime residents. As part of an ongoing process of community study, life histories can bring a personal quality to the dynamics of ethnicity and enhance students' awareness of cultural diversity at the local level (Cortes, 1981).

## Media Analysis

On a national level, information and ideas are communicated in a variety of forms including television, films, radio, magazines, and newspapers. These constitute an educationally powerful force within society. Media use accounts for a significant proportion of students' time away from school; by the time they graduate, for example, average high school seniors will have spent more time watching television than in the classroom—about 20% more (Cortes, 1983). In addition, the media are "multicultural educators." In this role, the media contribute to and reflect existing societal view regarding diverse groups (e.g., ethnic, racial, regional, religious,

To be "multicultural media literate," children must be active, informed, selective, and critical consumers of media as sources of information and ideas.

gender, class) within American society and in foreign countries. For example, in one second-grade classroom, the teacher discovered that her pupils believed "all Indians were dead" because no one they knew resembled the "image" of Native Americans evoked by television westerns.

The pervasiveness of the media in American society and their ability to shape users' attitudes and beliefs pose an important challenge for teachers. Culkin (cited in Los Angeles County Superintendent of Schools, 1981a, p. 1) describes this challenge as follows:

> The communications revolution has given us a new student and new means for communicating with that student. . . .We must acknowledge the existence and influence of this new media culture and enable the child to master its codes and to control its impact. We should want them to be active, intelligent, appreciative, and selective consumers of the total media culture.

As a primary source of ideas and information, both the fictional and nonfictional media should be examined analytically, a process that can improve critical thinking. From a teacher's perspective, the purposes of including media analysis in the curriculum is to help students develop the following (Cortes, 1980):

- An awareness of the multicultural content conveyed by the media and its impact on how individuals view themselves and others as members of specific groups.
- "Media literacy" (i.e., critical skills in evaluating the various media as sources of information and ideas).
- An understanding of how previous knowledge, attitudes, and experiences influence individuals' ability to interpret and respond to what they encounter as readers, listeners, and viewers.

Cortes (1980) has outlined four approaches teachers can use in teaching media analysis in the context of multicultural education; these approaches focus on content, communication structure, causation, and self as viewer. Each approach deals with a different aspect of the media and requires its own set of strategies for classroom analysis.

**Media Content**   Analysis of media content from a multicultural perspective has two major components: (a) to examine how various groups and foreign nations are portrayed in different media and (b) to identify the underlying viewpoint of various presentations. As with other sources of information, presentations in the media—even "factual" accounts of events—are subjective. Overtly or covertly, they mirror a particular point of view; intentionally and unintentionally, they are subject to varying degrees of distortion.

Having students do a content analysis of a television program is a good initial eye-opener in developing their media literacy. Subjecting a program to analysis is a much different experience than watching it solely for its entertainment value. In examining how different groups are portrayed, many elements such as the following are relevant (Banks, 1977; Cortes, 1983; Smith & Otero, 1982):

- Generalizations and stereotypes
- Representations of social status (e.g., class, occupation, profession, rural/urban)
- Attributions (e.g., intelligence, abilities, language, values, attitudes, behaviors, interpersonal relations, sense of humor)
- Problems and issues (e.g., types, scope, solutions)
- Degree of group identification
- Topic, theme, point of view, perspective (e.g., group members and nonmembers)

Numerous sources are suitable for content analysis, from children's literature and animated films at the elementary level to newspaper stories, television series, and movies at the secondary level (Cortes, 1980). In areas where television newscasts are available from other countries (e.g., Canada or Mexico) or in other languages, a comparative study of how the same events are covered for different audiences can be quite revealing. The selection of stories originating in Mexico City or Montreal, for example, use of film footage, and accompanying narration makes for a most interesting contrast with coverage on newscasts in the United

States. Such a project also can capitalize on ethnic language skills not often tapped in the regular curriculum. Using stories featured on the major network news, students can compare and contrast the treatment given the same individual, issue, or event as well as the time allocated for coverage (Cortes, 1983). Subsequent comparisons can then be made with coverage in print media (e.g, local newspapers and national news magazines).

**Media Communication Structure**    The various media differ in the communication modalities used to present messages. Some are visual, some auditory; others are multidimensional. When words, sounds, and images are juxtaposed, as in films and television, students must be able to recognize what each component contributes to the whole and how it does so. They also need to know how the various components can be examined separately.

Teachers can use several strategies to facilitate an analysis of visual and auditory messages. Cortes (1980) suggests drawing attention separately to each element. One technique is to show a news story or documentary in which ethnic groups or foreign nations are represented. The account is presented to one group of students with the sound track and to another group without the sound track. After viewing the story or documentary, students are asked to compare how their group interpretations differ and to assess the influence of the narration on how the visual material is interpreted.

Other strategies also can enhance students' ability to critically view films (Los Angeles County Schools, 1981b). For example, teachers can show a 2- or 3-minute excerpt from a film, directing students' attention to the visual material. In discussion, students are asked to summarize information and highlight main points. When the same segment is shown a second time, students are instructed to focus on the narrative, concentrating on what is said and how (e.g., wording and attitudes). An alternative approach is to contrast the spoken text and film sequence by taking an excerpt and recording the two messages side by side in separate columns for comparison. Some questions to consider when using films that portray cultures and populations are presented in Table 8-2. Having students analyze and compare several films, using these questions as a guide, will sharpen their critical viewing skills.

**Causation**    To be multicultural media literate, students must be aware of the reasons for variations in the treatment of different groups and foreign nations. This awareness comes from knowledge of the historical forces and societal conditions that influence media and account for changes in treatment over time (Cortes, 1980). How groups and nations are depicted is sensitive to war, international diplomacy, ethnic politics, economic conditions, and changing social attitudes. For example, the September 1941 issue of *Time* magazine carried an article offering "guidelines" for distinguishing between individuals who are Chinese and Japanese (Smith & Otero, 1982). Polls consistently reveal shifts in public attitudes toward different groups nationally and internationally.

At this level of analysis, relevant activities include the following (Cortes, 1980):

**Table 8-2**   Questions for Critical Viewing Skills of Films

---

**Overall Presentation**

*Does the film:*

1. Offer a positive image of cultures or populations portrayed?
2. Show basic similarities among all groups of people without making value judgments?
3. Present factual information objectively?
4. Portray one segment of the population and their activities as representative of the entire culture or population?
5. Provide a comprehensive view of cultures and populations which allows students to identify and appreciate characteristic modes of behavior and adaptation?
6. Present information in a manner that is balanced and unambiguous, (i.e., present positive and negative elements as appropriate, avoiding distortions and stereotypes)?
7. Provide an accurate and balanced representation of the historical development of the cultures and populations depicted?
8. Examine historical and/or contemporary forces and conditions contributing to advantages and disadvantages faced by the cultures and populations portrayed?
9. Explore intergroup conflict and tension in a balanced and objective manner?

**Photography**

1. How do the camera angles, types of shots, distance, and movement affect the way information is communicated by the camera? What is the message communicated through the photography?
2. How and when are long shots used? Are they supported by appropriate close-ups?
3. How and when are close-ups used?

**Sound Track**

1. Are "buzz" words used to describe people, living conditions, heritage?
2. To what extent does the narration convey a sense of respect for the culture?
3. To what extent does the presentation of content in the film depend on narration as opposed to visual material?
4. What words does the narrator emphasize? How is this done?
5. How is point of view reflected in the choice of words used in the narration?
6. How are music and sound effects used to enhance the message, set the scene, and affect the pace?
7. To what extent does the film appear to be authentic and accurate?

---

**Source:** Adapted from J. N. Hawkins and J. Maksik, 1976, *Teacher's Resource Handbook for African Studies* (Occasional Paper No. 16). African Studies Center, University of California–Los Angeles. Cited in Los Angeles County Superintendent of Schools (1981b).

- Identification of the period in which something was written or produced.
- Investigation of the social conditions of the period using other sources (e.g., historical accounts, literature).
- Examination of changes in the treatment of groups within a single genre (e.g., westerns in television and movies).
- Comparison of the treatment of specific groups or nations in different media during the same historical period or within a particular type of media over time.

**Self as Viewer**   Individuals' own knowledge, attitudes, and experiences influence how they perceive and interpret messages conveyed through the media. As Cortes (1980) has observed, the media are only part of the experience; "viewers and readers are the other critical aspect of the complex process of communication" (p. 45). How individuals respond to media messages is in many ways a reflection of themselves.

In the classroom, teachers can use different types of media to promote student awareness of their own reactions to media as viewers and readers. Cortes (1980) has found media presentations involving foreign areas, multiple ethnic groups, and intergroup relations especially useful for this purpose because they tend to generate a diversity of responses. As different group perspectives emerge, students can compare and contrast these reactions and explore why reactions differ.

## Did You Know That. . .?

Studies suggest that the relationship between television usage and academic achievement is complex. For example, 2 to 3 hours of viewing per day has been positively associated with school performance for students in rural areas and those who are Hispanic. In communities characterized as "poor," students who watch television seem to outperform those who do not. In affluent suburbs, however, students who do not watch television surpass those who do. At all levels, watching more than 2 to 3 hours of television daily appears to be negatively associated with performance (Sewall, 1988).

In a 1982 study, Coleman, Hoffer, and Kilgore (cited in Coleman, 1987) found that students in parochial and other private schools had higher levels of achievement in mathematics and verbal skills and lower dropout rates than did their counterparts in public schools. Their analysis suggested that these differences in achievement were not attributable to factors *within* the schools but to differences in the relation of the schools to the parental community.

## Summary

Getting to know their students is an ongoing process for all teachers. One part of this process involves learning about students' families, interpersonal relationships, communication styles, cultural traditions, and various aspects of their belief system. Another part involves becoming more familiar with the environment experienced by students, the neighborhoods and community in which they live.

To integrate students' educational experiences *inside* and *outside* the classroom—to make a connection between school and "real life"—teachers need to apply relevant cultural and societal insights in their teaching, thus relating curriculum content to the world outside the classroom. Parent involvement through school- and home-based activities provides an effective vehicle for promoting home-school relations. Although school-based activities appear to be influenced by factors such as socioeconomic status and teacher efficacy, this is not the case with activities based in the home. With appropriate school support and direct teacher involvement, activities like home tutoring can provide a rewarding and worthwhile experience for parents, students, and teachers alike.

Students are exposed to both a societal curriculum and a school curriculum. The societal curriculum is shaped by the home, peers, community, institutions, and mass media. In terms of multicultural education, the societal curriculum can have both positive and negative effects. The key question is how teachers deal with this facet of students' educational experience.

Teachers can make important and relevant aspects of the societal curriculum a part of the formal school curriculum in various ways. First, students can be made aware of the existence of the societal curriculum. Second, using techniques such as life histories they can learn about their community and the individuals in it. Through these personal stories, the commonality and diversity of family and community experiences can be easily incorporated into a variety of content areas. Finally, by examining various aspects of the mass media, students can become adept in dealing critically and intelligently with the multicultural content conveyed through visual, written, and spoken text. In the final analysis, they acquire the skills necessary to be multicultural media literate.

## References

Anderson, J. (1979). Community analysis field study. In H. P. Baptiste, Jr. & M. L. Baptiste, *Developing the multicultural process in classroom instruction* (pp. 208–212). Washington, DC: University Press of America.

Banks, C. A. McG. (1977). A content analysis of the treatment of Black Americans on television. *Social Education, 41*(4), 336–339, 344.

Coleman, J. S. (1987). Families and schools. *Educational Researcher, 16*(6), 32–38.

Cortes, C. E. (1980). The role of media in multicultural education. *Viewpoints in Teaching and Learning, 56*(1), 38–49.

Cortes, C. E. (1981). The societal curriculum: Implications for multiethnic education. In J. A. Banks (Ed.), *Education in the 80's: Multiethnic education* (pp. 24–32). Washington, DC: National Education Association.

Cortes, C. E. (1983). The mass media: Civic education's public curriculum. *Journal of Teacher Education, XXXIV*(6), 25–29.

Cortes, C. E. (1986). The education of language minority students: A contextual interaction model. In California State Department of Education, *Beyond language: Social and cultural factors in schooling language minority students* (pp. 3–33). Los Angeles: Evaluation, Dissemination and Assessment Center.

Cummins, J. (1984). *Bilingualism and special education: Issues in assessment and pedagogy.* San Diego: College Hill Press.

Elner, E. (1981). A neighborhood walk. In W. E. Sims & B. Bass de Martinez (Eds.), *Perspectives in multicultural education* (pp. 104–108). Lanham, MD: University Press of America.

Etlin, M. (1988, May/June). To teach them all is to know them all. *NEA Today, 6*(10), 10–11.

Felling, Nancy (Ed.). (1985, September 28). Oral history gives you "a place in space and time" (interview with J. Grenier). *Chico (CA) Enterprise-Record*, p. 6A.

Gibson, M. A., & Arvizu, S. F. (1978). *Demystifying the concept of culture: Methodological tools and techniques.* Monograph II. Sacramento: California State University-Sacramento, Cross Cultural Resource Center.

Grant, C. A. (1981). The community and multiethnic education. In J. A. Banks (Ed.), *Education in the 80's: Multiethnic education* (pp. 128–139). Washington, DC: National Education Association.

Hays, O., & Hays, S. (1981). A neighborhood walk. In W. E. Sims & B. Bass de Martinez (Eds.), *Perspectives in multicultural education* (pp. 101–104). Lanham, MD: University Press of America.

Hoover-Dempsey, K. V., Bassler, O. C., & Brissie, J. S. (1987). Parent involvement: Contributions of teacher efficacy, school socioeconomic status, and other school characteristics. *American Educational Research Journal, 24*(3), 417–435.

Los Angeles County Superintendent of Schools. (1981a). *There's more to television and films than meets the eye.* Unpublished annotated list of films. Coordinated by P. Seeley. Los Angeles: Office of the Los Angeles County Superintendent of Schools, Educational Services Group.

Los Angeles County Superintendent of Schools. (1981b). *Films on Africa. . .Another Look.* Project of the Administrative Committee for Program Development. Coordinated by J. B. Perez and P. Seeley. Downey, CA: Author.

Mehaffy, G. L. (1984). Oral history in elementary classrooms. *Social Education*, Vol. 8, No. 6, 470–472.

Saville-Troike, M. (1978). *A guide to culture in the classroom.* Rosslyn, VA: National Clearinghouse for Bilingual Education.

Sewall, G. T. (1988). American history textbooks: Where do we go from here? *Phi Delta Kappan, 69*(8), 552–558.

Simich-Dudgeon, C. (1987). Involving limited-English-proficient parents as tutors in their children's education. *ERIC/CLL News Bulletin, 10*(2), 3–4, 7.

Smith, G. R., & Otero, G. (1982). *Teaching about cultural awareness.* Denver: University of Denver, Center for Teaching International Relations.

Stenmark, J. K., Thompson, V., & Cossey, R. (1986). *Family math.* Berkeley, CA: University of California Press.

Swisher, K., & Swisher, C. (1986). A multicultural physical education approach. *Journal of Physical Education, Recreation and Dance. 57*(7), 35–39.

Wallace, G. (1981). Cultural awareness: Interaction of teachers, parents, and students. In W. E. Sims & B. Bass de Martinez (Eds.), *Perspectives in multicultural education* (pp. 89–112). Lanham, MD: University Press of America.

# Name Index

Adler, P. S., 21, 40
Alameda County School Department, 25, 40
Alatis, J. E., 88, 102
American Association of Colleges for Teacher
　　Education, 9, 16
American Association of Retired Persons, 165,
　166
American Council on the Teaching of Foreign
　　Languages, 91, 102
American School Board Journal, 149–150, 166
Ames, C., 61, 64, 73
Ames, C., and Ames, R., 61, 62, 63–64, 73
Amos, O. E., and Landers, M. F., 108, 113,
　135
Anderson, J., 204, 216
Appleton, N., 28, 32, 33–34, 39, 40
Arvizu, S. F., Snyder, W. A., and Espinosa,
　P. T., 20–21, 40
Association of American Publishers, 142,
　156–157, 166
Au, K. Hu-Pei, and Jordan, C., 50, 73

Baca, L. M., and Cervantes, H. T., 81, 85,
　101, 102, 108, 111, 112, 113, 114, 133,
　135
Baker, G. C., 10–11, 14, 16
Ball, S., 61–62, 64, 73
Banks, C. A. McG., 212, 216

Banks, J. A., 12, 16, 28, 40, 192, 161–163,
　166
Banks, J. A., Cortes, C. E., Gay, G., Garcia,
　R., and Ochoa, A. S., 176–177
Banton, M., 30, 40
Baptiste, M. L., and Baptiste, H. P., Jr.,
　12–14, 16
Barbe, W. B., 126, 135
Barbe, W. B., and Milone, M. N., Jr., 126,
　135
Barker, D., and Morrisroe, S., 100, 102
Batchelder, D., and Warner, E. G., 190, 192
Beebe, L. M., 55, 73
Bennett, C. I., 29, 30, 40, 64, 65, 73, 147, 166
Boehnlein, M., 132, 135
Bordelon, K. W., 150, 166
Britton, G., and Lumpkin, M., 150, 166
Brooks, N., 19, 41
Brophy, J. E., 51, 69–71, 73
Brown, P. R., and Haycock, K., 11, 16
Bullard, B. M., 156, 167

California State Department of Education, 4,
　17, 170, 173, 176–177, 183, 190–191, 192
Campbell, R. N., 77, 91, 103
Cantoni-Harvey, G., 100, 103, 150,
　167, 188, 192
Carbo, M., 127, 135

# Subject Index

## WE VALUE YOUR OPINION—PLEASE SHARE IT WITH US

Merrill Publishing and our authors are most interested in your reactions to this textbook. Did it serve you well in the course? If it did, what aspects of the text were most helpful? If not, what didn't you like about it? Your comments will help us to write and develop better textbooks. We value your opinions and thank you for your help.

Text Title _____ Edition _____

Author(s) _____ .

Your Name (optional) _____

Address _____

City _____ State _____ Zip _____

School _____

Course Title _____

Instructor's Name _____

Your Major _____

Your Class Rank _____ Freshman _____ Sophomore _____ Junior _____ Senior

_____ Graduate Student

Were you required to take this course? _____ Required _____ Elective

Length of Course? _____ Quarter _____ Semester

1. Overall, how does this text compare to other texts you've used?

_____ Superior _____ Better Than Most _____ Average _____ Poor

2. Please rate the text in the following areas:

|  | Superior | Better Than Most | Average | Poor |
|---|---|---|---|---|
| Author's Writing Style | _____ | _____ | _____ | _____ |
| Readability | _____ | _____ | _____ | _____ |
| Organization | _____ | _____ | _____ | _____ |
| Accuracy | _____ | _____ | _____ | _____ |
| Layout and Design | _____ | _____ | _____ | _____ |
| Illustrations/Photos/Tables | _____ | _____ | _____ | _____ |
| Examples | _____ | _____ | _____ | _____ |
| Problems/Exercises | _____ | _____ | _____ | _____ |
| Topic Selection | _____ | _____ | _____ | _____ |
| Currentness of Coverage | _____ | _____ | _____ | _____ |
| Explanation of Difficult Concepts | _____ | _____ | _____ | _____ |
| Match-up with Course Coverage | _____ | _____ | _____ | _____ |
| Applications to Real Life | _____ | _____ | _____ | _____ |

Circle those chapters you especially liked:

1  2  3  4  5  6  7  8  9  10  11  12  13  14  15  16  17  18  19  20

What was your favorite chapter? _____

Comments:

4. Circle those chapters you liked least:

1  2  3  4  5  6  7  8  9  10  11  12  13  14  15  16  17  18  19  20

What was your least favorite chapter? _____

Comments:

5. List any chapters your instructor did not assign. _____

6. What topics did your instructor discuss that were not covered in the text?_____

_____

7. Were you required to buy this book? _____ Yes _____ No

Did you buy this book new or used? _____ New _____ Used

If used, how much did you pay? _____

Do you plan to keep or sell this book? _____ Keep _____ Sell

If you plan to sell the book, how much do you expect to receive? _____

Should the instructor continue to assign this book? _____ Yes _____ No

8. Please list any other learning materials you purchased to help you in this course (e.g., study guide, lab manual).

_____

9. What did you like most about this text? _____

_____

10. What did you like least about this text? _____

_____

11. General comments:

May we quote you in our advertising? _____ Yes _____ No

Please mail to:   Boyd Lane
                  College Division, Research Department
                  Box 508
                  1300 Alum Creek Drive
                  Columbus, Ohio 43216

Thank you!